THE DESERT HAWKS

THE
DESERT HAWKS

Leo Nomis with Brian Cull

GRUB STREET · LONDON

Published by
Grub Street
The Basement
10 Chivalry Road
London SW11 1HT

Copyright © 1998 Grub Street, London
Text copyright © Leo Nomis with Brian Cull

A catalogue record is available on request from the British Library

ISBN 1-898697-82-5

Typeset by Pearl Graphics, Hemel Hempstead

Printed and bound in Great Britain by
Biddles Ltd, Guildford and King's Lynn

CONTENTS

	Acknowledgements	vi
	Introduction	7
	Preamble	20
CHAPTER I	The Volunteers	23
CHAPTER II	Operation Balak	40
CHAPTER III	Budejovice	50
CHAPTER IV	The Squadron	60
CHAPTER V	A Time In The Sun	73
CHAPTER VI	Herzliya	83
CHAPTER VII	The Interlude Actions	94
CHAPTER VIII	Death Of A Hero	104
CHAPTER IX	Winter Of Victory	113
	Appendix I	118
	Appendix II	120
	Appendix III	121
	Appendix IV	123
	Dramatis Personae	125
	Further Reading	127

ACKNOWLEDGEMENTS

Brian Cull wishes to thank his wife Val for her invaluable support during the preparation of this book, which entailed much editing and re-typing. He also thanks his friend and fellow author Shlomo Aloni for supplying additional information and photographs, as he does Frederick Galea, Hon Secretary of the National War Museum Association of Malta and long-standing friend, who also supplied some photographs.

Despite poor health, Leo Nomis has gamely continued to embellish his original account with additional anecdotes.

We both congratulate artist Chris Thomas for his excellent dustjacket illustration, and we thank our publisher, John Davies of Grub Street, for this first-class production.

INTRODUCTION

FROM FLEDGLING EAGLE TO FIGHTER PILOT

I was born [on 9 March 1922] and educated in the Los Angeles area of California, where the usually mild weather permitted sport flying the entire year. My father, after whom I was named, had qualified as a pilot with the US Air Service in 1917 but was held back as an instructor on Curtiss JN4s at Kelly Field, Texas. Before he could apply for overseas duty he was involved in a serious crash which killed the student and put my father in hospital until after the Armistice in 1918. He was discharged the following year as a Captain. He became a Hollywood stuntman and was killed in 1932 while performing aerobatics. I do believe he had influence on my decision later to fly myself, although I never flew with him. I had early on learned the primary elements of aviation by frequenting the airports on the outskirts of the city and obtaining odd jobs for which I would be rewarded with flying time. During the summer of 1940 I logged a certain amount of solo hours in this manner.

By the end of 1940, a growing number of American volunteers were being attracted into Royal Air Force service in spite of the US official status of neutrality. Many others had already actively entered into the war through the Canadian forces and, in the spring of 1941, by British-American accord, several training fields had been established in the United States specifically to prepare American pilots for duty with the RAF. Though the British Government had obvious political reasons behind creating these contingent bases in the US, the move expedited the enlistment of scores of American pilots who had hitherto been delayed in their quest to fight a foreign war. The requirements for acceptance into what became known as the Clayton Knight contingents were considered lenient and a total of 75 flying hours was the standard minimum for the applicants. Some who entered upon the adventure, however, had much less previous flight experience than the suggested quota.

Although experienced on only light aircraft of the era, I had, by the beginning of 1941, been accepted into one of the RAF training courses at Glendale, California. After a three-month interval in which we were instilled, by civilian instructors, with the principles and procedures of basic and advanced flight techniques on Harvard trainers, I left for Ottawa, Canada with a group of ten others. We were all young, some being under 20 years of age, and like most emerging pilots of that time we were looking for action with no serious idea of the grim realities that lay ahead. I think all of us, with very few exceptions, were simply adventurers and romanticists, and perhaps idealists. Few were patriots, but it probably worked into that later for those who got a real taste of what the war was, and who were permitted the chance to view liberty from a distance. Most of us had a vague conviction that America would eventually enter the obviously worsening conflict and we rationalized that we were merely getting a head start. It turned out, in essence, that this over-simplified reason for volunteering was to become perfectly true.

In Ottawa, though technically civilians, we were commissioned Pilot Officers in the RAF Volunteer Reserve at the British Liaison Office in Government Building. We did not receive our uniforms until we arrived in London three weeks later. A preview of what the future held was presented to us that August of 1941 when we were shipped out of Halifax, Nova Scotia on a North Atlantic convoy. Within a week we were witness to the sinking of several ships by German U-boats. Three of the American group were missing presumed killed in this attack.

Our arrival in Britain was heralded by an air raid and on our first evening in London we were rapidly becoming aware that we were in a war. However, the excitement of being in England rekindled our spirits and within two days we were sent to 56 Operational Training Unit at Sutton Bridge in Lincolnshire. Our position at the time was rather unique because, although we were already commissioned officers in the Royal Air Force, we had yet to endure any actual training under the British code of discipline and the OTU at which we arrived was to be our first encounter with this delight. Our closest association with British military rules to this point had been when we pledged obedience to the King's Rules and Regulations, a document whose contents were completely unfamiliar to us at the time.

At the airfield we were fascinated with the countryside and strange customs, and we were anxious to get into the air again. This desire was not long denied us. The first day we were checked out in the Miles Master advanced trainers by seemingly bored Battle of Britain veterans, and within a week we were airborne in Hurricane Is which, too, had been through the Battle of Britain. Summer was ending but the weather was good and with the flat checker-board terrain spread away beneath the wings of the aircraft, life seemed marvellous indeed. The instruments and controls of the British machines were strange to us at first but we soon learned to master the illustrious hump-back fighters, although the accident and fatality rate at the OTU was alarmingly high. Like most who finally face war close up we seemed to develop the fatalistic point of view that we personally were not going to die in the debacle and so we treated it as a huge and precarious game. This mental adjustment, however, did not prevent each day from providing a certain amount of apprehension and anxiety.

As the autumn of 1941 approached and the clouds and fog were increasing above the Midlands, we completed the six-week course and were, in a loose sense, certified as fighter pilots. We were forthwith posted to operational units and I found myself, along with one of the other Americans, assigned to 71 (Eagle) Squadron. After a two-day leave in London's West End, which apparently was the meeting place for all services in those days, we boarded the train out of Victoria Station for RAF North Weald in nearby Essex. There was probably not another city quite like London in the war. The bombings and the blackout did nothing to restrict the revelry that the masses performed on a nightly basis, as if it were the last chance for hilarity and companionship. The Regent Palace Bar was probably the single most popular spot for the cast of thousands who then passed that way. An officers' bar, this was to become the general headquarters for most Eagle Squadron members when on leave.

Our blue dress uniforms still had the appearance of newness and when the train stopped at the North Weald station we were in high spirits because 71 Squadron was in the RAF's famous 11 Group, from whence most of the offensive sorties over enemy territory were being launched. We thought we were ready for action. 71 Squadron was the first of the three units in the RAF which were composed entirely of American volunteer pilots, and it was to achieve the distinction of being the highest scoring squadron in 11 Group for the month of October that year.

Our quarters were comfortable at North Weald and within a week we went on operations, though it was first necessary to be checked out on the Spitfire V which the Squadron was operating. The Spitfire was quite different from the Hurricane in many ways but we were soon assigned to convoy patrol duty [first operational flight in AB812 on 7 December 1941], which at best was a monotonous task where our worst enemy was the weather. However, it gave us the opportunity to become acquainted with the remarkable capabilities of the Spitfire and if the weather seemed bad that autumn, the devastating winter – which would be recorded as the most severe in two decades – was fast arriving. The fighter sweeps and bomber escort missions over enemy-held France that had occupied the summer and autumn months were cancelled because of the weather. The dangerous low-level sorties known as Rhubarbs were still authorised periodically as volunteer missions but the Wing activities that winter were sharply curtailed by Group Operations. The Rhubarbs, however, could always be counted on to provide unlimited excitement or tragedy, or both. The CO of 71 Squadron, Sqn Ldr Chesley Peterson, was an excellent leader and at 23 was the first American Squadron Leader in the RAF. Not a high-scoring ace by other standards, he was nevertheless an exceptional pilot and was to lead well over 100 missions before the Eagles were disbanded. His job was none the easier when the first snow fell. The pilot quality in 71 Squadron was basically good, including several pilots with exceptional potential, but the Eagles were conspicuous by the fact that they did not produce any really high scoring aces, though several were to reach this plateau while serving later with other squadrons.

When America entered the war there were rumors that we would be immediately transferred to the US Command. This theory proved to be laughably premature. American forces were, at that time, far from being ready for any actual operations in Europe and it was to be ten long months before the Eagle Squadrons as a unit would be absorbed into the USAAF as the 4th Fighter Group. The majority of Americans who served with RAF or Dominion air forces did not necessarily see duty with the Eagle Squadrons, but were in reality scattered among the many and diverse units and commands of the day. Most of these had transferred to US authority by the summer of 1943 but a few served out the entire war with British squadrons. Some who were with the Eagles at one time or another were posted out east – the Mediterranean or Middle East – before the mass transfer of the following autumn was effected.

Meanwhile, losses due to weather, accidents and Rhubarbs began to mount as we sat out that winter at RAF Martlesham Heath in Suffolk [to where 71 Squadron had moved], and when spring came around in the fateful year of 1942 we had learned that flying was no longer just fun. It was duty, survival and oft-times fear. At any rate the actions of the Eagle Squadrons during that first winter were forgiveably unillustrious, although 71 Squadron had, in January 1942, one of the first real encounters with the Luftwaffe's newly introduced FW190 which was rapidly replacing the Messerschmitt 109 on the Western Front.

If one remained at the Squadron for several months one was assigned a personal aircraft and by April I had acquired a Spitfire [BL287 XR-C] which I rather adolescently adorned with a Red Indian head to signify that I was, to a certain degree, of Sioux Indian ancestry. My father, born in 1889 in Indiana, was one half Irish and one half Sioux Indian [inevitably, due to this ancestry, Leo was known to his colleagues in 71 Squadron as The Chief]. I had an accident with my new machine a short time later during a high wind.

During this period [on 17 April 1942] I was involved in an interception of a Ju88 which had made a hit and run attack on a convoy east of the Suffolk town of Felixstowe. My companion, JJ Lynch, attacked from dead astern. I saw black smoke coming out of Lynch's engine and he pulled away to port, saying on the R/T that he had been hit*. Again I closed in, firing, until the bomber suddenly reared on its tail, hung quivering for a moment, then whipped over and dived straight into the sea. My own aircraft [BL287 XR-C] was hit but I just managed to return to Martlesham Heath with an almost empty tank [Leo had, in fact, opened his account a few weeks earlier while flying AB907 when, on 11 January 1942, he engaged a Ju88 off Lowestoft which he damaged before it managed to escape in the prevailing murky conditions: see Appendix I].

By April the large fighter sweeps resumed over the continent and 71 Squadron moved from Martlesham Heath to RAF Debden in Essex, and became part of 153 Wing. An interesting sidenote on this particular RAF Wing was that in July 1942 it was actually scheduled, as a token force, to go to Russia and participate jointly with the Soviet Air Force at the Battle of Stalingrad. The move had to be cancelled when the preceding convoy to Murmansk, which carried Spitfire IXs for the entire Wing, was almost totally destroyed on the run past Norway. There is no way to contemplate what might have happened or how different everything might have been had we gone out there that terrible year.

Fighter sweeps increased with the arrival of summer and varied with the whims of Fighter Command Operations. All of the squadrons in 11 Group were involved and Spitfires were generally employed in a bomber escort role or simply for fighter attrition. The German High Command was understandably preoccupied at this stage with the enormous campaign on the Eastern Front and the Luftwaffe force in the West was primarily relegated to defense squadrons which, although comparatively thin, were of a high quality as far as veteran flying personnel was concerned, and were unrelenting in their aggressiveness against the RAF strike missions. One of these German units in particular became quite familiar to us at the time and was known for the remainder of the war as the 'Abbeville Boys' [this was the Messerschmitt Bf109-equipped Jadgeschwader 26, based at Abbeville, south of Le Touquet on the Channel coast].

I, among others, was intrigued, somewhat naively, by the reported actions at Malta and in the Western Desert. I volunteered for an overseas posting at the end of July, along with another 71 Squadron pilot, Plt Off Art Roscoe, and received orders to report to Glasgow in Scotland. We said farewell to the Eagle Squadron and the same evening were on a train north. We had no idea of our new destination until after we boarded the aircraft carrier HMS *Furious* with the rest of the overseas contingent at Glasgow and were notified that we would be proceeding to Malta. The *Furious,* which was anchored in the Clyde, was to transport us to a point

---

* Leo's companion, Plt Off John Lynch, managed to reach the coast where he crash-landed his damaged aircraft, suffering facial injuries. Lynch was later posted to Malta where he commanded 249 Squadron, gaining the DFC and Bar for ten victories plus a further seven shared.

in the Mediterranean from where the new Spitfire Vs, which were stowed below decks, would take us on the final leg to the besieged island. It was the beginning of another part of the war for us, and was to be accompanied by hardships we had not been exposed to in England. *Furious* was a short-decked carrier which catered normally to Swordfish and Albacore biplane torpedo-bombers, and there was some concern about the Spitfires having enough running room to get off the flight deck, a theoretical problem that was soon solved by fitting the fighters with the powerful but sometimes faulty hydromatic propellers.

The carrier glided down the Clyde and quietly out to sea on the afternoon of 5 August 1942, escorted by the heavy cruiser HMS *Manchester*, and we felt a certain homesickness at leaving the UK and travelling once more toward the unknown. The group of 20 pilots [there were, in fact, 38 pilots aboard *Furious*] included the usual mixture of British and Commonwealth ranks and, as we headed south through the Irish Sea, we began temporarily to adopt the Navy life. By coincidence, the senior officer in the flight party was Grp Capt Churchill, who had been the first leader of the infant 71 Squadron in the waning days of 1940. Churchill, an excellent officer and personally a fine gentleman, was en route to a base commander assignment at Malta and would take the first section off the *Furious*. With only the company of the *Manchester* on the vast expanse of sea we continued southward without incident and three days later rendezvoused at Gibraltar with an awesome array of ships. The Malta convoy was codenamed Operation Pedestal, and in later years historians of World War II would connect its role in the relief of Malta to the major Axis setbacks in both the Mediterranean and North Africa.

On the night of 9 August the convoy slipped out of the shelter of Gibraltar and when the sun rose on the clear morning of the 10th, the spectacle which became visible in the early light was, in effect, extraordinary. The score of merchant vessels which were bound for the distant island fortress were in the center of an armada of fighting vessels, among which were five aircraft carriers including the US Navy's *Wasp*, two battleships, the *Rodney* and the *Nelson*, and untold numbers of outlying cruisers and destroyers. Oddly enough, the only participants in this famous flotilla who were actually supposed to land at Malta were the merchantmen and the Spitfires from *Furious*. Because of exposure to enemy air attacks, which could be hurled forth incessantly from bases on Sardinia and Sicily, the bulk of the powerful Navy escort would begin turning back for Gibraltar at the midway point of this perilous voyage. At the time, we Spitfire pilots knew nothing of the strategy and were aware only of our own departure hour and air route. As we settled into our cockpits, German high-level bombers were actually in the sky directly above us. The *Rodney*, which was close by the *Furious* at that moment, nearly blacked out the noontime sun with bursts from its anti-aircraft guns. Then, shortly before the third section was due off the windswept flight deck, the convoy came under a determined attack by U-boats and, as I lifted from the *Furious* in my Spitfire [EP410], four torpedoes struck the port side of HMS *Eagle* and, by the time we had formed the flight above the now-harassed convoy, the stricken carrier had disappeared beneath the blue surface of the sea.

Others ships, including the *Manchester*, were to sink that day in the same attack and, of the merchant freighters and tankers, only half would survive the next three days to dock in Grand Harbor at Valetta. We, however, were soon away from the unsettling scene at 20,000 feet, paralleling the seemingly peaceful coasts of Algeria and Tunisia until we cut across Cap Bon eastward to where the waiting island lay. Using most of our fuel, which included 90 gallons in external belly tanks, we landed on the main airfield at Luqa at four o'clock in the afternoon.

Two or three minutes after landing on Malta, we began to entertain the thought that we had made a mistake in applying for an overseas posting. Fate had, nevertheless, decreed it and here we would stay until we departed, one way or another. It was a thought that was not particularly aided in its absence of tranquility by the words of a suntanned and wild-looking Wing Commander who informed us, before we had hardly emerged from our cockpits, that 'you have two weeks to live!' This grim and unkind estimate of our remaining life span was based on a current theory that the average length of a fighter pilot's existence at Malta was a fortnight. Surrounded by a visible atmosphere of death on that small white island, with its incongruous surplus of churches and blasted stonework in the middle of the sea, we believed him. It turned out that for many who were there that day his statement was surprisingly accurate*.

Malta. All who served there would never forget it. They should have awarded a medal for merely arriving at Malta. I have never been to another place with such an atmosphere of doom, violence and toughness about it at first sight. Coming out from England as we did, the filth, flies, diseases and near starvation absolutely fascinated us, the more so because the interception missions were not in the least deterred by these handicaps. It was oppressive, it was in many ways a daily tragedy, one was always hungry – one tin of bully beef and two pieces of stale bread per day, sometimes supplemented by incredibly tasteless local vegetables. The tiresome repetition of this diet was almost as hard to endure as the shortage itself. One was often ill and almost everyone went a little crazy out there. It was a solitary British bastion between Gibraltar and Alexandria and its torpedo-bombers and MTBs were the only

---

* Of the 37 pilots who accompanied Leo to Malta from the *Furious*, nine would be killed in action within a few weeks including Grp Capt Churchill, one taken prisoner and four wounded. Among the latter was his American friend, Art Roscoe (see *Malta: The Spitfire Year, 1942* by Chris Shores, Brian Cull and Nico Malizia, published by Grub Street).

obstacle in the path of Rommel's supply line to Libya. The island refused
to die. It was the only piece of land in the war to be awarded a medal (the
George Cross) and it was to be acclaimed as the most bombed section of
earth in the world. The Spitfires, nightfighters and anti-aircraft batteries
were its sole defense and the Luftwaffe and Italians continued to
pressure the island with admirable persistency. Their failure to neutralize
Malta totally, however, was ultimately to be a significant factor in the
Axis defeat in North Africa.

On the second day I was assigned to 229 Squadron which was
stationed at Takali in the north-eastern sector. The other unit on this
airfield was 249 (Gold Coast) Squadron, whose membership boasted the
presence of George Beurling, a Canadian who was proving to be a
phenomenal air fighter. During heavy enemy activity we were scrambled
six times a day at this base, and we sat in our cockpits on standby, taking
off when a red flare was fired from the duty hut. The field was wide and
covered with white chalky dust and bomb splinters, and when we
refuelled after a scramble we just stayed in the aircraft. The bomb craters
that regularly pocked the landing area were usually quickly filled by
ground personnel, but attrition was high and the pilot casualty rate was
so serious that one never got to know everyone in his own squadron. I
had been promoted to Flying Officer at the beginning of the month, but
rank at Malta had nothing to do with one's designation in the air. We had
to start all over again as wingmen to those who already had experience
in the different type of tactics which were used out there, and it was not
unusual to see Flight Lieutenants, Squadron Leaders and even Wing
Commanders who were just out from the UK, flying No2 to veteran
Sergeant Pilots.

In a skirmish over St Paul's Bay the day after reporting to 229, my
machine was hit by fire from an Italian Reggiane fighter and I nearly fell
victim to the stories we had heard in England that the Italians were not
really competent at air combat. This analysis was not necessarily true at
Malta and some of the Macchi pilots especially were experienced and
dangerous adversaries. The Germans, though, had most of the élite
fighter pilots based in Sicily and thus was the enemy force that
essentially took the highest toll on the island defenders. The yellow-nose
Messerschmitts had to be shown considerable respect and, if one was not
constantly alert, he could easily become the prey of these cunning foes.
The enemy bombers with the most lethal abilities in the siege were the
Ju88s, which were generally utilized as dive-bombers against the
airfields and the harbor area. The Junkers had one consistent trait to
which they seemed forever faithful in that if they were intercepted before
they arrived above the island, they would jettison their bombs and turn
back, but if once they had started the run onto their selected target
nothing but a direct hit would stop them.

It was mostly sunny at Malta, and sometimes there was haze that seemed to exaggerate the murderous rays of the Mediterranean sun. One never became accustomed to the strain and the hunger out there and the only valid reason for not reporting for duty was going down with a case of sandfly fever. With it all, some of the most spectacular air battles of the war were fought above the devastated island. Because of the bombing hazard the Squadron pilots were quartered several miles from the Takali base on a hill overlooking the terrain that led to the sea beyond the airfield. We lived in one of the old two-story dwellings of stone construction that were standard on Malta, and the upper rear section of the edifice possessed a lengthy porch-like balcony which had a view of the sloping terraced fields below. When we were off duty we would sit out there in wicker chairs and watch the parachutes descending. Sometimes the Ju88s would peel off far above and we always thought they were coming straight at us.

I had arrived at Malta during a relatively quiet period and quickly became frustrated with the lack of activity, so one evening I decided to carry out a lone, unauthorized sweep over Sicily. The night was very bright with a full moon. The sortie was, however, diverted about 20 minutes after becoming airborne by a direct order over the R/T from Fighter Control to return immediately to Luqa – the only base then with adequate night operations facility. Upon landing at Luqa, I was greeted after I had alighted from the cockpit by Wg Cdr Grant [the Wing Commander Flying], and informed that I was, to phrase it kindly, confined to quarters. I was returned to Takali the following morning, under escort, and was further informed that I was grounded and confined to quarters until told otherwise. Everyone at Takali, with the exception of the interrogators, regarded the incident as funny, and such was the state of mind and atmosphere at Malta in those days, no one (except the Inquiry Board) ever asked why I did it.

I soon discovered that I was charged with conducting an unauthorized sortie (at night in a day fighter), unnecessary expenditure of ammunition – I had tested the guns over the sea because we had been having instances of cannon jamming – and unauthorized consumption of petrol. There were several other related charges, but the final upshot of the whole thing was that about three weeks later I received summary disciplinary action through HQ Med in the form of a transfer to the Middle East. So, by October, I was packed off to Egypt, flying out in a Dakota. Everyone on board was apprehensive about German long-range night fighters which were known to venture out from Crete and patrol the very air lanes which we were travelling. We landed at Cairo before dawn the next morning. Even with its intolerable swarms of flies, Cairo took on almost the aspect of paradise after Malta, most noticeably in the realm of abundant food and exotic places and activities. I soon learned, however, that the natives were universally despised by the British and Empire forces and this dislike was, in turn, reciprocated at every opportunity by the Egyptians.

All this became academic after I reported to the Almaza transit camp out beyond Heliopolis. For some curious reason – considering the wretched living and operating conditions at Malta – a transfer to a Western Desert unit was considered as being sent to a 'punishment' squadron! As it turned out, the 'punishment' squadron I was posted to was the prestigious and high scoring 92 (East India) Squadron of the Desert Air Force's 244 Spitfire Wing. However, when I arrived at the landing ground, the terrain rivalled that of a moonscape in its desolation and made even Malta appear attractive in retrospect.

Two days later the British offensive known as Second Alamein or, more popularly, the Battle of El Alamein, began. There was no time to be concerned about the flies and the heat. We lived in tents and I had hardly been introduced to the other pilots when, flying the same type of tropical Spitfire V as we had in Malta, I went on the first sortie [on 9 November 1942, flying EP657]. The ground fighting had proved to be predictably fierce and the Spitfires, which were ordinarily reserved for escorting the Kittyhawk and Hurricane fighter-bombers, were ordered onto strafing operations but were pulled off the duty within the week because of losses and heavy damage to the aircraft. On one of these low level missions near Sidi Barrani we were attacked from above by some Messerschmitts of JG27 and lost two of the Spitfires. As we returned to base on the deck there were burning hulks of armored vehicles and lorries nearly as far as one could see across the arid landscape. That same week Montgomery's Eighth Army broke completely through the enemy resistance and the long Axis retreat out of Egypt and across Cyrenaica and Tripolitania had begun. Many cold nights in the desert lay ahead.

As the Afrika Korps and what was left of the Italian forces withdrew, the Desert Air Force moved forward behind the army units. We usually occupied the former Luftwaffe landing grounds after they were technically cleared of mines. On the airfields immediately beyond Alamein there were hundreds of abandoned enemy aircraft in every form of dismal disarray. The strains of 'Lili Marlene' began to fade and die.

By mid-November 1942 we were nearing Tobruk and the Squadron was joined by another pilot who was to become a distinguished British ace, Flg Off Neville Duke. At the time that he arrived at 92 Squadron, which incidentally was a Battle of Britain unit and one of the highest scoring in the RAF, Duke had already completed one operational tour in the Middle East and had downed eight enemy aircraft. At the end of the campaign he would have raised that figure to 19 and would add even more in the Italian operations of the following year. I had the opportunity that autumn and winter to fly in company with him. As with George Beurling, I was forever impressed with the natural qualities he exhibited in air fighting; the keen instincts, the exceptional eyesight, the total co-ordination, qualities which as a whole were denied the average fighter pilot of that era. A middle-class Englishman, 21-year-old Duke was quiet and deceptively unassuming and at times displayed a sense of humor toward the absurd, as if laughing at the monumental farce in which fate had cast us.

In January 1943 the new year found us at Misurata in Tripolitania and during this period we were plagued by Messerschmitt fighter-bombers. They would come in low and fast and sometimes they would catch us without warning; when we did scramble in time we had to be quite cautious because they were always escorted by a high cover. We lost one pilot over the airfield because of this arrangement. When February arrived, 92 was stationed at Castel Benito and I had nearly completed my first operational tour. We were conducting escort missions to the Mareth Line in southern Tunisia and on one of these sorties I was attacked by a Messerschmitt, which admittedly I did not see, and hit in the head by a shell fragment. In a way the incident is somewhat strange in its own context. I was with four other 92 Squadron Spitfires and a couple from 601 Squadron on patrol south-west of the Mareth Line. We began to get a considerable amount of ground fire at about the same time someone reported 109s going into the sun at eleven o'clock. I had no sooner looked in this direction when I was struck in the right side of the head with what was later proved to be either 15mm or 20mm shrapnel. I didn't see anything and had no idea where it came from except that it sliced parallel from the top of my ear to my left eyebrow, slitting my helmet somewhat and cutting my goggle straps. I began to bleed profusely from that side and instinctively took evasive action in a sharp downward turn to port. The strange part was that I saw no other aircraft at the time, not even Spitfires let alone 109s. The other strange factor was that there seemed to be no other damage to the aircraft, as indeed was the fact as I found out later. At any rate I proceeded to our advanced base west of Tripoli where I landed and was greeted with a certain amount of curiosity and apprehension by the groundcrews. After being conveyed to a field hospital where a couple of pieces of shrapnel were still in the wound, I was transferred to a rear base hospital in Cairo where I remained for two weeks. By that time the wound was considered to be healing and there were no more shrapnel splinters to be removed although I was cautioned by one doctor that I had possibly received nerve-ending damage to some of the trauma leading to my right eye.

At Cairo in March I was finally discharged from the military hospital and was scheduled for an instructor's assignment at an OTU near Port Said. At the time I was approached by an American Colonel who was a

Leo was involved in two successful combats during January 1943. On the 7th, in a fierce dogfight with Bf109Gs of II/JG77 which cost 92 Squadron two Spitfires, he claimed one Messerschmitt probably destroyed while flying ER473. The following day, when flying EP788, he engaged a number of Bf109Gs ten miles west of Tamet and after a tough dogfight eventually shot one down into the sea.

liaison officer with General Brereton's US 9th Air Force Headquarters and induced to transfer to the USAAF. I was, to a certain extent, reluctant to leave British service because by that stage I had become immersed in the RAF tradition and the American procedures seemed quite foreign. However, a deadline had been set by the US authorities for RAF transfers that spring and, on the last day of March, I was released from the RAFVR and inducted into the Army of the United States (Air Corps) with the rank of Captain.

The 9th Air Force in the Middle East at the moment contained only one Fighter Group, the 57th (Black Scorpions) which was equipped with P-40 Warhawks and had served at the front since July 1942. We had escorted them at intervals when I was with 92 Squadron and they were later to figure prominently in what became known as the 'Palm Sunday Massacre' off Cap Bon in April 1943. I was initially assigned to this Group but before I reported back to Tunisia the orders were changed and I was returned to the US in the role of combat instructor. So ended my two years with the Royal Air Force and as I boarded the transport flight and said goodbye to the sights and smells of Cairo, many reminiscences occupied my thoughts. Though the British did not actually record missions by the number, I had participated in about 110 operational sorties since that first day with the Eagles at North Weald. Curiously, circumstances were to dictate that I would never return to operations for the remainder of World War II.

As it is with all who return from a journey, I was happy to arrive home again, but with the war had come changes and it was not outwardly the same country that I had departed in the summer of 1941. The conflict, of course, was not at the nation's doorstep as it was in Europe and Asia but the aura of war was everywhere and the military forces were esteemed by civilians to such a degree that as a former RAF combat pilot I suddenly found myself to be, however briefly, a celebrated curiosity.

The time I spent with the USAAF during the rest of the war was really an anti-climax after all the actions of the early years, but combat instruction on fighters in those days was not without its excitement and tragedy. I also met many of the American pilots who would play a vital part in the air war over Europe in the final phase. Assigned to the 81st Fighter Squadron of the 50th Fighter Group (cadre OTU) at Orlando, Florida, I settled rather awkwardly into the the new routine but I soon became accustomed to the much larger fighters (P-47 Thunderbolts) with which the Squadron was issued. In time I learned to like them, though they did not have the same qualities which attracted me to the Spitfire. The pilot training programme in the US had grown to mammoth proportions by 1943 and personnel turnover in the OTU courses was seemingly endless. An average loss of one pilot a week was considered normal and most of these training fatalities were usually related to midair collisions or while performing aerobatics at low altitude. The part played by instructors in these cadre units was both nerve-wracking and dangerous because of the high amount of hours flown daily on all sorts of missions in conjunction with accompanying inexperienced pilots. But my only serious confrontation with disaster in this category came as the result of colliding with a tree-top during ground-target gunnery practice. The Thunderbolts were so sturdy that I landed without any problem with a large portion of the tree embedded in the leading edge of the port wing.

I was joined at this unit, whose specific purpose it was to ready pilots for operations in the European Theater, by other fighter veterans including a few from the former China Volunteer Group, the Flying Tigers. When, in March 1944, the 81st itself was ordered to England (later to be involved in air cover for the D-Day landings), I was transferred to the 438th Fighter Squadron at Fort Myers, an organization that also flew P-47s and had a similar OTU programme, but I was then hospitalized for several months following an accident. Upon convalescing I was assigned to another Thunderbolt fighter unit (53rd Fighter Group) and was due for embarking back to the UK, but by then the war was dissipating to its termination in Europe. I did not wish to remain with the peacetime service, so I returned to civilian life. After the roar of the past five years there seemed to a deafening silence.

The immediate postwar years were, for many who had served, a period of sometimes difficult adjustment to civilian life. If not disillusionment, then certainly frustration became a daily experience. I stayed in the aviation field because I had no other trade, and after a time as a demonstrator for a light aircraft company in California, I supplemented my subsistence with employment as a crop-duster and by performing aerobatics at small town air shows with a pre-war Stearman biplane. I was pursuing this uncertain profession when, in the spring of 1948, the Palestine issue and the formation of the Jewish State of Israel came into world-wide focus. It seemed clear that after what had happened to the Jews in Europe during the war and by the fact that they were, in Palestine, surrounded by hostile Arab nations who had vowed their annihilation, that here was not only a political and military crisis but a moral issue that one could not, in conscience, ignore. It also became obvious after 14 May 1948 [the official date of the ending of the British Mandate in Palestine] that the Jews were in desperate straits in their lack of military aircraft and of qualified personnel with operational abilities. By the end of the first week of the escalating conflict I had offered my services by letter through the Jewish Agency in New York and on 30 May 1948 I was accepted as a [non-Jewish] foreign volunteer in the Israel Defense Forces.

PREAMBLE

When the Jewish national homeland of Israel became a reality in mid-May of 1948, the problems which had accumulated for the new State were manifold and formidable. Defense of the partitioned Palestine boundaries against attacks by Arab bloc countries, whose alliance advocated destruction of the Jews, was the immediate and primary concern – and containment of the invaders in the initial stage was due in large measure to the resourcefulness and individual courage of the meagre Israeli forces. The serious lack of advanced war material and of arms in general caused the situation to be critical during the first weeks, and determination became a virtue that was almost mandatory within the defense units. An absence of co-ordination among the Arab armies afforded some respite but the position of the emerging nation remained precarious as the month progressed. Although the UN had assigned a mediator and a force of peace-keeping observers to the Middle East in an attempt to settle the dispute and end the fighting, it was recognized that the ultimate security for the Jews lay in military strength.

In addition to external pressures, the new government was plagued from within by increasing dissension between Haganah* and the extremist Irgun Zvai Leumi* (IZL) faction. David Ben-Gurion's moderate Haganah, supported by the internationally active Jewish Agency for Palestine, was firmly established as the ruling body but there was an ever-widening ideological gap between the two political elements and there was no hint of reconciliation on the horizon. As the month of May continued, the problems demanded a rapid solution because it was not only victory or defeat at stake, but the survival of the Jewish nation itself. One of the pre-requisites to this survival was to build an air force.

---

* Haganah was the military arm of the Jewish Agency; Irgun Zvai Leumi (National Military Organization) was classified as a terrorist organization by the British, as was the breakaway Lohamei Heruth Israel (Fighters of Freedom of Israel), better known to the British as the infamous Stern Gang, named after its notorious founder Avraham Stern, killed in a police raid in 1942.

When April ended that spring and the termination of the British Mandate loomed, Haganah was faced with preparing for the defense of the Yishuv (the Jewish population in Palestine) against the impending threat of Arab air attacks. With no suitable warplanes available, the multitude of complexities inherent in organizing an air force from nothing became obvious and dismaying. The Jewish leaders knew that concerted efforts must be made to procure combat aircraft and experienced personnel from abroad. The foreign volunteers who responded during these crucial months were to become part of what can only be described as a gallant band.

At a time when the Allies of World War II were scrapping guns and planes, the British blockade of arms to Palestine prior to May 1948 made the delivery of any aircraft almost impossible. Although the American [and British] public was generally sympathetic to the Jewish cause, the United States government was strict in its enforcement of the embargo which forbade arms exports to belligerents and, mainly as a result of British pressure, most European countries followed suit.

Parked on airfields in the United States were thousands of war surplus aircraft which were being sold at a fraction of cost. A limited number of transport planes (C-46 Commandos) among these were secretly purchased by Haganah and flown out during May under Panamanian registry. The air cargo carriers which were an element of this episode were to prove providential in the months to come and were, in fact, to be the nucleus of the Israeli Transport Command.

The arms embargo by the Western powers, however, which they had foreseen, had prompted the realistic Israelis to search elsewhere for the vitally needed arms and machines. These provisions were to come from the newly formed Communist state of Czechoslovakia. A month before the Declaration, an underground purchasing mission had negotiated for some Messerschmitt fighters which the Czech factory at Prag-Cakovice had manufactured for the Germans during World War II. After the hostilities started in Israel, the question of how to get these machines to their destination was resolved by the decision to dismantle them and transport them inside the cargo carriers, thus at once solving the matter of secrecy and the dilemma of how otherwise to fly short-range fighters across thousands of miles of unfriendly European territory.

The first Messerschmitt to be sent to Israel in this manner was transported by a chartered American Skymaster (C-54) on the airlift route which became known as Operation Balak. In conjunction with the arrival of the initial fighters, the first group of foreign volunteer and Palestinian Jewish pilots, who had been hurriedly trained on the difficult-handling Messerschmitts at Budejovice, were returned to Israel. Czech technicians accompanied the early aircraft deliveries to supervise their re-assembly at the Israeli airbase at Aqir. The C-46s from the deal in the US, which were then arriving in Europe, were immediately put into service on the Balak run and, by the end of May, four of the Messerschmitts were operational. Israel's first fighter squadron was born.

From 15 May to 29 May, the date that the Messerschmitts went into action, Jewish airspace had been completely controlled by the Arab air forces. While it was true that the Syrians and Iraqis in the north and central sectors were rather primitive as far as air power was concerned, the Royal Egyptian Air Force operating from the south possessed some of the requirements for a modern air war. Trained and partly supplied by the RAF, the Egyptians had, on the eve of the invasion of Israel, two fighter squadrons composed of 40 Spitfires and two Dakota (C-47) squadrons. Some of the Spitfires had been converted to fighter-bombers and most of the Dakotas were designated for bombing duty as well. The Egyptian base at El Arish in the Sinai became the operational headquarters for the air attacks on the Jewish State.

At the beginning of the conflict on 15 May, the Israelis had, in opposition to the Egyptian force, three flights of light aircraft which were known as the Palestine Flying Club. The majority of these planes were ex-RAF Auster liaison machines and though they were useful in carrying supplies and supporting the isolated settlements, in any type of sustained action they were at the mercy of the Egyptian pilots.

The arrival of more foreign volunteer pilots and the presence of the Messerschmitts were factors that were soon to change the scenario. On 3 June 1948 the Israelis won the first of the aerial victories which in time would produce a measure of air superiority never to be seriously threatened.

* * * * *

This book is a personal account of the author's experiences in Israel's War of Independence, based upon notes maintained at the time, and is essentially a story of the founding of an Air Force and of those who served in it during the first desperate year.

Leo Nomis

CHAPTER I

THE VOLUNTEERS

The noontime sun glares from the pale architecture and dances on the blue surface of the Mediterranean beyond the sea wall. The air is warm and smells of the sea. The city has a holiday atmosphere. Crowds fill the cafes along the beach road and there is the sound of laughter. There are old men in white shirts. They walk slowly and look at women in faded dresses bargaining with shopkeepers in the shade of doorways. But mostly there are soldiers in desert khaki. Sometimes the soldiers are walking arm-in-arm with girls who are also soldiers and always there is laughter. The rifles slung casually, the holstered pistols, the military vehicles on the streets taking nothing from the carnival mood. Colored streamers snap briskly in the breeze above a pavilion near the beach and bathers lie on the ground. It is Tel Aviv in the summer of 1948 and everyone knows that the war is not far away.

I sit at the sidewalk cafe with Bieberman. We drink Palestinian cognac and watch the sunlit street that passes in front of the Gallim Yam. We are volunteers. At the tables about us there are many people and most of them are volunteers too. Music comes from a gramophone inside the cafe. We listen to the music. We have just arrived in the city. It has been two weeks since the day at the Jewish Agency in New York. Now the sea at Tel Aviv sparkles before us. Time and distance have merged the days together – the journey to Rome and Haifa and the ride to Petah Tiqva with the others...

* * * * *

It was humid in New York and at the Jewish Agency office on 58th Street there was a crowd and we had to wait around for a while. I meet Bieberman. We aren't in the same group but we talk and then we are interviewed by the Agency man with the thick-lens glasses. He gives us some subsistence money and assigns four of us to a room at Claridges. Bieberman had taken a train from Cleveland and I was with the boisterous Schwimmer party from California which had arrived at

Millville, New Jersey, in one of Haganah's surreptitiously purchased Constellations. Everything had been rumor and when we had come up from Philadelphia that morning there was a lot of talk about what was happening in Israel. Everyone still calls it Palestine.

Bieberman is slightly built and he has a thin, well-trimmed moustache which makes him appear dapper. At the hotel he smiles politely and listens to Berger and Goodman. We had ordered drinks in the room and the ice is noisy in the glasses. There are 20 volunteers going through New York in this group and as soon as someone's passport is cleared they are sent out to Rome on the first available airline. The speculations persist about what lies ahead of us. Bieberman is an aircraft engine mechanic. Most of the others are groundcrew also but the curly-haired Berger is a bomber pilot. He and the thin-faced, bespectacled Goodman are talking about the situation. Goodman says that when he volunteered on the West Coast he didn't know whether the Jews even had any airplanes. Berger laughs. He says that Schwimmer has already smuggled some transports out of the States. Goodman looks unimpressed and I think of my meeting wih Al Schwimmer. Smiling and unworried, the heavy-set Schwimmer had ushered me aboard the Constellation at Burbank [California] after the Agency connection in Los Angeles had sent me out there. He had looked at a paper he was holding and, grasping my hand, said he was always happy to see fighter pilots.

The placid-mannered Schwimmer had been a flight engineer with the US Transport Command and after World War II he had formed an aircraft renovating company at Burbank. When, in the spring of 1948, it became obvious that the soon-to-be-declared State of Israel was going to have to obtain aircraft at any cost, Schwimmer approached the Haganah purchasing commission through the Jewish Agency. His proposal, which had initial success, was to buy up surplus transport planes and fly them out to Israel by a multitude of routes after 14 May. The machines subsequently were to be of vital significance in the early operations and most of them served the Israeli military command throughout the war under Panamanian registry. Schwimmer's role of procuring aircraft and crews in the US was to continue into the first months of the summer but it was a precarious role at the time and was soon to have its final performance.

None of us know anything for certain and we are travelling toward the unknown. There is no reason to ask why anyone volunteered. We are all nearly the same age and we are products of World War II and have all endured the disillusionment of its aftermath. It is simple. The Jews are fighting for a homeland in Palestine. They are alone. They can use all the help they can get. Goodman swirls the liquid around in his glass. Berger says he heard that the Jews have German Messerschmitts in Israel. They are getting them from Czechoslovakia. Bieberman looks at me and I look down at the design in the carpet. Two years with the Royal Air Force and another two with the Americans. I look up at the others. We are going to a different war now.

We stay in New York for three days. When Bieberman and I report to the Agency office on the third morning they tell us to be ready to leave that evening. They give us tickets to Rome on BOAC and hand us our passports with Italian visas stamped in them. We don't see Berger or Goodman again. At La Guardia that night we wait to board the overseas flight and we buy a newspaper and read that the UN has managed some kind of ceasefire in Palestine. The evening is warm and we are in shirt sleeves. It is 10 June 1948.

The Jewish Agency for Palestine, originally inaugurated under the British Mandate to mediate Jewish affairs, was the single most efficient body in organizing the immigration of the foreign volunteers to the new State of Israel. With the approach of the summer, expediency in transporting the volunteers to the war was its basic task. Nobody told us what to expect when we got there.

* * * * *

The stars in the dark void over the Atlantic shine brightly and I watch them through the window of the plane. Bieberman sleeps in an aisle seat. Part of the past comes into my thoughts and I remember the other war. The campaigns in Europe and the Mediterranean and North Africa. I look away from the window. I have never been to Palestine before.

We stop over at Bermuda and when we get to Paris the next afternoon we have an hour to collect our bags and change planes for Rome. The airport at Orly is packed with summertime travellers and on the Rome flight the passenger cabin is full. We sit in some rear seats and drink from the bottle of Hennessy we bought at Orly. Bieberman says there is political friction in Israel. The Zionist extremists want a hand in the government but Haganah won't have anything to do with them. Bieberman lights a cigarette. He says that Irgun is too radical. They were underground fighters against the British and a lot of Jews are afraid of them. He says there might be trouble. This observation was to be surprisingly prophetic.

It is night and the city is glittering with lights when we land at Rome. We go through Customs and after we pass the line of uniformed Italians we are met by an Agency man and one of the Haganah contacts. Our passports are returned and we go into the airport lobby. The Israelis are professional and we are told that arrangements have been made for us at the Hotel Roma. The Agency man gives us each 20,000 Lire. Bieberman smiles and the Haganah contact looks at him and says its not worth very much in US currency. They put us in a taxi because they have to stay and meet others and they give us a card with a telephone number on it. The taxi rushes down the boulevards and after we survive the ride into town we feel that we have nothing more to fear from the future.

For some reason we are in Rome for five days and, as in New York, we are told little. They say we will find out in Israel. The postwar influx of tourists and students has converged on the city and the cafes are crowded. We spend most of the time in the cafes or drinking cognac in the hotel room. The second evening, at sunset, the room is filled with soft light and at the table near the window I pour a drink from the bottle and think of why we are in Rome. The incongruities that have taken form in the Palestine war seem almost laughable. The Egyptians with air supremacy! In the Cairo of 1942 the idea of the Egyptians as fighters would have been funny. And the Jews flying Messerschmitts! My mind wanders and other thoughts intrude. 1943. I was shot down by a Messerschmitt 109 over the Mareth Line in Tunisia. I drink the cognac and set the glass in the center of the table. Beyond the window the distant rooftops are all tinted red.

On the fifth morning the Agency man is waiting in the lobby of the Roma. He gives us the usual 20,000 Lire and says that we will be leaving for Haifa tomorrow. The street sounds are loud through the open doors and the Agency man beckons us closer. He says we are not over here for fun. In the afternoon we go to a cafe for lunch. We are finishing the meal when Stein comes in. Stein is one of the mechanics who was with us in New York. He pulls out a vacant chair and sits down. He says he has heard the story on the Messerschmitt deal from one of the volunteer transport pilots. Bieberman orders ice cream. Stein is swarthy and has a bull neck and he says that the Israelis bought 25 Messerschmitt fighters from Czechoslovakia and are delivering about four of them a week to the airfield at Aqir [see Appendix II]. They are transporting them in the C-46s that Schwimmer smuggled out of the States. Stein has more information. He says the arrangements for the Messerschmitts were made two months ago but they couldn't get them down until May. A fighter squadron has already been activated in Israel which consists mostly of foreign volunteers and eight of the Messerschmitts are now in service. Stein says that the commander of the fighter squadron is a Palestinian Jew who shot down two Egyptian bombers over Tel Aviv on 3 June. Stein stands up. He has to go because in the evening he is travelling to Czechoslovakia. He is going to take a course on the modified Junkers engines. He says that the Jewish pilots are trained on Messerschmitts at Budejovice. He wants to know where we are going. We tell him Haifa.

At Urbe airfield on the outskirts of Rome the morning is clear. We take our bags from the taxi and go into a wooden flight shack. Our passage is booked on an unscheduled airline called Pan African which is due out for Athens and Haifa. Inside the shack we meet Meyer Bernstein and an Israeli girl, Sarah. Bernstein is from Chicago and he was a machine-gunner on heavy bombers in World War II. He has been in

Rome for a week but we have not seen him before. Sarah is a Palestinian Jewess who is on a special assignment in Rome and is returning to Israel. Her Haganah service job is with the airborne medical corps and she has been asked to escort us as far as Tel Aviv. Sarah is quiet and plain and she is wearing a military blouse over a light skirt. She sits down in one of the corner chairs. The rest of us go outside and stand in front of the shack in the morning sunlight.

Bernstein is tall and dark and he displays a certain nervousness. He points down to the far end of the airfield. He say that is where Beurling was killed on 20 May. Beurling, a Canadian Gentile, was flying one of the Norseman reconnaissance planes out to Israel and when he took off the aircraft blew up and became a ball of fire, and it crashed into the middle of the runway. Bernstein waves his arms. He says it could have been sabotage. I look over toward the runway. There is still a charred spot there. I look away. I think of Malta that terrible summer [1942] when we never had enough to eat. We were in the RAF then. Beurling was the leading ace out there and he was young and blond and skinny, and everyone called him Screwball.

The flight crew arrives. They are British and they are laughing about something. Without knowing what it is, we laugh too. The aircraft for the trip is a dirt-streaked DC-3 parked down the line. Some mechanics are still working on it.

An hour later we leave Rome behind and climb toward the Adriatic. Bieberman and I sit together and Bernstein and Sarah have the seat in front of us. There are five other passengers but none of them speak to us and all of them are looking out the windows. Bernstein talks for most of the journey. He asks Sarah what she thinks about the ceasefire. She speaks so softly we can't hear her answer. No one thinks the ceasefire will last. Both sides are violating it every day.

Haifa appears off the port wing in the late afternoon. It has the look of all Middle East cities, white in the lowering sun. The transport cuts across the harbor and there are ships at the docks and then we come around to the south and sink onto the chalky surface of the airfield. We are in Israel.

It soon becomes evident that the British are still here. When we arrive at the line in front of the white Customs building there is a British sentry on duty near the entrance. The engines become silent and everyone moves to the rear door. We take the bags from the empty seats and Bernstein asks Sarah what the British are doing here. Sarah smiles and looks at her watch. She says they have authority at the port and the airfield because they are guarding the oil refineries in the north. We get out of the plane and pass by the sentry. He is tanned and his shirt and shorts and beret are dusty. He has flat blue eyes and he glances briefly at us when we go in. His rifle, which has a short bayonet fixed to it, is planted in the dirt at a forward angle and he stands with feet apart. We

walk inside and Sarah takes our passports to a long counter where some
Israelis are busy checking papers. We look at one another. We seem out
of place. Our American slacks are baggy and Bieberman has on a white
dress shirt. A khaki-clad Customs man is speaking with Sarah. They
speak in Hebrew. We don't know what they are saying because none of
us understands Hebrew. Sarah comes over with our passports and says
there is transportation outside to take us to a military hostel. We look
inside the passports. They are not stamped.

We ride to the hostel in the back of a lorry that swerves through
narrow streets and up hills for 20 minutes. The driver is a young Jew in
an undershirt. When we get to the hostel we discover that it is an old villa
in the eastern section. There are two large wings to it and wide steps lead
up to a terrace. There is an untended garden on one side. Sarah stays in
the truck and goes around to the womens' compound. Dusk is over the
city when we take our bags and go up the steps. The air is warm.

Inside we enter an enormous room that is full of talking people. Most
of the occupants are lying on straw pallets on the floor. We put the kit in
a corner which is already piled high with personal gear of every
description. Everyone in the room is in various stages of undress.
Bernstein motions to one who is reclining in only a pair of shorts and
asks him what this place is. The one in the shorts leans on his elbow. He
says this is a transit camp for foreign volunteers.

We find the mess hall and get a tin plate of lentils and a piece of rye
bread and take seats at a wooden table. The mess hall is crowded. We sit
across from two South African Jews who have been here for a day. They
know more than we do. The room is illuminated by shaded overhead
lights and all of the windows are open. The South Africans ask us what
we do. We tell them. They smile. They say that they are here to join the
Palmach. They are refering to the name given the Haganah front-line
defense units. One of them says that there are volunteers here from all
over the world. The other one says he saw an Oriental Jew yesterday.
Though it is night we have to wave flies away from the food. Bieberman
brushes violently at one. Bernstein says that we are from the States. The
South Africans smile and say they have already noticed that. We finish
the meal and get up. The South Africans continue to smile at us. Their
tropical army shirts are wrinkled and show damp streaks down the back.
We go out and near the mess hall entrance they are selling seltzer water
for five mils. We don't have any Palestine money. Bieberman buys three
bottles for a 25 cent piece.

Some of the lights have been turned off by the time we find vacant
pallets. We lie down and take off our shoes. Ceiling rafters travel the
length of the white-washed walls and I stare up at them for a while. It
seems a long time since morning.

We awaken at daybreak. It is not voices that wake us but the flies
alighting on our faces and feet. The windows at the far end of the room

are open and screenless. Many of those in the room are over on the southern side where there is a wash trough and latrines. The early light shows through the windows and it is already hot. Bernstein is four pallets away but Bieberman has the one next to me. I look at Bieberman. He is sitting up and holding his hands to the side of his head. I get up and make my way to where we left our gear and change into some khakis. I change leaning against the wall. I watch the scene. There are rich and poor, good and bad here. They are all veterans of some war, some army, some oppression. Survivors of concentration camps are here. Nice Jewish boys from affluent families are here. Jews from the ghettos and from every section of any city are here. Christians are here. It doesn't matter who anyone is or who they were – what matters is that they are here. They are volunteers.

We have some tea and bread and then walk out to the terrace. The bright rays of the morning sun flash through the leaves of the trees in the garden. Bernstein joins us and in a few minutes Sarah comes around through the garden. Bernstein asks her what we are supposed to do. Bieberman is still wearing the same clothes as yesterday and Bernstein has on a bright orange polo shirt. Sarah smiles weakly. She says there is a jeep here to take us to Tel Aviv. There is something about her which causes one to feel sorry for her without knowing why.

When we get down to the road with the kit there are lorries parked on the embankment. Some are already loaded with people and they shout back and forth between the vehicles. A jeep is near the head of the line and Sarah motions us in. The driver has a creased, brown face and he is wearing a tattered British Army beret. He speaks English with a heavy Hebrew accent. We all get in and Sarah sits in front and we lunge out in front of the trucks and curve down the hill. We go behind the city and onto a sloping road and we can see the oil storage tanks to the north. The sun has climbed higher and it is warm on our backs as the jeep turns out toward the coast. We come to a stop where the road intersects the Haifa-Tel Aviv highway near Cape Carmel. Off to the right are rows of barracks. The road has been rushing past and I don't see the checkpoint until we halt at the barricade. Bernstein is talking and Sarah turns and motions us to be quiet. Four British soldiers have emerged from an open hut next to the barrier. Three of them have tommy-guns on slings and the other is an officer who has a revolver in a holster. The officer's mouth forms a contemptuous smile which curls downward and the faces of the others are blank. Their appearance is tough and unfriendly and when I see the green berets I whistle under my breath. The British must consider the Haifa area a priority to have the Royal Marine Commandos down here. We are close to the sea and I look across the beach and far out over the blue water. The sky is bright and some gulls are settling on the sand where the tide has made a wide arc. I don't look at the British commandos. It is a different time. Another country.

The officer wants to see the destination papers. The driver looks in a dusty map case on the floor of the jeep and hands a folded chit to the Englishman. The officer, still smiling, looks at it and makes a complete circle of the vehicle. He seems amused with the situation. He returns the paper and turning his back, thumbs us on. One of the soldiers impassively raises the barricade arm and we pass through to the open highway.

On the south road the sea stretches away to one side and inland the brown hills rise beyond the coastal plains. We pass Israeli lorries but the traffic is not heavy and at midday we stop at the beach town of Natanya. We park on a narrow street behind some army trucks and the driver produces a cardboard box containing knishes. One of the Haganah soldiers in the lorry ahead of us yells in Hebrew. The jeep driver makes a gesture and pushes his beret to the back of his head. He gets out and goes into one of the stores across the street. The store has a sign in Hebrew and English. When the driver comes back he has some bottles of seltzer. We eat and drink and we stay in the town for an hour. We can hear the rolling of the surf beyond the beach front. It is hot. Sarah says that the Arab salient is across from us at Tulkarm. The enemy is only ten miles away.

We pull out of Natanya and continue down the coast toward Tel Aviv. Several times we see people in Arab dress tending goats beside the highway. I look over at Bieberman. He shrugs. The terrain becomes flatter and we swing eastward on a dirt road. It is afternoon and on both sides the ground is shaded by a line of trees. We pass a village that has seen fighting. There are heaps of rubble about and, farther along, a burnt-out vehicle. A larger town lies ahead. It is Petah Tiqva. Before reaching the town we turn onto a road that is bordered by an olive grove. Behind the olive grove are some low white-washed buildings. The tyres of the jeep throw out a trail of dust as we turn through an open barbed-wire gate into a large compound. We are waved to a stop by an Israeli sentry in worn British fatigues. We are at the Haganah security barracks at Tel Litvinsky.

The compound is not as crowded as the hostel was and we drive around to an administration hut where we are met by a Haganah official. The Israeli has thin legs revealed by his tropical shorts and he is bald. He indicates that we are to take our kit to the nearby barracks room. The motor of the jeep continues to run and we get out. The driver has one foot propped against the dashboard. Sarah says goodbye. They are going on to Tel Aviv and when she leaves in the fading afternoon light she looks back for an instant and then the jeep disappears behind the trees.

The barracks are hot. We are assigned cots and Bieberman sits on the edge of one and stares out at the compound through a window. Half-naked men are lying on some of the cots and others are coming in from an outside shower beyond the rear door of the barracks. We go out and wash.

Before the evening meal we sign papers. We sit at a narrow table in the administration hut and sign the rules and regulations of the Haganah military forces. When we sign them the bald Israeli gathers the papers and takes them over and puts them on a bridge table that is being used as a desk. He looks at us. He has a naturally cynical expression but he also has an indefinable quality which causes him to be likable. He says our passports were not stamped at Haifa so as far as anyone else is concerned we are not here. He smiles wryly. He says that since we are serving with the Haganah forces we are, militarily, Israelis and we will report to Service Headquarters in Tel Aviv tomorrow. He nods and we get up and we all smile automatically and we go out and find the mess hall. After dark we lie on the cots in the barracks and we talk for a while and Bernstein wishes he was back in Chicago.

In the morning the olive trees shimmer in the rising heat of the day and we wait beside the barracks for transportation. Five others are also waiting and everyone is dressed in a different combination of desert khaki. We are the only American volunteers in the group. A lorry stops near the administration hut and we walk over to it. The lorry is an open-back British type with a gun swivel on top of the cab and the windshield is covered with a film of dust. There are four people in the rear section already and we climb up over the tailgate with the others. Bernstein is the last one and he hands the bags to us and then vaults up into the back. The driver has a handkerchief tied around his head. He is wearing sunglasses and he leans from the cab and talks in Hebrew with someone in front of the hut. In a moment the gears grind and we lurch toward the gate and out of the compound.

The distance to Tel Aviv is not far but we stop three times to pick up hitchhikers. When we get to the suburbs the truck is jammed with people and equipment. Soldiers, girls, rifles, knapsacks. I sit next to Bieberman against the side railing. Bernstein is standing at the front near a dark-haired girl whose skirt is too short. He is trying to talk above the rushing wind. No one is wearing any insignia or rank and there is a shortage of headgear. I look at the rifle someone has propped on the railing. It is a German Mauser.

Through the spaces in the side I watch the streets pass. The streets are tree-shaded and the structures are neat and symmetrical. The sun is so bright that the shadows beneath the trees look black. We move through the suburbs and into the congested activity near the beach front. The traffic is heavier here but no one seems to slow down. We turn off into a motor pool area near the sea wall and everyone jumps down and merges with the crowd. We take our kit and jump down also. Across the beach road we can see the water and the salt spray drifts over to us. The driver comes around from the front. He points to a large grey building a half block away. He says that is the Yarkon Hotel. The Yarkon is the Service Headquarters in Tel Aviv.

At the sandbagged main entrance to the Yarkon the sentry can see that we have just arrived. He waves us in. The first floor is crowded and we leave our gear at the doorway and try to find someone who can tell us where to report. The tiled walls are cool but the air is heavy inside and perspiration is beginning to roll down the side of Bieberman's face. There are a lot of volunteers standing around and Bernstein questions some of them. I look at the crowd. Many are wearing side arms and some have the holsters but no guns. The sound of voices is loud. We are directed to the second floor by one of the American volunteers who had arrived yesterday. He wants to know if we have much patience.

The hotel rooms have been converted into offices. Some are double offices and none of them have any identification on the doors. We wait in the white-tiled hallway for two hours. We wait in a line of volunteers and everyone tries to make jokes and no one knows what they are talking about. When we get into the office we are issued a handwritten Hebrew identification card and a book of meal tickets and then we are sent to a second desk for some Palestine currency. The two Israelis at the desks go about the business methodically and a girl with short hair is counting the money. The room is not large and there are too many people packed into it and sounds from outside are coming in through the north windows. We are assigned temporary quarters in Tel Aviv and they tell us to report to the Air Force section in the morning. We get out of the office and into the hall and Bernstein wants to go back and ask more questions. Bieberman and I leave and go out into the summer air and find the Gallim Yam and drink cognac.

The Gallim Yam Cafe was a second home to many of the foreign volunteers that June and it was to become so for us in the days that followed. Across the sea wall on the beach road, it was a block from Headquarters and its bar and tables were always occupied. Some of the outside tables were shaded by red and white umbrellas and when the breeze came in off the water it passed all the way through the open bar. There was music and laughter at the Gallim Yam and sometimes there was sorrow.

We are at the Yarkon early the next day. The hour does nothing to diminish the size of the crowd inside. Bieberman and I are billeted in a small hotel near Allenby Road and we have already had a breakfast of sardines and a glass of tea at the Gallim Yam. Bernstein was sent to a room in a pension house behind Ben Yehuda Street. We have not seen him today. On the third floor at Headquarters there is another line of volunteers at the Air Force screening office. When we go in, an official is at a desk that is piled with papers and he has an accent like Sarah. He tells us to be patient – it will be another day before we can be processed. He says to go see the sights and report in tomorrow. He writes our names down in Hebrew. We go back to the Gallim Yam and find a table near the sidewalk. Bieberman looks at his hands and I watch the blue-green breakers roll in behind the sea wall. At Headquarters we heard that the Egyptians had advanced to Isdud before the ceasefire. Isdud is 25 miles from Tel Aviv.

The noon crowd begins to arrive and we order cognac. The tea we had been drinking during the morning hours remains unfinished in the glasses. Two American volunteers sit down in the extra chairs at the table. A waiter brings our drinks and Bieberman pays for them with one of the Pound notes we were alloted. The American Jews eye Bieberman's stateside clothes. They order beer from the waiter. They are young and dressed in khaki and their teeth appear exceptionally white against the tan of their faces. They receive their beer and they drink and say they have been in Israel since the end of May. They are stationed at the airbase at Lydda, ten miles south-east of Tel Aviv, above the dangerous Latrun Junction. They say the town was taken from the Palestinian Arabs the first week of the war. They say the fighting will start again soon. We tell them that we just got here. The volunteers laugh and talk about the problems they had and say we will have them too. They are with the groundcrew at Lydda and they say the Messerschmitt squadron is farther south at Aqir.

Bieberman goes to the bar and gets two more steins of beer and brings them to the table. The volunteers smile. They begin to tell us stories about the Egyptian fighter-bomber raids. They say two soldiers were killed near the sea wall not far from where we were sitting. They say that the bodies were mangled and were not removed for a while and a lot of flies had gathered. Bieberman looks at me. His mouth is turning upward on one side in a twisted smile. The groundcrewmen say that there haven't been any daylight raids since the two Dakotas were shot down. That was over two weeks ago. They say that Mordecai Alon shot them down and that he is the first air hero of Israel. I look down toward the beach. The war is little more than a month old. One of the volunteers is describing the Dakota incident. He says the Dakotas bombed the central bus station. They simply rolled the bombs out of the side door of the transport plane. Then a Messerschmitt had appeared in the sky. The Dakotas tried to get away but both were shot down. One crash-landed beyond Jaffa and the other caught fire and went into the sea. The volunteer lifts the beer stein. He says that everyone was cheering in the streets.

I was to hear the story in detail in the months to come. How only one of the Messerschmitt fighters had been serviceable at Aqir that morning of 3 June. One Messerschmitt for the air defense of the new State of Israel. The commanding officer of the just activated Israeli fighter squadron took off down the long hot runway of the advanced base some time after the Dakotas were reported coming up the coast from El Arish. The CO is the Palestinian Jew, Mordecai Alon. The Egyptians had appeared unconcerned and methodical. The fact that they were continuing the use of unarmed and unescorted transports as bombers not only displayed an ill-advised contempt for the Israeli defenses, but indicated very uninformed Intelligence sources. The Dakotas reached Tel Aviv and rolled their bombs out and killed some Jews. They were returning home when the Messerschmitt intercepted them.

When the Egyptians became aware of the Israeli fighter's presence they took separate courses toward the south but, climbing above them, the faster Messerschmitt attacked the nearest Dakota and sent it crashing earthward. Mordecai Alon was hampered by the fact that only two machine-guns on the fighter were operating, but it didn't make any difference. The second Dakota crossed the coastline and the Israeli plane closed in behind and fired. A bright flame appeared beneath one of the wings of the Egyptian aircraft. The blaze grew and enveloped the wing and everyone in the streets below could see how bright the flame looked against the blue of the sky. The doomed machine rolled down toward the calm surface of the sea and pieces began to fall from the fiery wreckage. A plume of water and spray and black smoke briefly marked the place where it disappeared. They had met their fate and the drama had unfolded in the cloudless sky above Tel Aviv before ten thousand pairs of eyes. It was a turning point.

In the afternoon we walk back to the Yarkon and we see Sam Lewis coming around the sandbags at the sentry post. Sam Lewis is the pilot who took the Constellation into Millville on the New York run from Burbank the first week of June. He remembers me and smiles. We stand to one side of the Headquarters entrance to avoid the flow of people. Lewis says that the same Constellation is down at Aqir. He is going back to Czechoslovakia in the evening and he is in a hurry to get over to the Park Hotel. He says that Schwimmer was in Miami and that Goodman and Berger are at Zatac.

After Lewis leaves we stand in front of the Yarkon. We are wondering what to do when Bernstein comes out. He says he has his swimming trunks on under his clothes and he wants us to go down to the bathing beach with him. We all walk to the north end of the sea wall where it slopes into a wide stretch of sand. There are others there but it is not really crowded and we sit on the sand. The sand is hot and the tide rushes in farther down. Foam from the waves glides inward and then recedes. The breeze sometimes carries a trail of mist from the tops of the incoming breakers. People splash in the surf. Bernstein takes off his trousers and shirt and begins to sun himself. He received the same news as we did at the Yarkon except that it was embellished by the information that they didn't have a bomber for him to be a machine-gunner in yet. But he is optimistic and cheerful because he has heard a rumor that some B-17s might be smuggled in from the States, and they are considering sending him up to the airfield at Ramat David near Nazareth where they are planning to organize a bomber squadron.

Bieberman and I sit on the sand and watch the bathers. Bernstein goes in the water and when he comes out he starts a conversation with a girl sitting nearby. She comes over and joins us and she can tell that we are volunteers before Bernstein informs her of the fact. The girl is laughing. Her name is Ruth. She is wearing a black bathing suit and she is eighteen years old. She is a sabra. All of the Palestinian Jews are called sabras. Bernstein introduces us. The girl laughs again. She has a nice laugh.

We lie on the soft, flat surface and talk. I can see the jetty at Jaffa curving out into the blue water down the coast. Sunset is near and in a little while Ruth says that she has to go. She wants us to come and meet her parents who have an apartment over beyond Rothschild Boulevard. Bieberman doesn't want to go but Bernstein does, and he and Ruth insist. We all stand up. Ruth ties a skirt around her waist and Bernstein gets dressed and we walk back to the sea wall. Some of the shops and cafes along the beach front are already showing dim lights from the interiors. There is only a partial blackout in effect in Tel Aviv and on Allenby Road a lot of people are on the sidewalks. We pass two cinemas and both are showing Eddie Cantor films. Most of the time we have to run across the streets because of speeding vehicles. We turn up a side road and come to a block of flats with trees in the front yard. Ruth and Bernstein are walking ahead and when we get to the door of the second floor apartment the parents smilingly greet us and gesture us in.

Bieberman looks at the mezuzoth on the door frame as we pass through into the main room. The place is small and has old leather furniture, and there are old vases on the tables. We all seat ourselves at a round lamplighted table in the center of the room. The mother is frail and courteous and the father is courteous too. He has sallow skin and he limps when he walks. They insist that we have some cakes and sweet wine, and while it is served they all talk. The father is a watchmaker and has a shop off Allenby. They had the foresight to get out of Germany in the twenties and Ruth was born in Palestine. So was one of their sons. He is serving with the infantry at Jerusalem. The father pours more wine. He says he was in the British Army with the Jewish Brigade and he was wounded in Italy in 1943. He joined the Haganah Palmach in 1946 but had to give it up the following year because of his leg wound. He says they had too few weapons on account of the British blockade. Bernstein asks him about Irgun. The father and the wife don't change expressions. They shrug. Then the wife says that her family was killed by Hitler. There is a silence for a moment. Ruth gathers the empty plates. She says she is going to join the army next month.

We are back at the hotel. The single room is neat and the two beds are close to the floor. There is a wash basin in one corner. The toilet is outside on the ground floor. From the second-story balcony we can look out on the street below. It is quiet now. Bieberman switches on the lamp between the beds and we talk about what the father said and how all the Jews here are convinced they will win. We have prepared for bed when

Bieberman wants to go down to the Gallim Yam for some ice cream. We go back out.

The street is empty when we walk down toward the beach front. We can hear the surf hissing at the bottom of the road and then we walk into a Stern Gang road block. We are shouted at in Hebrew and we stop walking. In the half light there are two lorries backed up near the end of the street and we don't see them until after we are shouted at. Two soldiers, both short and one wearing a beret, rush up to us. They are carrying Enfield rifles and they both have glowing cigarettes in their mouths. They ram the rifle bolts home and point the barrels in our faces. They persist in Hebrew. They are excited and they act tough and right away we know they are Irgun. Bieberman tries answering in English and then Yiddish. They respond in Hebrew and prod us with the rifles. Bieberman resorts to the ancient gesture of sinking his chin into his chest and raising his palms out. We are nervous and almost laugh. The Stern Gang soldiers don't laugh. They point toward the street entrance behind us and it becomes obvious that they want us to get out of there. We turn around and walk back the way we came. The street is dark and there is silence now but we know that they are there watching us. We turn the corner and the way to the hotel is deserted. When we get to the room Bieberman looks pale and his hands shake and he curses. We are speculating about the incident when a burst of automatic rifle fire echoes down the road outside. A bullet hums above the roof of the hotel. We decide that this is either a normal night in Tel Aviv or that the Arabs may have infiltrated the city.

In the morning the early sun casts an orange glow on the walls opposite the balcony of the hotel room. There is increased gunfire in the streets and toward the beach. We dress and wash and leave the room. We go down the steps to the front of the building. We start out for the Gallim Yam. A soldier with a Sten gun in his hand crosses the road ahead of us, running in a crouch. We begin to run also. We take a narrow street that leads to the beach front and when we reach the first intersection, bullets ricochet from the pavement on the far side. We turn into the rear entrance of the Gallim Yam. More bullets hit out in the roadway and pieces of the surface disintegrate in tiny puffs. There are others already at the cafe and everyone is sitting at the sidewalk tables and looking down toward the bathing beach. Bernstein is there and we join him under one of the red and white umbrellas. We look where everyone else is looking and we can see an LST* lying in the water a hundred yards from shore. Bernstein tells us what happened. It is a clash between Irgun and Haganah and it has gained momentum during the night.

Bernstein points to the ship. The distance from where we are sitting

---

* The LST was the *Altalena*, a former US tank landing ship of the type used during World War II.

is 300 yards but it seems nearer because the air is so clear. The LST is full of arms and Irgun tried to run it up onto the beach and unload it in the darkness of last night. They grounded it on a shoal too far out. Bernstein is incredulous and he says the Jews are fighting each other. The accuracy of his statement cannot be denied. As we watch, a longboat rises on a heavy swell and starts out from the side of the LST. The longboat is white and it contrasts sharply with the dark hull of the larger craft. People and wooden boxes fill the inner space of the longboat and it sits low in the water. The oars begin to pull for the shore. Rifle fire commences from the rooftops down the seafront road and the firecracker sound of a machine-gun comes from the same direction. Simultaneously, automatic weapon fire begins to flash from the Irgun beachhead in the lee of the sea wall. We can see spouts of water rising beside the longboat as it attempts to travel the distance between the LST and the rolling surf. Other flashes wink sporadically along the side of the landing craft. We are all out in the open and exposed to the fire but nobody moves. It is like we are in front row seats at a theater and the play has already begun. We look across at the stage. The Haganah gunners are picking off the men with the oars and the longboat is now drifting aimlessly just beyond the breakers. They are not rowing anymore. As often happens in war, we watch more in fascination than in horror and I am reminded of a line of Spanish poetry – 'Death came and, with a leaden finger, pointed to her victims one by one'.

The confrontation between Irgun and Haganah had been, evidently, inevitable. The continued friction had finally erupted into violence that spread from the beach into the streets of the city. In a move calculated to strengthen their military position and, consequently, their political bargaining position, Irgun had arranged to have a large quantity of arms landed at Tel Aviv. With considerable secrecy the LST operation had been organized at a southern European port and the crew were volunteers. Under the cover of night the vessel, loaded to capacity with weapons, was steered in from the Mediterranean toward the bathing beach. Certain things began to go wrong almost immediately. The craft, which was supposed to be maneuvered directly onto the shore, became stranded on a sand bar a hundred yards out. Other factors intervened. The Irgun vehicles near the seafront, which were to receive the transfer of the arms from the ship, were discovered by Haganah patrols. By then Irgun had passed a point of no return and so decided to fight. Before dawn the Stern Gang had occupied some strategic points around the city. Road blocks and barricades were in turn set up by the Haganah forces and, as the sun rose, it appeared that a Jewish civil conflict, in the midst of a current war of survival, was not going to be avoided. Although the fighting was not really widespread or prolonged, the very existence of the confrontation created tragic overtones and, in the end, the challenge failed. Destiny did not decree it would succeed.

Another burst from the beachhead and some of the bullets sing through one of the umbrellas at the Gallim Yam. Everyone jumps up and runs toward the rear exit. There is a strong smell of gunpowder cordite in the air. A table is overturned in the rush and when we get to the street we keep running. Others are already going down the block. The long shadows cast by the rising sun are stretching out behind them.

The rest of the day is strange. Nothing is normal. The crowds are gone from the streets, the shops are closed. The only vehicles are the lorries taking defense troops to positions. We go around to the Yarkon and the ground floor is full of people and everyone is subdued. We can still hear the firing and then two Mills bombs [hand grenades] explode at the end of the street. The detonations are loud and shrapnel whines shrilly past the doorway. We go down to the latrines. Bernstein stays in the latrine too long. Bieberman and I go upstairs to report. We walk up the stone steps and when we get to the third floor there are people lying down in the corridor. We don't know why they are lying down but we find space near a window and lie down too. The window is open and there is a Haganah defense soldier on the roof of the building across the street. Every time someone tries to pass through the corridor he motions them down. No one knows the reason for this but since the soldier is waving a rifle, no one questions it. We lie with our shoulders against the wall. Bieberman tries to light a cigarette but the match goes out. He is upset over what happened at the beach and about the affair last night when we ran into the Stern people. He says we could have been killed.

Two girls in light tan skirts come up the stairway. They both have fair complexions and one of them wears glasses. They don't lie down. They step over everyone and go to the window above us and begin to shout in Hebrew at the soldier on the roof. Those on the floor exhibit consternation and tell them to shut up. The girls laugh and ignore the ones on the floor. The girl with glasses steps on Bieberman's hand. Bieberman curses and everyone looks at him. The girls continue to shout and finally they make the soldier angry and he raises his rifle and puts a round through the upper pane of the window. Glass flies inwards and showers those in the hallway and the bullet ricochets above our heads for a seemingly interminable length of time. The girls lie down.

It is an hour before we get to the office to report and when we go back downstairs there are many waiting to get out at the main door. The sentries are letting them go two at a time and telling them to stay off the roads. We don't hear any gunfire at the moment but someone says the Stern Gang is over on the next street. Our shirts are wet with perspiration when we get outside. There is a Haganah roadblock on the corner and we turn around and walk down past the Park Hotel. At the far side of the hotel three people have been killed. There is no one else around and the scene seems suddenly eerie. Two of the bodies are on the sidewalk and one is in the middle of the street. They look as though they had fallen while they were running and there is equipment scattered about. The body in the street is lying face down and a ribbon of blood has travelled an irregular course over to the gutter. The blood has turned dark brown in the mid-morning sun. We stand at the curb in silence. A warm gust sends a dust swirl down the empty roadway. The pavement is hot and we turn away and walk on until we find a cafe open on Allenby Road. We go in and drink cognac.

Bieberman is preoccupied and he stares transfixed at the table top in the cafe. He talks again about how we could have been killed. He says he didn't come over here to be killed by a Jew. Bieberman wasn't the only one in Tel Aviv that day who was upset about Jews killing Jews. Everyone felt it. Some were angry, many were fearful and all were gripped by sadness. After the Holocaust and the exodus and the underground fighting, it was Jew against Jew. The future of the national homeland was in the balance and they were fighting each other. Regardless of the ideologies and differences that led to this day, it would remain a day of regrets.

By evening the crowds have returned to the streets but we are kept away from the beach by the barriers and the patrols. A pall of black smoke is drifting over the city. We are standing on a corner a block from the Yarkon and when one of the patrols comes by Bieberman asks them what happened. The two Haganah soldiers hold their rifles carelessly and their shirts are soiled with dirt and sweat. They tell us that a Haganah gunboat has shelled the LST and the landing craft is burning. It was also shelled by a howitzer artillery piece that was dragged onto the beach road. They say the fighting at the beach is over.

Except for a few skirmishes and several armed jeep rampages through the streets by the Stern Gang, when the fighting ended at the seafront it was over. The entire Irgun party was either killed or wounded at the beachhead. The weapons on the LST were destroyed or confiscated and only a hulk remained of the ship. There were casualties among the Haganah forces and an American photographer was one of those killed near the Park Hotel. The episode was not easily forgotten but everyone turned back to the war.

There was never another threat to Haganah. The clash resulted in Irgun being outlawed by the Ben-Gurion government and the Irgun leaders who could be found were arrested. The faction, however, remained in force and they were to play a part in other incidents with their independent actions during this eventful year.

In a few days the beach is serene again and soon the only reminder that fighting has passed that way is the hulk of the LST. It was to remain there, silent and pointing inward at the city, during the long summer and into the autumn and winter of the war. Waves would break along its sides and bathers would sometimes swim out to it. Sometimes one would remember the volunteers who brought it to this place and died.

CHAPTER II

OPERATION BALAK

At the end of the week I receive orders to go out to the airfield at Sde Dov for a flight check. Bieberman gets an assignment to the maintenance section at Lydda the same day. We walk to the hotel room from the Yarkon and Bieberman gets his suitcase. I go with him to the motor pool near the beach. We don't say much and he gets on an army supply lorry that is due to leave for Lydda in five minutes. When he gets into the back of the truck Bieberman reaches down and shakes my hand. There is a bullet hole through the tailgate where he is standing. It is afternoon and the sea breeze is fluttering the collar of his shirt. The lorry starts forward and turns into the street traffic and passes from view behind the Yarkon. In a little while I get a ride to Sde Dov.

The Messerschmitts have moved out of Aqir. They had trouble with the fighters on the paved runways and they are now operating from an auxiliary strip near Natanya. The unit has been designated 101 Squadron and a permanent base is under construction at Herzliya. The accident rate has been high. At Sde Dov it becomes clear that if I am to fly fighters I will have to go to Czechoslovakia for indoctrination on the Messerschmitt. The machines have a bad reputation because of certain handling characteristics and the Messerschmitts in Israel are restricted to operational sorties. They are having problems keeping enough of them serviceable. The ceasefire isn't expected to last much longer.

Mischa Keren leans back in the camp chair behind the desk in the operations shack at Sde Dov. He's the CO of the light plane base. He is slim and wears a British bush jacket with no insignia. Articulate and relaxed, he is formerly of the RAF and the Palestine Flying Club. He lights a pipe and sits forward. A paper is on the desk between and he writes across the bottom of it. I look out through the wooden-framed doorway at the field beyond. Sde Dov is on the northern fringe of Tel Aviv near the mouth of the low-ebbed Yarkon River, and the base is so close to the beach that the main strip leads into the sand. There are some trees on the northern border and the patches of short grass on the landing area are burnt brown by the summer sun. During the Mandate there was sport flying here. Now a collection of training craft and the fabric-covered Rapide transports are parked about the perimeter and near the hangar at the eastern end.

The air is clear except for some sea haze to the west and we taxi the Fairchild into the wind and stop near the field huts. The propeller continues its revolutions for a moment after the switches are cut and then it snaps to a halt in a diagonal position. Keren is still laughing about the landing. We had flown in the vicinity of the base for 20 minutes. Keren could see that I was able to fly the machine so he didn't bother to prolong the flight and when we came back in, the landing was too fast and we floated down to the sand. I had to go around and try it again. At the hut line we climb out of the cabin section of the aircraft and stand beside the brownish-colored fuselage. The Fairchild was not an unfamiliar type to me but it is prewar and it is a long time since I operated one. Keren taps the wing strut and laughs. He says it was captured from the Egyptians two months ago. They were smuggling hashish in it when it developed engine trouble on a night flight from Lebanon and was forced to land in the Negev. The Egyptian pilot was interned when the aircraft was confiscated by the Israelis. The Fairchild was initially put into Jewish service with the 3rd Palmach Galil Flight but was later transferred to Sde Dov. It has the blue Star of David on its side.

We walk back to the Operations hut and we hear the sound of a fighter turning high overhead. It is a Messerschmitt and its silhouette is sharply defined against the azure background of the upper atmosphere. Keren squints into the sun and smiles. He says it's still odd to think of the German machines as friendly. He takes his pipe from a pocket and nods toward the disappearing fighter. He says that some of the Egyptian prisoners of war call the Messerschmitts Desert Hawks. We are at the hut and Keren points to a British Auster down the field. They flew bombing raids in the tiny planes during the first days.

The original group of pilots at Sde Dov were already legendary. The base was a prime target for the Egyptian fighter-bombers in the early weeks and the field was shot up with persistent regularity. There was little anti-aircraft defense and the crews would lay on the ground with rifles and fire at the Spitfires, and when the Egyptian planes had gone the Israeli pilots would get in the Austers and take off on missions against the enemy concentrations. The Israeli raids with the light aircraft were ineffective and foolhardy but there was never any hesitation in launching them.

Keren looks toward the low fence on the southern edge of the field. Behind the barbed-wire enclosure of the maintenance area one can see the fuselage of a Spitfire, the green and white crescent and stars of the Royal Egyptian Air Force showing clearly on the dull camouflage of the body. He turns and looks at the Auster again. He talks about one of the missions in May. There were small home-made bombs on improvised racks under each wing of the sport plane. A report had been received that Egyptian motorized units were maneuvering north of Majdal along the coast and the Israeli pilot of the standby Auster took off and headed south, flying low past Tel Aviv and Jaffa. When he reached the enemy area, which was only 15 flying minutes away from Sde Dov, the Israeli pilot saw the vehicles and he circled at 3,000 feet and released the bombs. Bursts from the defensive ground fire began appearing close to the small craft and when the bombs fell they only dropped from one wing. The pilot had to reverse the controls in order to remain upright, The Israeli couldn't see where the departed bombs had hit and while he was struggling with the jammed lever he was attacked by a Spitfire. The Egyptian plane came in so fast it overshot the Auster and, while the Spitfire was turning, the Israeli shook the stubbon bombs loose and dove for home. He frustrated the Egyptian with evasive tactics and when he got over Jaffa the Spitfire broke off the pursuit. The Israeli landed at the Sde Dov base and when he alighted from the aircraft they told him to get ready for another mission to the same target. Keren laughs. In a war of unsung heroes the men of Sde Dov would remain high on the roll of honor.

At the Operations shack two pilots were looking at a wall map. Keren goes around them and at the desk he writes again on a paper in Hebrew. He hands me the paper. He says that he is recommending that I go on up to the fighters but then he looks at me and shakes his head. He says that I will be told at the Yarkon that I have to go to Czechoslovakia to check out on the Messerschmitts. We shake hands and he wishes me luck.

When I return to Headquarters that day I am sent in to see Boris Senior, the sophisticated South African Jew who has a reputation for charm and organizational ability as well as being an experienced pilot. Boris Senior has taken Israeli citizenship and he is to play an important part in Air Force affairs this first year. In the office he stands beside a table and reads the note I brought from Sde Dov. He politely gives it back and, walking to the door, he points out another office farther down the hallway. He says to see Aharon Remez.

Aharon Remez is dressed in a plain khaki shirt and tropical shorts. There is no protocol when I go into the room. He waves an arm at a chair and I sit down. He is to be the first Commander of the Israeli Air Force. He is an inscrutable Palestinian Jew who conducts business with a stern approach that discourages familiarity. Having been a fighter pilot in the RAF, he is only a few years older than I but gives no sign that we have anything in common. He sits at the desk and looks at the wall for a moment and then glances at the paper. He says the CO at Sde Dov has recommended that I go to 101 Squadron but that I will have to go to Budejovice first. Remez gets up and goes to the window and looks at the street. He says the Messerschmitts are bastards and if I am not properly checked out I could be killed quite easily. I will go out on the Balak run from Aqir tomorrow. When he turns away from the window he picks up a telephone and speaks in Hebrew. He hangs up the receiver. He smiles but the smile lacks congeniality.

I stand up. As I start to leave, the CO of 101 Squadron comes in and Remez motions me to stay. Israel's first air hero has fair hair and a strong jaw and blue eyes and he could pass as a German fighter pilot. One of the Messerschmitt pilots is with him. Remez introduces them. Mordecai Alon and Ezer Weizman. Tall, rail thin with classic Hebrew features, Weizman has a debonaire quality which is absent from the personalities of both Remez and Alon. The CO of 101 Squadron looks at me. His face shows nothing. He is reserved, cool. He is undoubtedly a dedicated man. He says he will be happy to have me in the Squadron when I return from Budejovice. He is sorry that I can't be checked out at Natanya but they can't risk the machines. The ominous implications of this statement seem to be considered normal by everyone else in the room. Weizman is sitting in one of the chairs and watching the rest of us with an amused smile. No one talks about operations but Alon asks me what I know about the Messerschmitt. I look toward the window. I think of 1942 and the captured Messerschmitt 109s at El Daba and how we used to sit in the cockpits and manipulate the controls. I remember the cockpits always had a peculiar odor. Alon smiles thinly. He says I will have to know more than that.

* * * * *

The rays of the setting sun slant through from the balcony archway and create a bright patch on the floor of the hotel room. I pack a worn travel bag. It seems strange without Bieberman. We had only been together for three weeks but it seemed longer because of everything that happened. I sit on the edge of the bed. There is a copy of the *Palestine Post* on the other bed and I pick it up – 'Arab Legion Violates Truce in Jerusalem' – 'Bernadotte Leaving Damascus Today' – 'New Stamps Due' – 'Truman on Campaign Tour' – 'Louis Retains Title' – 'The Ordeal of the Negev Settlements' – 'Road Junction Sniping' – I put the paper down. It is yesterday's. I stare at the floor and think about the recent days. They have a different kind of patriotism here. It is not emotional on the surface. It is a determination. It is the all-encompassing confidence and determination that is impressive. It is the mass energy and intellect of a people applied toward a single goal. I go out and stand on the balcony and look down to the crossroad. A pushcart vendor is arguing with someone who is inside the cab of an army truck. The truck is up on the sidewalk. I turn back into the room and finish packing the bag.

I see Bernstein at the Gallim Yam the next day. I left my kit at the Yarkon and was informed that I leave for Aqir in the evening. There was talk at Headquarters about a hospital plane that went down somewhere.

At the Gallim Yam I sit down at the table where Bernstein is having tea. He is due to go up to Ramat David tomorrow and he still talks about the B-17 rumor. He has also heard the story of the missing hospital plane. A Rapide light transport carrying some wounded from a field near Jerusalem failed to arrive at Sde Dov. There were five aboard including a girl and it is assumed that the aircraft made an emergency landing along the coastal flats somewhere north-west of Isdud. There is an air and ground search under way. The tower at Aqir last heard from the Rapide at dawn and then the radio transmissions from the aircraft had ceased. Bernstein pushes his chair back from the table. He says the area where they think the Rapide went down is reputed to be pretty desolate and it isn't occupied by either side. Bernstein says that the pilot of the hospital plane is an American Gentile.

It is almost midnight when the jeep gets to the transport operations building at Aqir. Two of the C-46s are parked near the adjoining hangar and the only light is coming from the interior of the Flight hut. There are three others in the jeep who are crewmen returning from leave in Tel Aviv. It was late when we leave the Yarkon motor pool and we ride in silence on the dark roads. I am the only one getting out at Ops and I take the bag and walk to the doorway. The stucco on one side of the hut is pock-marked from bomb fragments. The air is cooler now. Inside, the Flight hut is busy and it is noisy. Flying equipment is scattered about on the chairs and tables. A blackboard on the far wall has names and numbers written on it. Some Americans, who fly the chartered C-54 for Northern Air Lines out of Czechoslovakia, are lounging on a fabric-covered couch in a corner. Two of the C-46 pilots come over to where I am standing. They know who I am. They are both American Jews and their short-sleeved shirts have grease on them. They say the aircraft isn't ready yet. I put the bag near a wall of the hut and lie down against it.

It is three hours before the co-pilot comes by and says that they are preparing to leave. We go through the field door and the cargo carrier is directly outside. Off to one side in the darkness are piles of crates that were unloaded from the C-54. Most of them are Mauser ammunition boxes. When we get to the loading door of the C-46 we are joined by the pilot and navigator. An intellectual-looking German Jew, the navigator has a small monkey on his shoulder. The monkey jumps up to the top of the navigator's head. The others laugh. There are no other passengers and I wait by the belly steps while they inspect the aircraft. Even in the dim light the Panamanian flag is conspicuous on the tail fin. Operation Balak. The C-46s are the workhorses of the Balak run which brings in the war material from Czechoslovakia. I look up at the wide fuselage and remember the unpopularity of the machines. They were unstable and generally unreliable but in this war they are the backbone of the Transport Command.

One of the groundcrew comes by. He is a foreign volunteer who was with us the first day at the Yarkon and he stops and comes over to where I am waiting for the others. I tell him that I am going to Zatec. The mechanic rests a foot on the extended steps of the cargo compartment. He says they found the hospital plane. They saw it from the air in the afternoon and then a Palmach patrol finally reached it after dark. One of the engines had failed and the Rapide had made a landing on the flats. The plane was intact but everyone on it was dead. Saudi Arabian irregulars had found them. Saudi Arabian irregulars. It was one of the common names applied to the independent guerilla bands who were not under any regular army command, and who had been engaged in actions against the Jews since before the end of the Mandate. The crew of the aircraft and the wounded casualties aboard had been shot and some, particularly the Israeli girl, had been mutilated. The bodies were taken out by the patrol and brought up to Tel Aviv. The pilot was identified as an American. The mechanic is silent after he tells the story and I look past him at the diminishing night beyond the hangar. They were 20 miles from home.

The sky is light with the breaking dawn when Tel Aviv passes behind us and we are on course over the Mediterranean. The cargo space is empty and I sit back against the cabin bulkhead. I can feel the engine vibrations through the panels. In a while the pilot comes back from the cockpit and sits down next to me. He has alert dark eyes and a scar runs jaggedly through one of his eyebrows. He spreads a map on the floor beside us and points to the course. The Balak run is oddly roundabout. Our first stop is at Ajaccio, Corsica. The pilot laughs. He says it's the only place the Jews could make arrangements for refuelling on the route. The French think we are from Tangiers. The pilot's finger traces a line on the map which leads north-east out of Ajaccio and across Italy, passing east of the Alps and then upward until it reaches Zatec in Czechoslovakia. The pilot brushes back his hair. He says he brought one of the C-46s over from the States in May and they had a lot of trouble. The United States Government is depending on the UN to settle the Palestine issue and they are putting pressure on the Jews with the arms embargo. We get up and go into the cockpit section.

There is coffee in a cognac bottle and it tastes bitter but I drink some. The navigator is in the co-pilot's seat and the monkey is perched on the compass above the instrument panel. The monkey studies me with an unblinking stare. The pilot is acting as engineering officer and he sits down in the side seat and lets the co-pilot fly. The engine noise is loud in the cockpit and the pilot raises his voice when he talks. He says they lost their engineering officer on another trip. They were coming into Aqir with a load of guns and ammunition and a dismantled Messerschmitt aboard and when they touched onto the runway the landing gear collapsed. The engineer was taking a nap near the front bulkhead in the cargo compartment and the Messerschmitt fuselage broke loose and crushed him against the plates. No one else was even hurt but it killed the engineer. The pilot lights a cigarette and looks out of the port window. Beyond the wingtip, far to the south, there are broken white clouds close to the sea.

Corsica appears on the horizon and when the craggy mountains of the island become discernible we begin to descend from 10,000 feet. We are on the ground at Ajaccio before noon. The French refuel the C-46 and we go over to the airport cafe for the midday meal. We sit at a wide table in a corner and the food is good and we drink white wine. Fresh air flows through the busy room from the open doorway. Everyone eats and the navigator pours some wine in a glass for the monkey.

When we get back to the aircraft the pilot signs a form that a French mechanic hands him and then, when the engines are started, one of the propellers won't change pitch. The pilot shuts the engines off. He gets out on the wing and lays on top of the nacelle and toys with the propeller mechanism. The co-pilot gets out on the wing also and the navigator and monkey watch from the ground. They try it with the engine running three more times and the third time it works all right, and we all get in. At the front of the runway we wait for a few moments and then the vineyards at the end of the field are falling away beneath us and we are airborne over the sea. It is 1 July.

The airfield at Zatec is 30 miles east of Prague and during the summer of 1948 the Czech base was codenamed Zebra by the Israelis. The weather had begun to deteriorate over Austria and when the runway lights appear there is a steady rain beginning to fall from the darkening sky. We touch down on the wet surface and the lights are yellow through the mist. We turn onto a concrete ramp and swing to a stop near a large hangar. As soon as we drop from the belly steps I see one of the Schwimmer Constellations parked on the apron and, behind a fence beyond the hangar, there are three B-17s. Through the rain, the shapes of the bombers are unmistakeable and I think of Bernstein at Ramat David. The Czech groundcrew and some of the Jews gather around the C-46 and they talk with the flight crew and then we walk over to a wire mesh gate where we are met by two of the Israelis from the Embassy. The crew is going to the Stalingrad Hotel in Zatec and I say goodbye to them and get into a small black sedan with the two Israelis. The Israelis are both silent and they both have on raincoats. I sit in the back seat of the car with my bag and we start out for Prague. The windshield wipers swish monotonously as we go through a guard barrier and on to a slippery two-lane highway. The Czech soldier at the post has a Skoda sub-machine gun slung on his shoulder upside down.

The Israeli arrangement in Czechoslovakia was conducted in an efficient and rather secretive fashion. If the general populace knew anything, there was no outward indication and no one asked questions. The government officials in this most recent of Russian satellites were in

control of all the dealing, and the Jews were paying for everything they
got. Still, Czechoslovakia, regardless of motive, had to be looked upon
as the primary benefactor of Israel, militarily, during this period.

In July 1948 the Israeli Embassy in Prague was comprised of several
suites of rooms in a top floor wing of the Flora Hotel. The hotel still had
a certain elegance in the old European style but time and wars and
austerity had all taken their toll and now, like the Gothic architecture of
the city, it was becoming a faded reminder of what used to be. The Flora
is near the central railway station and, after almost an hour's drive in the
rain, the black sedan stops at the side entrance of the hotel. It is early
evening but there is not much vehicle traffic on the streets. Everyone is
walking. The taller of the Israelis motions me out and we go through the
lobby and up a red-carpeted staircase. Those at the desk pay no attention
to us. The Israeli says that I have been assigned an Embassy room for the
night.

The room is comfortable but there is something about it that reminds
me of the war and I go to the window and watch the rain for a while. I
wash and change clothes and the tall Israeli returns and asks for my
passport. He leans against the door frame. I give him the passport and
he hands me a book of food ration tickets. He never smiles. He says that
it won't be necessary to see Ehud Avriel. Ehud Avriel is the Israeli
Ambassador to Czechoslovakia. The tall one turns away from the door.
He says that I will meet Lichter at dinner. George Lichter is the
designated Israeli instructor on the Messerschmitt course at Budejovice.
An American Jew with a calm, studious appearance, he had been a
fighter pilot with the US 9th Air Force in World War II and he came
through Czechoslovakia with the early group. He was held over after the
course because a need was discovered for a Jewish liaison pilot at the
Czech base. Lichter was considered an excellent pilot but he hadn't been
down to Israel yet.

In the dining room off the hotel lobby the driver of the black sedan
waves me over to a table adjacent to the entrance. There are two people
seated at the table and the driver points to the stocky one and says this is
George Lichter. The other is Red Flint. The driver leaves and I sit down
and Lichter calls a waiter and orders dinner for me. Flint has
exceptionally white skin and he looks too young to have been in the war
but he was a US Navy pilot in 1945. At first I don't think he is a Jew but
he is. Lichter leans back in his chair and studies me for a moment. He
has a short black beard and his eyes are serious. He says that Flint and I
will be the last Israeli contingent at Budejovice. The Jews aren't going
to buy any more Messerschmitts.

In the morning the weather front has passed and it is clear and bright
and we prepare to take the midday train south. A communist parade is in
the process of forming on the streets and a group of Russian officers are
in the foyer of the Flora. Everyone ignores them. It is four blocks to the

station and we take a taxi and from the windows we can see uniforms from everywhere in the Red Alliance. At the depot Lichter buys the tickets for Budejovice and we board one of the trains on the west end of the station. We are all dressed in sports jackets with open neck shirts and we all sit together on one wide seat. Lichter raises the window and leans out and, after the train pulls out, he sits back down next to Flint. The trip takes two hours and the car is full of people and at every stop they sell beer through the windows. We buy some beer and hold the paper cups on our laps. Lichter says that there were ten pilots in the previous group. They were American and South African volunteers. They left for Israel two days ago. Budejovice is not a large city nor is it essentially industrial. The farmland which surrounds the town stretches away to the hills and then to mountains and forests. The countryside is inclined to be picturesque. It is called Budweis in German and the airfield is a mile from the outskirts. We were to be at the Czech operational training base for three weeks.

We are issued Czech identification cards when we arrive and the same afternoon I fly with Lichter in the Arado. The flying suits and parachutes have Luftwaffe insignia on them but Lichter doesn't seem to notice it. He has been here before. I sit in the rear cockpit of the high-powered trainer and I experience a sense of uneasiness because the airspeed is indicated in unfamiliar kilometers and the altitude is registered in meters. The horizon suddenly slants to vertical and then it is inverted as Lichter takes the controls and performs a series of rolls. We come around to land from the unobstructed southern approach and we drop close above the single-seaters parked along the perimeter. We bounce lightly when we settle onto the wide flat surface of grass.

In the evening Lichter takes us around to see Colonel Hlodek who is the base commander. Hlodek isn't at his quarters, but outside the officers' barracks we encounter Captain Bilek. Bilek is the Czech instructor assigned to the Jewish contingent at Budejovice. He had served for five years with the Royal Air Force during the German occupation of his homeland. He is short with Slavic features and is apparently imperturbable. He laughs and says that most of the Czech officers speak English and he assures us that one of them will be in the control tower when we are airborne.

He is possessed of a disarming candor and he speaks freely about the present political situation. He says that he himself eased obediently into the communist fold because not to do so meant professional suicide with worse to come later. Colonel Hlodek lurches out of the latrine which adjoins the barracks buildings. When he sees us he smiles broadly and since he knows Lichter quite well he comes over and hugs him. Heavy set and red-faced, Hlodek has his blue tunic unbuttoned and he insists that we come into his quarters for vodka. Hlodek was a veteran of the Soviet Air Force but there is no mention of flying except that when we finish our drinks Captain Bilek says that we will check out in the Messerschmitt two-seater tomorrow.

The Israeli section was never referred to as such at Budejovice. It was not a clandestine operation but neither was it publicised and most of the Czech personnel treated it with studied nonchalance. They would not be obliged to do so much longer. Israel had purchased 25 of the Messerschmitt fighters and the last five were waiting at the factory field at Prag-Cakovice. Their delivery during July would conclude the first chapter in the story of an Air Force.

CHAPTER III

BUDEJOVICE

The Israeli Flight at Budejovice was now four aircraft. They are parked into the prevailing wind on the edge of the grass apron at the south perimeter. A path leads from the quarters at the officers' block of buildings, past the white-frame mess hall, along a row of elm trees and emerges onto the airfield at the western boundary where the slant-roof hangars face outward to the landing ground. Far across the field on the eastern border the huts of the Czech student pilots lie flat against the background of the distant meadows. A line of fighter planes squat impassively in front of the huts and along the utility road that runs to the forest at the north barrier.

Bilek is leaning against the side of the two-seater when I get out to the Israeli line. I wear the Luftwaffe flight suit again but Bilek has his parachute harness buckled over his uniform. He points to the nose of the Messerschmitt and indicates that this machine has a Daimler engine. We get into the cockpits and when we are strapped in I look back. The rear seat is so restricted that Bilek seems to be in a half-standing position. He looks over my shoulder and prompts me on the strange procedure. When I am ready Bilek motions to the mechanics who are by the leading edge of the port wing. They insert a heavy crank into the side of the engine cowling and begin winding the inertia starter. I watch them through the windscreen panel. The initial turns are difficult and both crewmen have to pull on the handle together but, as the momentum increases and the whining sound reaches a high pitch, one of them lets go while the other continues to rotate the crank with accelerating ferocity.

Bilek taps me on the back of the helmet and waves his other hand at the crewmen. When the mechanic disengages the handle I switch on the magnetos and press the starter button. The propeller begins to windmill and then the whirring of the inertia is obliterated by the blasts of the exhausts. I look through the canopy glass at the wing surfaces. The Czech national markings are bright against the mottled-grey camouflage. The wheel blocks are pulled away and we move forward, the exhaust popping and backfiring with the sound that is peculiar to the German

engines and which was to become so familiar in the months ahead. The
machine shudders and vibrates when the engine is revved on the
boundary path and I stare for a moment at the quivering starboard
wingtip. I turn to the instruments, tighten the throat microphone and call
the tower on the radio. A green light flashes from the elevated wooden
structure beyond the hangars. Bilek hasn't said anything on the cockpit
intercom. I look behind and he adjusts the goggles on his forehead and
nods. I check the elevator trim control on the left of the seat and open the
throttle. The earth blurs beneath the wings and then we rise into the wide
sky above the dark border of the forest.

It is two days before I fly the Messerschmitt fighter. For all the
unfamiliar qualities of the two-seater, I don't have any undue trouble
with it but both Bilek and Lichter recommend caution with the fighter.
Because of the engine modification it has some unique desires. Officially
called the Avia, the single-seater was in fact the German Messerschmitt
109G powered by a Junkers engine instead of the Daimler-Benz for
which the aircraft was originally designed. This change necessitated the
re-modelling of the installation mountings and the utilization of the
broad-bladed wooden propeller. With these differences, and with the
lesser horsepower, the machine was found to have high take-off and
landing speeds, while the narrow gauge of the undercarriage, along with
a monstrous torque, frequently caused dangerous direction deviations on
the ground. The aircraft was considered worthy once airborne buts its
potential for unmanageable behavior was indicated by the name Mezec
(Mule) which was standardly applied to it.

The Messerschmitt is a short-range fighter. It holds less than 90
Imperial gallons of fuel and it has a flight endurance of something under
two hours at a cruising speed of 310 kph. The Czech versions are armed
with two 20mm cannon which are oddly underslung beneath each wing
and two 7mm machine-guns are mounted along the engine, under the
cowling panels, and are synchronized to fire through the propeller. Racks
to accommodate 250kg bombs could be employed also and for all its
other faults it was a formidable war machine.

There is a high, thin overcast and the wind has risen when I taxi the
fighter the short distance to the take-off area. The safety belt and
shoulder harness are tight and the odor of petrol is blended with the
unsavory smell of the interior varnish which is vaguely reminiscent of
the smell of decaying fruit. The cockpit beneath the square-cut canopy is
narrow, compact, almost too small and the rudder pedals are on a line
with ones' stomach. The seat is flush above the central fuel tank. I apply
the brakes and stop the machine at the south marker. The extensive turf
spreads away before me to the trees at the north end. Over to the left I
see the activity around the maintenance hangar. I turn in the seat and
look back through the canopy. The short grass is rippling in the wash of
the propeller. Tiny white flowers are mingled with the grass. The leather

helmet is too tight and I pull at it. Then the tower light blinks and I turn the Messerschmitt into the wind. The popping of the exhaust becomes a steady roar when I push the throttle forward and after a seemingly endless run on the ground, the machine gets into the air.

* * * * *

The clouds are lowering. After the midday meal we are in the quarters at the officers' barracks. The sauerkraut and dumplings and beer that we had for lunch have barely settled when we hear on Lichter's radio that the truce has fallen apart in Israel and fighting has started again along most of the fronts. We are lying on the cots in the big room and we hear the relay from the US Armed Forces Radio in Germany. Lichter and Flint sit up. The red-haired, sleepy-eyed Flint has a balled-up piece of notebook paper in his hand and he throws it toward a basket beyond Lichter's cot. It bounces off Lichter's head. Lichter doesn't smile. He gets up and goes close to the radio on the table in the center of the room and listens to the end of the report. He has been giving us our pay in Czech kronen and now he pulls a roll of bank notes from his pocket and holds some of them toward us. I sit up. After he gives us the money Lichter goes to the small four-paned window and looks out at the elm trees. Gusts of wind are swaying the branches. He says if it rains hard he is going up to Prague for a couple of days.

The weather is threatening when we get to the Flight line in the afternoon but I go up again in the fighter. Flint is having problems with the two-seater. He and Bilek take off ahead of me and when I am half-way down the run the fighter begins to swerve 45 degrees off course. The north boundary is looming closer and I push the rudder hard, like Bilek said, and the nose of the aircraft jolts back to center. In the air I stay below cloud base near the field and when I come in to land some raindrops bounce off the windscreen. I swerve again when I get on the ground but I catch it in time and then a crosswind carries the plane close to the students' line. I roll slowly back to the Israeli section and wonder if I'll like it in these machines. I watch the ground passing under the wing and memories of the other war come unbidden into my thoughts. It seems strange to be flying the Messerschmitts.

At four o'clock we are ready to take off on a two-plane formation flight. Lichter is in the other fighter and the sky to the north-east is ominous. We are preparing to start the engines when Lichter waves off the mission. A red light shines from the tower. The storm front is moving along the mountains and soon the rain falls across the summer fields. It drums hollowly on the wing surfaces of the aircraft and descends in slanting patterns onto the canopy. The wind increases in velocity and drifting sheets of moisture move steadily over the trees down the perimeter. Everything is suddenly wet. We run with our jackets over our heads toward the row of barrack buildings and the damp earth smells good.

The rain falls intermittently for two days and the fighters have to be grounded. We ride into Budejovice the first evening and Lichter takes the train up to Prague. I go with Flint to a cafe in the square and we have dinner. The beer is strong and afterward we go to another place and there is a violinist. No one speaks English. Flint leans across the table so that his face is close to mine. He says that he is afraid of the goddamn Messerschmitts. The violin plays and the rain falls and we can hear the thunder rolling above the sounds of the bistro.

At the end of the week the skies are clear again and when Lichter gets back from Prague the programme continues. The first day the surface of the field is soft and hazardous and some of the Czech students damage aircraft with ground loops during the afternoon. Lichter sends Flint to Bilek for more dual instruction in the two-seater and then we walk to the fighters. The horizon is pale beyond the forest. To the west I can see a long line of washing blowing in the wind at a distant farmhouse. I put on the parachute and get in the cockpit and close the heavy side-hinged canopy. A few yards to the right Lichter starts his engine and the noise is loud. I switch the radio on and the sound dims amid the crackling of the static in the helmet earphones. I work the fuel primer pump and the Messerschmitt rocks gently while the mechanics wind the inertia. The engine starts and the rhythmic rumbling creates a relaxing effect. I look over at Lichter and he moves forward from the line with rudder fishtailing. I turn out behind him and we take off into the bright air.

Lichter handles his machine deftly. We have a simulated dogfight at 10,000 feet and I watch as the patchwork of the earth below tilts diagonally. Then the wings of the aircraft in front flash upward and the windscreen is filled with the blue above. Lichter rolls while climbing, tightens the roll into a turn and drops out behind me. I smile to myself. It is two years since I have flown fighters. The propeller of Lichter's Messerschmitt throws off some vapor as he cuts across underneath. Beyond him, far below, the multi-colored fields merge with the hills and then disappear into the range of mountains. Lichter comes up off the port wing and gestures and we roll down together and, gathering speed, we pass quickly above the hilltop castle that looks down upon the town of Budejovice.

In the evening the clouds return and when we finish supper in the mess hall we go back to the quarters. The barracks seem dreary and the shaded overhead light leaves the corners of the room in shadow. Lichter goes out and when he comes back he says he was on the telephone to the Embassy in Prague. He takes off his jacket and throws it on the cot. He says the Jews have bombed Egypt with the three B-17s that were at Zatec.

It developed that sometime in June the enterprising Al Schwimmer had actually acquired four B-17s at a surplus field in Florida. Though stripped of armament and some of the instruments they were considered to be in fair flying condition and, because of the urgency which prevailed in the situation in Israel, they made plans to smuggle the bombers out of the States as quickly as possible. On 12 June three of the planes with volunteer flight crews were ready at Miami. The fourth had engine problems and after some delay it was decided to leave it behind. The others took off and, apparently without attracting attention, flew up to Millville. The New Jersey airfield had been used frequently in the covert transactions in May because there was no Customs authority at the facility and fuel could be bought for cash without official inquiry. The B-17s refuelled at Millville on the evening of the 12th. It was the first stop on a flight that took them over Greenland and around the British Isles and on down to Czechoslovakia. They completed the journey without mishap and after they arrived at Zatec the Jewish groundcrews began refitting the bombers and arming them with machine-guns on improvised mountings.

Ray Kurtz, an American Jew and a former squadron commander with the USAAF in Europe, was flown up from Israel on the Balak run to take charge of the operation. This operation was at first considered to be the relatively simple one of ferrying the B-17s out to Aqir but, when the ceasefire ended in July, orders were received to bomb Cairo en route. Though viewed by some as impulsive and vulnerable to international censure, the scheme was nevertheless welcomed with enthusiasm by the bomber crews. The aircraft, however, were far from ready for an actual combat mission. Of the three machines, only one had a bomb-sight and none of them had adequate oxygen systems. They were all provided with crude projectile releases and a collection of welding oxygen tanks. The replacements for missing instruments and parts were equally innovative. By the time the selected departure day arrived, the aircraft displayed such a lack of operational readiness that Kurtz almost aborted the project as too precarious. After a meeting in which the Jewish morale factor was weighed against everything else, they resolved to fly the mission despite the difficulties and uncertainty.

There was a final briefing at the Stalingrad Hotel in Zatec and then, on the afternoon of 14 July, the crews shook hands, embraced and then boarded the bombers for the flight into history. Most of them were from the original Miami group. The B-17s were loaded with the maximum capacity of fuel and bombs and they ran into trouble as soon as they were airborne. Right after take-off, Kurtz lost an engine in the lead machine but he was able to restore partial power to it from the cockpit. He was determined to continue the venture and he was still manipulating the carburetor/air mixture on the faulty engine when they flew into bad weather. The problems began to multiply after some of the flight instruments malfunctioned and, as they neared the Alps, the three planes lost sight of each other entirely in the heavy turbulent clouds. After fighting the controls for hours and maintaining contact with the others by radio, Kurtz finally got below the weather along the Albanian coast. Here they were fired on by suspicious anti-aircraft batteries and had to change course to the middle of the Adriatic. Nearly exhausted by flying through what seemed to an endless storm, the pilots emerged into clear skies over the Mediterranean and within the next hour were able to regroup the formation. They reached the Greek islands at dusk and Kurtz slid the side window open and waved goodbye. His B-17 was the only one going to Cairo. The other two would make bomb runs on Egyptian bases in the northern Sinai and the Gaza-Majdal area on their way into Aqir.

After the two trailing aircraft had turned away, Kurtz began to climb the B-17 up to the flight lanes used by the airlines going into Egypt. When they reached 25,000 feet the navigator fell unconscious over the chart table. Within minutes other crew members collapsed as Kurtz himself experienced a gathering blackness. He instinctly realized that the oxygen pressure from the substitute devices was inadequate for that altitude and he dived the plane back down to 13,000 feet. When the others had recovered from the effects of the thin air they all resorted to the emergency oxygen bottles which someone had the foresight to bring along on this strange odyssey. Kurtz regained the lost height but he didn't know whether the air supply in the small receptacles would last through the run over Cairo.

It was dark when they reached the North African coast a hundred miles west of the Nile Delta and everyone took their stations. Homing on the RAF Fayid radio beacon in the Suez Canal Zone they soon saw the lights of Cairo glowing on the horizon. The city was obviously unaware of their presence and Kurtz set the course on a line over the Farouk Royal Palace. The bombardier then took charge and, directing the B-17 onto the target, he released the cargo of high explosives. Kurtz felt the sudden rise when the machine became lighter and, pushing the nose down, he turned toward Israel as the detonations of the bombs began to light up the sky behind them. They landed at Aqir at 1030 on a clear evening.

The actual damage caused by the raid was comparatively small although 4,000 pounds of explosives had been dropped around the Abadin Palace in the Cairo affair. The psychological impact, however, was far reaching and was, in fact, of infinitely greater value than any physical destruction that could have been delivered by the B-17s at the time. Though it would not be recorded among the great feats of war, the mission was a valiant effort.

* * * * *

Lichter turns out the light and the room becomes dark and, lying on the cot, I think again of Israel and the beach at Tel Aviv. It seems long ago. The rains return sometime during the night. When the rain was heavy the grassy landing area would turn to mud and it was too dangerous to fly the Messerschmitts. We would lie on the cots in the barrack room and listen to the passing storm. A week passes before the sky is blue again.

Lichter says that I will be leaving for Prague tonight. I bank the Messerschmitt onto the final approach and, as usual, I have difficulty rolling the manually operated flaps all the way down. I stare at the handwheel that parallels the seat and pull on it again. The flaps drop another inch. Everyone wears a glove on the left hand in these machines to avoid blisters from this necessary but disconcerting task. The landing field is now large in the center of the windscreen and I begin to put back pressure on the control stick. I drift fast across the perimeter above the Israeli section and the tail starts to drop and I hold it off for a few seconds and then jolt onto the ground. Mud erupts and flies past the canopy and I try to keep the trajectory straight. Way down the field I turn off at an angle to the pine forest. The road that runs along the boundary is ridged with ruts that lead into pools of water.

At the southern line I shut off the engine. The canopy is open and I can see the groundcrew pointing to something at the north end of the take-off run. In the cockpit I lean to the left and look along the side of the cowling. One of the Czech student pilots has just become airborne and the Messerschmitt is hanging perpendicular to the turf a hundred feet in the air. Someone forgot to set their elevator trim forward. The scene seems frozen for an instant and then the aircraft falls off on one wing and hits the ground. There is a loud crack but there is no fire, no smoke, just a spray of mud and then a crumpled pile of metal. People start to run down the field. I stay in the cockpit and idly toy with the control stick. It was always a surprise that a life could end so easily.

Lichter and Flint accompany me to where the path turns onto the perimeter when I leave for Prague that evening. They are staying on at Budejovice for another week because so far Flint had proved particularly ungifted in handling the obstinate traits of the Messerschmitt. I carry the bag and we stop near the gate road. Lichter gives me some extra money for the train ticket and they turn and go back toward the barracks. They say that they will see me in Israel. I wait until they pass behind the elm trees and then I follow along the edge of the perimeter toward the main gate barricade. Bilek is coming down from the hangar and he crosses over by the Spitfire revetments and walks with me. We stop for a moment in front of one of the British fighters. There are five of them at this post and they were a gift from the RAF at the end of the war. Bilek smiles. He says that the Israelis want to buy them but the Czechs haven't agreed on a price yet. He raises his eyebrows. The sun has set and the sky is red and we walk on and talk about the winter in England and the

Spitfires in the snow. At the last revetment there is a soldier standing guard. To the side near the sandbags is something covered by a parachute panel. The center of the silk is bloodstained and muddy boots are sticking out at one end. Beneath this shroud is the body of the student pilot who was killed in the morning crash. The guard salutes as we pass. We walk down to the sentry post at the gate and I go over to the Czechoslovakian Air Force monument at the barrier and look at it one more time. The monument is an entire Messerschmitt set on top of a granite pedestal.

I ride the two miles to the railway station in a Czech service van that Bilek flags down for me, and it is after dark when the train gets into Prague. I go to a room in the Embassy section of the Flora again and when I walk down to the hotel bar I see Sam Pomeranz. The pleasant-faced American Jew is not only a good pilot but he is the chief Israeli engineering officer on the Czechoslovakian end of the operation. He beckons me over to a seat at the bar and we drink German schnapps. Pomeranz is stationed at Zatec but he is in Prague for the night and he laughs and tells me about Al Schwimmer. The airplane procuror is in Israel. After the B-17s left the States illegally, the Federal authorities closed in and Schwimmer had to abandon his business and everything else he owned and get out of the country. He left a day ahead of an indictment charging him with violating the Embargo Act.

I stay in Prague until the next evening and there is a rumor at the Embassy that the UN has arranged another ceasefire in Israel. By the time I leave for the train depot the rumor is confirmed. It is night when I arrive in Zatec.

At the small station a cloud of steam drifts from under the locomotive. Girls in summer dresses pass by. I walk outside and an Israeli technician from the base directs me to the Stalingrad Hotel. The obviously re-named hotel is down a narrow street a hundred yards from the station. It is old and not well lighted. It is the Headquarters for the Zebra operation. There is a cargo carrier crew at a table in the lobby and one of them arranges quarters for me. They are American Jews and I have some beer with them. They say that we won't leave for the south until morning. They know that I am from Budejovice and they talk about the recent fighting in Israel. The fighter squadron had been active since the truce was broken on 8 July. They had used the Messerschmitts as bombers and they had lost one of their pilots in action. Ground support missions had been flown against the Faluja pocket and there were other strikes that ranged from the Negev to Mishmar Ha'Yarden in the north. A volunteer American, Bob Vickman, was the pilot who had been killed and Mordecai Alon, the CO, had shot down an Egyptian Spitfire.

The C-46 crew start to talk about some of the action in early June – the time when only four of the Messerschmitts had been in service. A raid against the Egyptian Sinai base at El Arish had been organized but

before they got off the ground it was cancelled and they were told to
attack an enemy column which had advanced to a point along the coastal
road, 20 miles south of Tel Aviv. The four, which included Mordecai
Alon and Ezer Weizman, flew out to sea initially and then cut back in
across the beach and strafed the Egyptians. Two of the aircraft were
carrying wing bombs and though the strike was not extraordinarily
devastating, the disruption that was caused succeeded in halting the
advance. During the sweep, however, a South African volunteer, Eddie
Cohen, was shot down and killed and Alon had to crash-land at Aqir.
Eddie became the first fighter pilot in the Israeli Air Force to die in battle
and on the one mission the newly appointed Fighter Command had lost
half of its strength. The following day it was down to one aircraft when
another Messerschmitt was lost near Natanya. This machine was hit by
fire from an Iraqi armored force which was trying to push to the coast
from Tulkarm. The pilot in this instance was an American volunteer
named Rubenfeld who had since transferred from the Squadron. When
he was forced to parachute from the out-of-control plane over the Jewish
settlement of Kafr Vitkin, he had the presence of mind to shout loudly
and persistently in Yiddish as he descended because the farmers in the
area at the time considered anything in the air to be an enemy. As with
many of the volunteers, Rubenfeld didn't speak Hebrew but his Yiddish
served the purpose in this case because when he was picked up by an
Israeli army unit the farmers hadn't hung him. The C-46 crew all laugh
and they order more beer. Someone says that it was the day after this
incident that Alon shot down the Dakotas with the one remaining
Messerschmitt.

   In the early morning we have coffee at the hotel and then ride to the
base in one of the Czech military cars. The cargo carrier we are taking is
on the flat concrete ramp by the main hangar. Inside the fuselage we
have to squeeze between crates to get to the forward section. A
Messerschmitt is lashed down on the starboard side and the disconnected
wings are jammed tightly against the frame of the transport
compartment. After what happened to the flight engineer at Aqir, I avoid
sitting near the front bulkhead and I get up on top of some weapons
boxes at the side of the narrow aisle. The pilot pushes through toward the
cockpit. He says the crew I came up with are back in Israel. There have
been changes since the month began. The Balak run has been closed
down and the Israelis are using a different route. It is now called
Operation Velveta and the fuelling stop is Yugoslavia.

   It is sunny when we clear the end of the runway at Zatec and we turn
on to the first leg which is a course almost directly south to Titograd. The
Yugoslav airfield is not far from the coast of the Adriatic and when we
land we find ourselves on a vast sod surface. There are mountains in the
background and the C-46 lumbers across the field until we arrive at a
number of frame buildings where we are met by the groundcrew. We

have been in the air almost three hours. Many of the Yugoslavs are around the aircraft when we get out and most of them are attired in worn uniforms and some in under shirts. They begin the refuelling and they show evident curiosity about the Panama insignia. We stand around and watch the procedure for a few minutes. The system they are employing is crude in its simplicity because they merely pump the fuel by hand from large drums. A thin, middle-aged officer comes over and we follow him down a muddy lane until we get to a hut where they are serving food. We are offered a substantial soup and strong Yugoslavian liqor.

The Velveta route was not only more direct but it had become, a few weeks earlier, a pressing necessity for the continued delivery of military supplies to Israel. The United States, which remained single-minded in its belief that the Jewish-Arab conflict could be ended by the UN mediation, had put diplomatic pressure on the French to deny the Ajaccio stop to the Israel-based transports regardless of the Panamanian registry. The Panama ruse had been suspected in May during the early Schwimmer procurements but no significant action was taken until a month after the B-17 episode at Miami. With the Balak operation thus blocked at Corsica, an alternate refuelling base between Czechoslovakia and Israel suddenly took on an aspect of extreme urgency. The deal at Titograd was the alternative and it was another example of the Israeli ability to resolve quickly the emergencies that were commonplace throughout this war.

After a two hour delay because of ignition problems in one of the engines, we leave the Yugoslavian scene behind. The afternoon is fading and in three hours night falls outside the cargo space windows and the sea turns sombre below. Tel Aviv is easily discernible as we approach the coast of Israel but inland the lights disappear until the runway at Aqir comes into view. It is nearly the end of July.

The C-46 goes to the far side of a corrugated hangar on the south boundary and, when we get out of the aircraft and walk to the Operations hut, we can see one of the B-17s inside the maintenance compound. As soon as we go into the shack Bernstein comes through the field door. His face is browned and he looks different and his khakis are soiled. He smiles and says they are down at Aqir to change a cylinder head on the bomber. We sit down in some chairs in a corner and Bernstein talks. He says he likes Ramat David and that they [the B-17s] bombed Damascus during the fighting in July. Transportation is leaving for Tel Aviv and I stand up. Bernstein says that Sarah was the Israeli girl who was killed on the hospital plane in June.

CHAPTER IV

THE SQUADRON

I stay that night at the aircrew quarters in the Tel Aviv suburbs and when we get to the Beit Dagan crossroads on the way in from Aqir, two jackals run down ahead of us in the beams of the headlights. In the morning I am assigned to 101 Squadron at Herzliya. The Yarkon is the same and it is good to be there again. When I leave the posting office I get my kit and go across to the motor pool. Some people are climbing into the back of a truck and they say they are going to Lydda. I ask one of the volunteers about Bieberman. He says that Bieberman was sent back to the States two weeks ago because he was disconsolate all the time. I leave my kit at the motor pool and go out to the beach road and walk down past the Gallim Yam. I think of Bieberman and Sarah and the day we arrived in Haifa.

It is even hotter that it was in June and at the sea wall I stop and look out at the LST. Nothing had changed. It was rustier but the spray still flew over it and the water was shining beyond it like it always was. I go back to the cafe in Allenby Road. The cafe is dark inside after the brightness of the sun and someone calls to me from another table. It is Al Freeman. We had been together in the same US fighter group for a while in 1944 but I hadn't seen him after that. He comes over and, smiling, sits down. An easy-going American Jew, Freeman is with 101 Squadron but he says he has applied to go home since the recent ceasefire. He says he heard I was coming down from Budejovice.

Al Freeman arrived with the previous group at the end of June and went into action on 8 July when the first truce was broken. He laughs and says that everyone got bullet holes in their planes on the low-level missions and that one of the flight commanders shot his own propeller blades off when the machine-guns became unsynchronized. The greatest attrition to the aircraft, however, was caused by the accidents which occurred on the ground. Freemen talks about one of the Messerschmitts that went over on its back with a bomb under each wing. The pilot got a fractured skull but the bombs didn't explode because the detonators hadn't been set. He stretches his legs out beneath the table. He says that on the mission when Vickman was shot down there was a lot of ground fire at the time. Three girls come in and sit down at the next table. Two are wearing army skirts and the third a yellow-print dress. The one in the print dress smiles at Freeman. He gets up from the table. He says he will probably be leaving Israel tomorrow. He touches my shirt and then edges between the chairs and into the passage way. The girls smile and say shalom and he nods and then is gone out into the sunlight.

Herzliya in 1948 was an average Jewish town in Palestine. It had some cafes and small stores and a cinema and outlying houses with gardens. It is eight miles north of Tel Aviv and a mile from the sea. Beyond the houses, which date from the early Mandate years or before, are open fields. Many of the fields are cultivated but one, to the south of the settlement of Kafr Shmaryahu, is being graded into an airbase. Kafr Shmaryahu sits atop some grassy hills at the northern end of the strip and below lie the tents and stone block buildings of the base camp. To the east and south are groves of orange and fig trees. Cedars border the road toward town. The camp is the home of Israel's first fighter squadron.

When the lorry slows at the Command hut I jump down with the duffel bag and the truck continues along the road to the airfield. It is late afternoon and there are not many people about. Two girls watch from the doorway of the Communications shack. One of the girls has red hair. Modecai Alon is alone in the hut and he is writing at a desk that has scars in the dark wood. His bush shirt is clean and well ironed. To one side of the room is a leather-covered couch and behind a semi-curtained partition is a smaller room with a cot in it. Flies buzz sporadically through the doorless entrance. The sound is curiously restful. The CO doesn't ask any questions.

There are no aircraft at the Herzliya base. Everything is up at Natanya until the new strip is ready. The pilots return to quarters at Kafr Shmaryahu at nightfall. I follow the CO outside and one of the jeeps is coming down the dirt road from Herzliya. The road runs for a quarter of a mile through the southern groves and passes the administration huts and the mess hall, and then curves down to the operations area at the strip. The jeep stops near the Command hut. All of the occupants are either talking or laughing. A few have on light cotton flying suits but others are wearing tropical shorts and some are stripped to the waist. They are casual with the CO. He is addressed simply as Moddy. No rank, no salutes, no military stance. Laughter and curses, yet one gets the immediate impression that they know their job. The driver of the jeep is an imposing South African Jew and he gets out of the seat and comes over to where we are standing. Moddy says that the South African is the commander of B Flight. It is Sid Cohen.

From the heart of Johannesburg, Sid was in most ways a South African but as a Jew his desire to see a secure Jewish State in Israel was as strong, perhaps, as the similar desires of the most dedicated sabra.

When World War II began he was starting his medical studies which he forsook to enter military service and he was accepted early into the South African Air Force. Although he was large physically, he was appointed to fighters when he finished his training and was assigned to P-40 Kittyhawks in the Western Desert in early 1942. The Kittyhawks were the goats of the desert campaign and while attached to 4 SAAF Squadron, he participated in most of the North African battles that year and into 1943. By the time he finished his second operational tour it was 1944 and the Kittyhawks were obsolete. He was transferred to Spitfires and was beginning his third tour when the war finally came to an end while he was stationed in northern Italy.

Though not one of the spectacular fighter pilots which that era periodically produced, Sid had a unique combination of skill, endurance, and the ability to lead with an almost uncanny calmness of spirit. Like all who have seen action, he was effected by it but it was a mark that was rarely visible in the nature of him and he returned to civilian life with an attitude that was probably more outwardly serene than most. He, as was the case with any who flew in the great conflict, never forgot the air but he settled into the routine of making a living on the ground and he went back to his medical studies in Johannesburg. It was three years before he would again offer his services and, this time his experience, to a nation at war. Though he didn't arrive in the new State of Israel as early as did Boris Senior or Eddie Cohen, his unmatched qualities as a pilot and a leader precipitated his immediate appointment as a Flight commander in 101 Squadron after coming in from Budejovice in late June. To Sid, the fact that we were flying Messerschmitts seemed forever ironic and comical.

He looks different without a beard. At El Adem that autumn of 1942, Sid had a beard. I think of the night when we [members of 92 Squadron] were looking for the landing ground where the Spitfires were and the flat desolation of the Western Desert all seemed the same. We drove up to the mess tent of the South Africans. They were having a party. The South Africans always had brandy and it was the first time I met Sid. At two inches over six feet, he was at the tent flap with tin cups in his hands and he ordered us to have a drink. He called himself Cohen the Jew and he led everyone in singing ribald songs. We stayed there all night. Now we stand in the dust beside a stone hut in Israel and face each other again. The beard is gone but there is the same flat nose, the wide face, the calm eyes. Remembering, Sid takes my arm and we go over to the jeep and I meet the others. Sid Antin, Aaron Finkel, Sandy Jacobs, Giddy Lichtman. They joke among themselves. Then Moddy gets his jeep and we go up to Kafr Shmaryahu.

The winding, rutted road that travels up the hill from the camp turns on to tar pavement at the top of the rise, and then passes the scattered dwellings of the settlement and ends at a lane near the pilots' quarters.

White plaster buildings with red tile roofs stand back from the lane and a hedge leads to an entrance where there is a garden area with a large acacia tree by a screened dining hall. The rooms in the two wings of the pension buildings are small and to accommodate all of the personnel a sleeping tent had to be set up at the edge of the adjoining maize field. On the other side of the lane are the fenced corrals of a farm and, back where the tar surface terminates, there are a few houses and a store. Down behind a vineyard is a beer garden. On the northern side the dirt lane trails off to a deserted Palestinian Arab village and then the hills slope west to the open fields and the sea. Beyond the beer garden in Kafr Shmaryahu the main road continues for a mile and, at the junction where it bends toward Herzliya, there is a roadhouse. Below the roadhouse is the white sand of the beach that runs beneath the sharply-rising coastal escarpment.

Before dark the remaining pilots arrive from Natanya and after the evening meal everyone sits around in beach chairs under the tree. I go with Sid Cohen to the tent. He and the South African Arni Ruch are the only other occupants and, after I put my kit under one of the cots, we walk back out to the nearby garden. There are fifteen pilots plus the adjutant and engineering officer at the Kafr Shmaryahu quarters. When the last group from the auxiliary field comes in, the Gentile Chris Magee is with them. He has a red handkerchief on his head and a pistol on one leg and a trench-knife on the other. Like everyone else he is burned dark by the sun.

Moddy goes into Tel Aviv after dinner and Ezer Weizman gets the other jeep and we go down to the beer garden. Some are walking down and Ezer almost hits two of them when he spins the jeep on the dirt. Everyone curses and laughs. The night is warm and at the beer garden we sit outside under the lanterns which are strung overhead. The daughters of the proprietor serve the beer in glass pitchers and we drink and everyone talks. They talk mostly about the flying and I look at the faces and try to remember the names. Lou Lenart, an affable American volunteer who led some of the missions in the first days, is sitting next to Sid Cohen. Across the planked table are three others from the States – Bill Pomerantz [not to be confused with Sam Pomeranz], Leon Frankel and Rudy Augarten. Directly opposite is the A Flight commander, Maury Mann. Short, heavy and curly haired, Mann is an English Jew. Beside him there is another English Jew, the tall, relaxed Cyril Horowitz. At the front of the table is the happy American Stan Andrews, and the irrepressible Ezer Weizman.

The youngest of the three sabra pilots in 101 Squadron, Ezer is cultured and witty. Coming from a distinguished Russian emigré family, he is the nephew of the legendary Chaim Weizmann, Israel's first President. Ezer is possessed of both intellect and a sense of humor and his command of the English phrase is enviable, but beyond this it is his personal nature that serves him best. He has an obsessive dedication to the cause of the State but he also has the gift of approaching issues with an unshakable light-heartedness. Trained in World War II by the Royal Air Force, he attained the rank of Sergeant Pilot, which was almost the universal rank for the handful of Palestinian Jewish candidates who achieved pilot status with the British during those years. He served until 1946 and, although he never saw actual combat operations with the RAF and was less experienced than Remez or the brilliant organizer Dan Tolkowski or than Mordecai Alon, Ezer had already achieved the reputation of being one of the most flamboyant of the Messerschmitt pilots.

There are night insects circling about the lanterns and one of them flies into a beer pitcher. Sid Cohen says that it looked like one of Giddy's landings. Someone retrieves the moth and throws it into the bushes bordering the tables. Sid pours some more beer into his glass. He is the pilot who shot part of his propeller blades off on a mission to Faluja and someone jokes about it. Sid smiles and drinks his beer. Giddy comes over from the group at the other table. From Newark, New Jersey, he stands next to Ezer and, holding a glass, he starts talking about the time they were scrambled after some Egyptian Spitfires in June.

Everyone was in Tel Aviv that day because none of the Messerschmitts were close to being serviceable. In the afternoon Moddy was contacted at their town Headquarters in the Yarden Hotel and was told by HQ Operations to get two of his pilots and scramble. There were reports of the Spitfires fooling around along the coast south of Jaffa and three of the Messerschmitts at Aqir had suddenly and miraculously become combat-ready. The only problem was that the Jewish pilots were 20 miles away from the base. Moddy hung up the telephone and ran out of the room. The first two he encountered were Lou and Ezer. When they all got out to the street they discovered that Moddy's jeep was missing, which, although it was an annoying development, was not an uncommon occurrence in Tel Aviv during this phase of the war. Ignoring the stares of everyone on the walkway, the trio sprinted the few blocks to the motor pool at the Yarkon to requisition some transporation but here a clash ensued with the Duty Officer because they had no written authorisation. Out of breath, Moddy and Lou were angry and Ezer was infuriated. He ran into the middle of the road and flagged down an ancient taxi and they all jumped in the back and headed out of town. During the entire trip to Aqir, Ezer and the driver argued over how much the fare was going to be and when they got to the base they had to run another hundred yards to the Ops shack, where they found out that the scramble had been called off.

When Giddy finishes the story everyone laughs and Ezer smiles down at his beer glass. This incident, like so many others that became part of the legends of that year, tended to be embellished upon and exaggerated

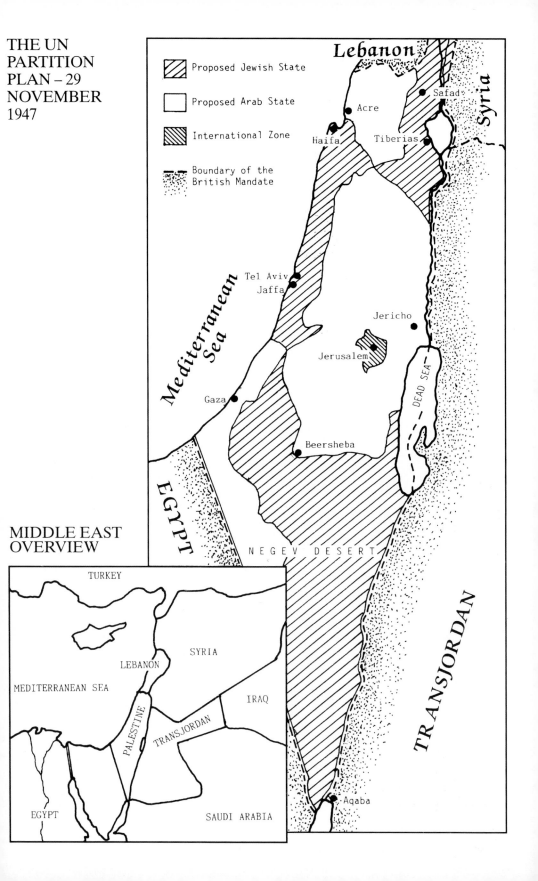

THE UN
PARTITION
PLAN – 29
NOVEMBER
1947

Proposed Jewish State

Proposed Arab State

International Zone

Boundary of the
British Mandate

MIDDLE EAST
OVERVIEW

Lebanon

Syria

Safad

Acre

Haifa

Tiberias

Mediterranean
Sea

Tel Aviv

Jaffa

Jericho

Jerusalem

DEAD SEA

Gaza

Beersheba

EGYPT

NEGEV DESERT

TRANSJORDAN

TURKEY

CYPRUS

SYRIA

LEBANON

MEDITERRANEAN SEA

PALESTINE

TRANSJORDAN

IRAQ

EGYPT

SAUDI ARABIA

Aqaba

Newly commissioned Pilot Officer in the RAF; Leo as a RAF fighter pilot with 71 (Eagle) Squadron, 1942.

(Leo Nomis via NWMA collection)

Top: Leo posing with his 'own' Spitfire (BL287 XR-C) while serving with 71 (Eagle) Squadron, 1942.

(Leo Nomis via NWMA collection)

Above: With 229 Squadron RAF at Takali, Malta, August 1942. Leo is standing seventh from left. Seated in front of him is Wg Cdr John Thompson, Wing Commander (Flying) Takali, and on Thompson's left is Grp Capt Walter Churchill, who was killed in action two days after the photograph was taken.

(Leo Nomis via NWMA collection)

Left: Plt Off Leo Nomis (left) with Plt Off Art Roscoe, both 71 (Eagle) Squadron, 1942. *(Leo Nomis via NWMA collection)*

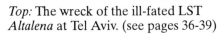

Top: The wreck of the ill-fated LST
Altalena at Tel Aviv. (see pages 36-39)

Bottom left: A pilot with two hats: Leo
after his transfer to the USAAF in 1943.
(Leo Nomis collection)

Bottom right: Leo in Israel, 1948.
(Leo Nomis collection)

Top: Messerschmitt D-107.
(Leo Nomis collection)

Above: 101 Squadron's first CO, Palestinian-born Moddy Alon (right) with American volunteers Lou Lenart (left) and Giddy Lichtman (centre).
(Giddy Lichtman collection)

Left: Left to right: Cyril Horowitz, Sandy Jacobs, Stan Andrews (killed in action 20 October 1948) , Lou Lenart, unknown, Bob Vickman (killed in action 9 July 1948).
(Maurice Mann collection)

Top: The irrepressible Ezer Weizman (centre) with Bill Pomerantz (left) and Maury Mann (right).   *(Aaron Finkel collection via Shlomo Aloni)*

Bottom: Aaron Finkel and Sid Antin with Messerschmitt D-108.

                                                                   (Aaron Finkel collection via Shlomo Aloni)

Top left: Sid Cohen, Giddy Lichtman,
Moddy Alon, Ezer Weizman, Arni Ruch.
(Aaron Finkel collection via Shlomo Aloni)

Top right: Group of 101 Squadron pilots
with Messerschmitt. On cowling, Maury
Mann, Ezer Weizman, Red Finkel; on

wing, Bill Pomerantz, Sandy Jacobs,
Sid Antin; standing, Sid Cohen, Chris
Magee, Giddy Lichtman, Leon Frankel,
Leo Nomis. *(Giddy Lichtman collection)*

Bottom: Same occasion, same group.
(Aaron Finkel collection via Shlomo Aloni)

Top: With the Squadron jeep at Ma'abarot, from left to right: Rudy Augarten, Cyril Horowitz, Red Finkel, Maury Mann, unknown, Leo Nomis, George Lichter.

(Aaron Finkel collection via Shlomo Aloni)

Bottom: Maury Mann and Sid Antin with Messerschmitt. *(Maurice Mann collection)*

Top: 101 Squadron pilots and administration personnel at Herzliya, September 1948. Left to right, standing: Sid Cohen, Coleman Goldstein, Maury Mann, Lou Lenart, Sid Antin, Ezer Weizman, Moddy Alon, Stan Andrews, Les Shagum, Rudy Augarten, Bill Pomerantz, Leo Nomis, Assistant IO, Dave Croll; front row, George Lichter, Chris Magee, Giddy Lichtman, Sandy Jacobs, Red Finkel, Kalman Turin, Provost Marshal, Arni Ruch. *(Leo Nomis collection)*

Bottom left: Prime Minister Ben-Gurion's visit to Natanya. Left to right, Giddy Lichtman, Moddy Alon, David Ben-Gurion, Mrs Ben-Gurion, Maury Mann, Sandy Jacobs.

(Giddy Lichtman collection)

Bottom right: Ezer Weizman, proudly displaying his newly grown beard.

(Leon Frankel collection via Shlomo Aloni)

Top left: Giddy Lichtman poses in front of a Messerschmitt.

(Giddy Lichtman collection)

Top right: Cyril Horowitz survived a take-off crash in Messerschmitt D-122.

(Maurice Mann collection)

Bottom left: Maury Mann, Bill Pomerantz, Sid Antin. *(David Baron collection)*

Bottom right: Ready for action – Giddy Lichtman; he shot down an Egyptian Air Force Spitfire and an Arab Airways Dragon Rapide during his service with 101 Squadron. *(Giddy Lichtman collection)*

Top: Dragon Rapide TJ-AAE of Arab Airways, sister aircraft to that shot down by Giddy Lichtman. *(John Havers collection)*

Bottom: Leo Nomis and Cyril Horowitz at Falk's house, Kfar Shmaryahu.

(Leon Frankel collection via Shlomo Aloni)

Top: Bill Pomerantz in the cockpit of D-120. *(Leon Frankel collection via Shlomo Aloni)*

Bottom: Ezer Weizman tries to 'outdo' the image on the Squadron badge.

(Leon Frankel collection via Shlomo Aloni)

Top: 101 Squadron's Technical Officer Harry Axelrod in front of D-123.

(Leon Frankel collection via Shlomo Aloni)

Bottom: Debriefing at Herzliya (left to right) Ezer Weizman, Maury Mann, Sid Antin, Dave Croll (IO). *(Leon Frankel collection via Shlomo Aloni)*

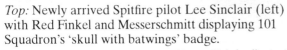

Top: Newly arrived Spitfire pilot Lee Sinclair (left) with Red Finkel and Messerschmitt displaying 101 Squadron's 'skull with batwings' badge.

(*Aaron Finkel collection*)

Above: Count Folke Bernadotte's UN-marked Dakota narrowly escaped becoming the victim of Messerschmitts flown by Giddy Lichtman and Leo Nomis. (*Al-Ahram Archive*)

Right: Maury Mann with the resurrected Spitfire D-130; while flying a Messerschmitt he shot down a Syrian Air Force Harvard.

(*Maurice Mann collection*)

Top: Messerschmitt D-120.

Middle left: Dov Ben Zvi, alias Baron Wiseberg, alias David Baron; a former Royal Navy Fleet Air Arm fighter pilot who flew a few operations with 101 Squadron early in the conflict.

(David Baron collection)

Bottom left: Moddy Alon, 101 Squadron's first CO who was killed when his Messerschmitt crashed on 16 October 1948.

(Leon Frankel collection via Shlomo Aloni)

Bottom right: Leo Nomis with Ezer Weizman in December 1986. Ezer Weizman commanded the Israeli Air Force from 1958 to 1966 and is currently (1998) the President of Israel. *(Leo Nomis collection)*

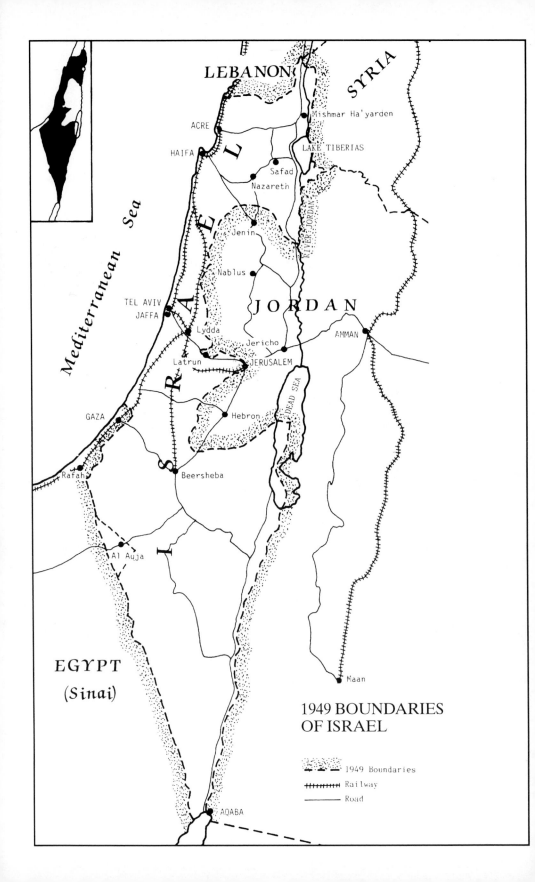

LEBANON

SYRIA

Mishmar Ha'yarden

ACRE

HAIFA

LAKE TIBERIAS

Safad

Nazareth

Jenin

Nablus

JORDAN

TEL AVIV
JAFFA

Lydda

Jericho

AMMAN

Latrun

JERUSALEM

GAZA

Hebron

DEAD SEA

Rafah

Beersheba

Al Auja

EGYPT
(Sinai)

Maan

Mediterranean Sea

RIVER JORDAN

I S R A E L

1949 BOUNDARIES
OF ISRAEL

AQABA

1949 Boundaries
Railway
Road

as time went on, and one version even had Ezer arriving at the base directly from a bar mitzvah and scrambling after the Egyptians in a tuxedo.

Giddy was one of the original group of foreign volunteers in the Israeli Air Force. Twenty-five years of age, he was of medium height, personable, cheerful and courageous. Arriving right after the Declaration, he was in the second contingent at Budejovice and he was at Aqir shortly after 101 Squadron was activated. He could handle the Messerschmitts better than most and by the beginning of the second month he had shot down one of the Egyptian Spitfires. The Jewish-Arab war was a crusade as far as he was concerned and he wouldn't accept the standard salary offered by the Agency to volunteers, receiving only the subsistence pay that was alloted monthy in Israel. With the US 9th Air Force in Europe as a P-51 pilot in 1945, he saw little action before World War II ended but he had come to Israel to fight. The truces and ceasefires annoyed him and during these periods he patrolled endlessly for the elusive shufti kites and stunted high in the sun. Shufti kite (shufti, from the Arabic word for 'look') was the popular term applied to those high-level reconnaissance aircraft of unknown nationality that daily made runs over Israeli territory. The quest to engage these seemingly unreachable machines was seriously hampered by the absence of oxygen equipment in the Messerschmitts, a situation that was mysteriously never remedied during their entire length of service that year. The shufti kites had been identified as British-built Mosquitos but the origin and homeland of the rapid-travelling planes has yet to be established.

There is a half-moon in the cloudless sky when I walk with Sid Cohen and Arni Ruch on the road back to our quarters. They talk in Afrikaans sometimes and the jolly-natured Arni laughs at everything Sid says. Arni isn't as big as Sid and he is fair-haired. He seems to be always smiling. We near the lane and Sid is talking about when they got up to Italy in 1943 and he had met a girl in one of the villages outside Parma. She wouldn't have anything to do with him romantically because she said he looked like Jesus Christ. Sid says he shaved off the beard after that. Arni laughs again and pulls at his tropical shorts. We turn through the garden and walk past the white buildings. In the tent Sid lights a kerosene lamp and our shadows appear large on the canvas. We get into the cots and roll the insect nets down and Sid extinguishes the lamp. We are all sleeping in our underwear. The voices from the buildings die away and the dogs behind the dining hall stop barking and then there is silence and darkness. A half hour later the jackals begin their wailing down the hill and the chorus is answered along the line and carried far off into the distance. The sound is like children crying in the night.

The morning at Natanya is clear and hot and a cloud of dust is hanging in the air at the north end of the field where one of the fighters is running up. Two miles to the west, beyond a line of cedars, the beach

town simmers by the sea. The trees continue across the southern edge of
the wide landing strip and turn back up the eastern side where they
separate the airfield from the inland road to Herzliya. The tents of the
groundcrew and the new covered aircraft revetments lie along the
perimeter to the north-east and, from a distance, they are distorted by the
heat devils which rise from the dry earth. The area is flat and there is a
perpetual crosswind. The approach from the north is directly over the big
fresh water vats of the fish farms. We had left Kafr Shmaryahu at dawn.
We could feel the heat of the coming day when we ate breakfast on the
screen porch of the dining room and then we got into the back of the
Squadron lorry. The ride to Natanya took 25 minutes. We were all
bunched together in the rear of the truck and everyone was quiet because
it was so early.

It is the first day of August and due to the ceasefire the flying at
Natanya is limited to line patrols; and futile attempts to intercept the
shufti kites. The cloud of dust on the north boundary is heavier now as
the single Messerschmitt swings around and, gaining speed, takes off
past us and roars down the strip. It lurches about but bounces into the air
farther along and barely clears the southern trees. Everyone turns their
backs to the rush of wind and we walk over to the Ops tent near the
maintenance area. I have been assigned to B Flight and Sid Cohen
arranges for me to go on a four-plane sector patrol. Giddy is appointed
to lead the formation and the others are Ezer and Sandy. The third of the
trio of sabra pilots in 101 Squadron, Sandy came over from the light
planes at Sde Dov and he has unsettlingly little fighter experience to be
flying the intolerant Messerschmitts. Small, almost frail, the
imperturbable Sandy is British-educated and speaks with the precise
intonation of the upper class but he says nothing now as we select
parachutes and gear from an assortment piled haphazardly on the floor
of the Ops tent. When we go back outside Sid unfolds a map on the
ground. He points to the salient created by the Partition and, indicating
that Tulkarm is the apex, he moves his finger along the approximate
positions of the Arab lines. He looks at Giddy and says that we will stay
away from them today. Tulkarm is eight miles due east of where we are
standing.

The Israeli and Arab positions along the fronts had changed little with
the comparatively brief fighting in July. In the diverse sectors the Galil
was still held securely against the Syrian attacks and the Alexandroni
Brigade had checked the Iraqis and Trans-Jordan Arabs in the west
salient. The problems with the Arab Legion in Jerusalem and along the
corridor supply route at Latrun remained and, because of the proximity
of the combatants in this situation, the area was forever involved in truce
violations. The Palestinian Arabs who had fled Israel's boundaries and
joined the invading armies were scattered generally among all of the
regular Arab forces, but they also had independent commands in the

salient and in the Negev to the south.

The major foe in the south was, of course, Egypt. This army had advanced into Israeli territory as far as Isdud, just north of what would become known as the Gaza Strip, and here they were stopped by the Jewish Givati and Negev Brigades and by the heroics of the people on the kibbutzes in their path. This latter Brigade also controlled the Egyptian forays to the eastern Negev and one unit, Chaim Bar Lev's 8th Palmach Regiment, proved to be particularly deadly in counter-attacking these enemy moves. Except for some advance patrol activity in earlier days, Isdud was to be the farthest penetration by the Egyptian ground forces and, as August arrived, their main invasion army was encamped there. Although they were halted, their presence was both morally and militarily intolerable to the Israelis, not the least of the reasons being that the airfield at Yasir (Hatzor) had to be abandoned because it was only two miles from the Egyptian artillery. To the extreme north, Lebanon had proved to be impotent from the first day and other than a rallying point for some of the Palestinian Arab groups it was considered neutralized. Lebanon, however, did provide a seaport for the Arab bloc countries which were landlocked and was looked upon during the war as more of an economic ally to the invaders than a military one. The situation as it stood on 1 August was far from being settled.

Ezer and Giddy are already in the cockpits and the shirtless crewmen are standing in the sun beside the planes when Sandy and I come out to where the four Messerschmitts are lined up. The mechanics are curious when I get there because they haven't seen me before. I climb onto the wing and the metal on the side of the cockpit burns my hand when I grasp the running edge for support. I stand on the wing and put on the helmet and fasten the parachute buckles. I look over at the Messerschmitts on the line. In contrast to the grey camouflage on those in Czechoslovakia, these are colored a solid pale tan with light blue under surfaces. The Star of David insignia on the fuselage is inordinately large and a thin blue and white band encircles the body in front of the tail section. Preceding the band is a Hebrew letter and a number in black. The Desert Hawks. As I get into the cockpit I look down the side at the number. It is 114.

We wait in the heat at the end of the field beyond the Ops tent. We wait with propellers turning idly for Sandy to pull into line. The inside of the cockpit becomes a furnace and perspiration drips onto the safety harness. The coolant temperature climbs to a dangerous point and Giddy comes on the radio and says we better get off the ground. Sandy swings around behind and when Giddy turns down field to take off, a hazy mist of dark smoke begins to come from Ezer's engine. It indicates an oil leak and he tuns in a wide circle and heads back to the maintenance area. Giddy signals with his hand that he is opening the throttle and I follow closely to his right so I won't be engulfed in the dust from his prop wash.

Sandy disappears behind us. We lift off near the south border and Giddy stays in a constant turn to the left. We come around low and parallel to the strip and then cut across so Sandy can catch up. The gear indicator light flickers and I check the handle. Everything seems all right and in a few seconds the light remains steady. When Sandy is in position on the port side, Giddy climbs to 9,000 feet and we can see scattered white clouds way off to the north. The cockpit is tolerable now as the cool upper air passes through vents.

Giddy takes the formation on a tour. Continuing north, Caesarea glides away under us on the coast and, across the narrow void between the aircraft, the illusion is created that we are all hanging suspended and motionless. We change course south of the Syrian-Lebanon frontier. The Israeli positions in the Galil string outward along the terrain and everything appears peaceful from above. We turn south over Lake Tiberius. Following the west bank of the Jordan River we come to where the salient cuts in sharply and Giddy clicks the R/T and points to the sector which is held by elements of the Carmeli Brigade. The lines are facing the ancient Jewish lands of Judea and Samaria and, down beyond Jenin, a veil of dust implies that there are troop movements by the Trans-Jordanians. We bank westward before we pass into enemy airspace and we are back on a course for the coast. Ramat David is off the starboard wing. We have been in the air for over an hour. When we approach Natanya we can see Tel Aviv clearly and away to the south-east lies sprawling Jerusalem.

Giddy has tired of the monotonous routine flying and he gestures for Sandy to change over. Sandy drops below us and comes up on my right wing. He is close in and the side engine panels of his aircraft are streaked with oil and dirt. As soon as we are in the echelon formation Giddy rolls down to the left. As I drop with him I can see Sandy from an inverted position for an instant and then ahead of me Giddy is rolling straight down at the earth. Kafr Yona is directly beneath us. The brown fields come closer and we pull up and the line of the sea passes by on the horizon. Giddy is rolling upward at the sky. I pressure the control stick strenuously. It is difficult to stay with him and the aircraft have become strung out. Sandy is now far below. After ten minutes of trying to catch up we come onto the approach at the Natanya strip and, one by one, make the turn over the fish farms and hold off into the crosswind when we land.

At noon a truck comes in from the Herzliya camp with lunch rations and we sit along the eastern row of cedars and eat sandwiches made of fig jam and rye bread. Giddy, Sid Cohen and Maury Mann are sitting side by side and Maury is talking about some problem he had with one of the machines during the morning. Someone is landing a Messerschmitt from the south because the wind has changed 30 degrees and we all watch as he settles and touches down on the strip. It is a good landing but then the aircraft suddenly swerves to the right and starts into a ground loop. The pilot is plainly using counter rudder but the Messerschmitt ignores it and begins to drag a wingtip. We stand up. One of the mechanics is urinating on a tree and he watches over his shoulder. The uncontrollable plane still has a lot of speed and it is now heading toward us at a rapid rate. No one moves and the only sound is the gunning of the engine. A billow of dust is streaming back from under the wing and as the machine's direction becomes apparent everyone on the line of cedars starts to run. Maury kicks over a tea mug that is on the ground in front of him and we begin to race toward the revetments down the perimeter. I look back and the mechanic is running behind us with his pants unbuttoned. The wayward Messerschmitt bears down relentlessly but before it gets to the perimeter it swings around to the west and one of the legs on the landing gear collapses. It comes to a stop 20 yards away, the wooden propeller churning the earth and throwing out giant splinters. The tail bounces six feet into the air and the engine dies. The dust settles and there is silence. Those who had been running come to a halt. Then, as is the case when one appears foolish in the face of danger, everyone laughs.

Moddy is at the Ops tent when we go back and his face is impassive. A Flight is sending out a two-plane line patrol and the tough, wiry, oft-times stoical Sid Antin and Red Finkel are gathering their equipment in the tent. They are both New York Jews and at thirty-two years of age they are the oldest pilots in the Squadron. Composed, sandy-haired, quiet, Finkel smiles to himself and carries his parachute toward the standby aircraft. I look at the maintenance board that is propped against the tent flap. There are nine Messerschmitts serviceable out of the fifteen at Natanya. Moddy tells Sid Cohen to bring me along and we walk over to a nearby revetment which, like the others, is covered from above by camouflage netting. The bright sun filters through the netting and onto a Spitfire which is suspended on wing jacks. Around the Spitfire are four mechanics and they are all wearing greasy shorts. None of them is wearing a shirt. Moddy calls the crew sergeant over and we go around and look at the engine. The aircraft is almost ready for operations. Moddy and Sid look under the eliptical wings and then go back and inspect the tail section. I stand next to Moishe the crew sergeant and look up at the nose spinner and then Moddy comes back to the front of the revetment. He nods to me and says the machine is an Egyptian Spitfire.

It was brought down in May, during the first week of the war. Hit by Bren gun fire on one of the Tel Aviv raids, the Spitfire was forced to belly-land north of Isdud and was captured by Israeli defense troops in the area. The pilot was taken prisoner and the machine transported first to the base at Aqir, where it was found to be repairable if enough replacement parts could be found. At the time there were discarded RAF maintenance supplies left by the British at Lydda, but whether or not there were enough miscellaneous Spitfire parts remained to be seen. A talented and industrious aircraft engineer, Freddie Ish-Shalom, took charge of the project of resurrecting the enemy plane and he and his mechanics began to comb the abandoned British depots for the essential material. They were soon directly aided in their search by the Egyptian fiasco at Ramat David which occurred shortly afterward.

In this incident, which many Israelis considered the most amusing of the war, the Royal Egyptian Air Force sent six Spitfires out from El Arish to attack the northern Palestine base at Ramat David, apparently without knowing that the airfield was still under RAF control. The Egyptians did some damage to the installation with the fighter-bombers and were on their way back across Israeli territory when Royal Air Force Spitfires caught up with them. The British pilots shot down five [sic] of the Egyptians and the wreckage was strewn across the plains. Most of the downed planes were demolished but one was salvageable after it made a crash-landing near the beach north of Natanya. Freddie Ish-Shalom would have his parts. Since the British, to a great extent, were supplying the Arabs in general and the Egyptians in particular with arms and aircraft, the Jews thought the episode not only funny but ironic. Moddy looks at the Spitfire which is now painted in Israeli Air Force colors. He says the Egyptian who crash-landed was a Squadron Leader [sic]*. He was the same pilot who had dropped a bomb on the main Tel Aviv post office in an earlier raid when 20 Jews had been killed.

In the afternoon I go on another flight with Giddy and this time Ezer accompanies us. After we rev the engines at the north approach, Giddy transmits on C channel of the R/T and asks if we are ready to go. Ezer is to the left of the undershoot warning marker and he sits high in the cockpit. He has on a cloth summer helmet and he holds an upward thumb toward Giddy. The R/T crackles again and Giddy, calling himself Blue Leader, contacts base radio. There is nothing resembling a control tower at the Natanya strip and base radio is a walkie-talkie device over near the Ops tent, where the operator has a Very pistol and a handful of red flares in case of an emergency. The range of the walkie-talkie is five miles and one quickly learned not to depend on it at any distance from the airfield. There is static on the control transmission and Giddy waves us on. He doesn't bother to give any unit call because we are the only ones on the frequency.

We are airborne and now we climb to the south until Tel Aviv is spreading out to the west of us. The sun is sinking lower and the rays flash a mirrored reflection from the canopies. At 12,000 feet Giddy turns east over Lydda. Ezer's Messerschmitt rises and falls in the clear air off Giddy's port wing. Ahead is Jerusalem. We hold the course and the city comes below us, bleached and majestic in the afternoon light. The Arab

---

* See *Spitfires over Israel* for further details of this incident.

lines run jaggedly across the Old City and the sun glints from the golden domes of the mosques. The dry, rocky hills roll away eastward and when we come around north of enemy-held Bethlehem, white anti-aircraft bursts blossom against the blue of the sky. They are some distance to the left, over Beit Jala, and Ezer dips a wing toward them. Giddy makes a profane remark on the R/T. We keep flying west and, far below, the railway line from the coast twists through the passes beside the corridor road. Southward, the Israeli outposts and settlements stretch across the arid Negev and we can see, away in the distance, where the Egyptians are stalled at Isdud. We pass above Aqir and Rehovot, south of Ramleh and Rishon-le-Zion, and go over the beach below Jaffa. Beneath the wings the sea replaces the varied colors of the land and we turn north and stay offshore because the Israeli fighters are restricted from flying over Tel Aviv unless engaged on an interception mission. When we pass Herzliya, Giddy peels downwards and light and shadow become blended as we slant in over Natanya. We go into the pattern singly and it is nearly dusk when we get on the ground. We are still in the cockpits at the revetments when a shufti kite buzzes above the airfield at 20,000 feet.

The early days of August pass slowly. The ceasefire remains in effect and everyone strengthens their position for the next round while the UN tries to negotiate a peaceful solution. Everyone knew there would be another round. In light of the situation three months earlier, the Israeli Air Force had made substantial strides. Though still operating under comparatively crude conditions and circumstances, the efforts of the Transport Group, the activating of a Bomber Command and the strong showing of the fighter squadron in the July operations, contributed immeasureably to the prestige of the young organization and to the spirit of the new State itself. The arrival of the Messerschmitts, regardless of their notoriety, had unquestionably changed the pattern of the war. Since the Dakota episode at Tel Aviv in June and the additional loss of some of their Spitfires to Israeli fighters, the Egyptains had, except for one unproductive naval sortie by two destroyers off Jaffa, relegated their raids to ineffectual night missions and strikes against isolated Negev settlements. The use of the Messerschmitts in an increased ground-support role the previous month had also created an adverse effect on the morale of the opposing armies but now, in the heat of midsummer, the fighters sat in the sun and waited.

101 Squadron countered the lack of combat activity during this period by continuing its efforts to intercept the shufti kites and by launching a photographic reconnaissance section. Military Intelligence at the Yarkon, which had only light planes from Sde Dov supplying them with limited information of enemy movements, had been anxious to have one of the fighters fitted with a camera. The captured Spitfire had already been tested by Boris Senior who, because of his abundant experience with this type, had come over to Natanya for the purpose. All had gone

well on the initial flight and with some minor adjustments it was considered operational by the end of the first week in August. It was designated as the PR aircraft. Dave Croll arrived from Intelligence and was assigned as the officer in charge of the reconnaissance operations. A heavy aerial camera was fitted into the vacant oxygen tank compartment behind the cockpit of the hybrid Spitfire and a hole was simply cut in the bottom of the fuselage to expose the lens. For several months the project would be known as the Spitfire Brigade.

To conserve fuel the Messerschmitts were assigned to alternating single-plane patrols and maximum-altitude flights were sent up for the shufti kite searches. The most dangerous part of these high-level missions without oxygen was the dependence upon the judgement and common sense of the pilot. There were no orders limiting the patrol altitude but anything beyond 18,000 feet was viewed as suicidal and everyone began to play a private game to see who could endure the highest climb. The Mosquitos were fast and they were probably lightly armed. Headquarters was inclined to believe that the RAF was conducting some of the sorties out of Cyprus and the Suez Canal Zone. Everything was theory until the intruders could be identified and orders came down to the fighter pilots to make every effort to ascertain the markings on the Mosquitos in lieu of shooting them down. Whatever their source, the shufti kites had acquired all the aspects of daytime phantoms.

CHAPTER V

A TIME IN THE SUN

It is the end of the week and I am on a two-plane patrol with Giddy. By
ten in the morning we are out of the heat at 11,000 feet and 40 miles
north of the base. We are turning west when we see a C-47 Dakota
heading down from Haifa at 6,000 feet. Giddy doesn't say anything on
the R/T and he slips downward so suddenly that I hesitate for an instant.
Then we are in a steep, curving dive that brings the C-47 under us and I
reach forward and adjust the gunsight. As the transport grows large in the
windscreen I can see that it is white with big red UN letters on the wings
and fuselage, but I stay with Giddy and wonder what he is going to do.
Abruptly he pulls up and his voice comes in over the radio. He says we
had better stand off. The Dakota is the personal aircraft of the UN
Mediator, the Swedish Count Bernadotte. The sky is almost turquoise
blue and we sit half a mile off the starboard wing of the Dakota as it
heads into the salient toward Jerusalem. When we pass into Arab
airspace, Giddy pulls his Messerschmitt over and flies upside down for
a while.

Back at Natanya I stay under the partial shade of the netting at the
revetment and talk to the groundcrew. Messerschmitt 108 bakes silently
in the sun in front of the mechanics' tent and down the line Giddy takes
his equipment toward the shade of the trees. Most of the groundcrew are
either sabras or European Jews who came in at the time of the 1947
exodus, or before. They all smile and Isaac the sergeant hands me a
canteen with warm water in it. The petrol truck pulls around in the dust
and two of the mechanics go over to refuel 108. The machine is one
which already has the new Squadron insignia on the engine panel above
the exhaust stacks. The decal depicts a helmeted skull adorned with
black bat-like wings imposed on a red circle. The design was principally
the creation of Stan Andrews and the Squadron had voted unanimously
to adopt it. Though it was totally devoid of any symbolic sentiment for
the State of Israel, it seemed singularly apt to represent the
undisciplined, war-scarred and unheralded collection of volunteers in
Israel's first fighter squadron.

I look across at the insignia on 108. Isaac says that the aircraft has a jinx on it. The others laugh. They say they have had a lot of trouble with it and that it has already crashed once. They call it the 'Harlot' and say that it is the one that killed the flight engineer on the C-46 at Aqir [this was *not* however the aircraft involved in the accident].

The sun has dropped below the rim of the sea when the jeep leaves for Kafr Shmaryahu. Sid Cohen is driving and there are six people in the rear section. Harry Axelrod is talking about the hydraulic system on the Messerschmitts. Harry is a volunteer from the States and he is the Squadron Engineering Officer. He is a good engineering officer and the burden of his job is unenviable. His facial expression is always serious. Hydraulic failures have become a persistent problem plaguing the maintenance crews, and Harry is telling everyone to operate the radiator shutter control if a hydraulic lock occurs in the undercarriage system. The resulting pressure reaction may unblock it. The jeep hits a rut on the dirt road and jolts harshly upward. Harry continues to talk about his theory. Everyone else is talking at the same time.

At the pilots' quarters there is boiled chicken for the evening meal. Sid Cohen and Arni Ruch go to the water spiggot near the tent and wash for dinner while others wait to get into the single latrine and the shower behind the porch. Considering the demands and restrictions of the war, life at Kafr Shmaryahu was comfortable that summer of 1948. When the operational duty was alternated between the two Flights those who remained at the quarters would go down to the beach beyond the roadhouse. The days were sunny and at the beach the wind was warm and the water was clear. You could see down where the sun made patterns on the sand of the sea floor. Sometimes the girls from Communications would come over from the camp at Herzliya and we would have drinks at the roadhouse on the way back in the evening. In the tent we change our shirts and then walk out to the screen porch. Mr Falk serves the chicken. Kindly and white-haired, he owns the pension house.

B Flight is off in the morning and when Moddy comes by in his jeep some of the pilots are sitting in the chairs under the acacia tree. Moddy calls Ezer over and then motions to me. When we get to the jeep he says we are going to see the commander of the army camp on the plateau north-west of Kafr Shmaryahu. He doesn't say why he is going there or why he wants us to accompany him. I sit in the back of the jeep and the breeze is in my face. We go down the tar road. Ezer is speaking in Hebrew and Moddy stares straight ahead. We are all wearing British desert shirts.

Moddy is the oldest of the sabra fighter pilots at 28 years of age. Like Ezer and Aharon Remez and others, he had been a Palestine volunteer with the Royal Air Force in World War II and he emerged as a Sergeant Pilot during the last year of the conflict. He and Ezer had taken their initial training together in Rhodesia but when they were assigned to fighter school, Ezer went on to the American-built Thunderbolts and eventually sat out the war at a base in India, while Moddy was designated for Spitfires. The war ended before he saw much action with the RAF, however, and he returned to Palestine to be demobilized and to find the smoldering friction between the Jews and the British, and the Palestinian Arabs and their allies of the Arab Bloc irregulars, ready to ignite. By 1947 he, along with the other native Jews with aviation experience, was engaged in what was known as 'underground flying'.

The situation at the time was that both Arab and Jew were unhappy with the pending Partition of Palestine and the British, who were in many ways responsible for the dissatisfaction, particularly where the Jews were concerned, were still officially in control of the country and were, in effect, in the middle. They had then thrown the future of the Jewish homeland into the lap of the UN. As the Security Council struggled with the Partition problem, the position of the adversaries worsened. Jewish settlements, especially those which were somewhat isolated, became in constant danger of hit and run attacks by the Palestinian Arabs and the irregulars, and the Haganah Palmach and IZL began to retaliate. Blood was spilling during the entire year before the Mandate ended.

In order to obtain aerial reconnaissance of these enemies and to maintain contact with the scattered Jewish underground forces, the small number of sport aircraft available to the Jews were secretly put into service. These mainly originated from Sde Dov where they were assigned to various areas. Ezer spent nine months in the Negev during this period, flying an Auster and co-operating with the recently formed Palmach units, while Moddy was with the Galil Flight in the north. At the end of April 1948 they were summoned by the Haganah leaders to a clandestine meeting in Tel Aviv and told of the Messerschmitt deal in Czechoslovakia. It was agreed at this meeting that the fighters be given the utmost priority and Ezer and Moddy plus three foreign volunteers were despatched to Budejovice. They arrived in Czechoslovakia the first week in May and three weeks later, in Israel, 101 Squadron was formed. Moddy was not immediately appointed as CO of this first squadron in the Israeli Air Force and early missions were led by the more experienced foreign volunteers, but after the destruction of the Egyptian bombers at Tel Aviv he became the unanimous choice for the CO, as well as the best known hero in Israel. Modest and introverted, fame didn't seem to mean that much to Moddy and he placed duty and final victory above popularity. Although he had little previous experience as a leader, he managed the Squadron with energy, wisdom and patience but no one was really close to him.

At the army camp we have tea with the commander in the officers' mess and he and Moddy talk for a while in Hebrew and then we all go out to the firing range. There is no shade. Some of the soldiers are testing one of the Czech machine-guns. They are using sandbags set against a rocky embankment as targets and we watch until the bullets have torn the bags to shreds. The commander smiles. He walks with us out to the jeep. He has a waxed moustache and his tropical shorts have a neat crease in them. On the way to Herzliya, Ezer inclines his head toward the back seat and tells me the reason for the visit to the army camp. He says Ben-Gurion is going to be at Natanya in two days and the army will supply some of the guards. It is never explained why I was invited on the trip.

At noon the next day I go on a shufti kite patrol. Leon Frankel, the black-haired, ex-US Navy pilot from Milwaukee has just landed. He says he saw nothing. When I get into the air I turn north and keep climbing until the altimeter needle passes 15,000 feet. I experience periodic sighing intakes of breath but I hold altitude and patrol for an hour on the line between Natanya and the outskirts of Haifa. I look upward most of the time and the brilliance of the sun creates dancing circles of light when I look away. The Mediterranean sun. I look around. The sky is vacant for a thousand miles.

In the afternoon I take Messerschmitt 113 on a test flight. 113 has just come out of maintenance and it is another machine considered to be an arch trouble-maker. It has been crashed twice and has a history of countless mechanical malfunctions. They call this one 'The Bastard'. After I run up the engine and check the instruments I turn up wind and it gets off the ground smoothly and continues to perform well during the half-hour flight. When I bring it back in the landing is not a good one and the Messerschmitt takes instant advantage of it by ground looping. Fortunately the wingtip stays clear of the dirt and the field to the right is open because I am unable to come to a stop until I am over by the western cedars. I sit facing down wind and my shirt is saturated with sweat. At the north end of the strip another Messerschmitt is taking off.

During this summer 101 Squadron was, in fact, an international squadron. The vast majority of the pilots were of Jewish origin but they had all served in the forces of other countries and none but the sabras were on their native soil. Emerging from the turbulent years of World War II, they had something in common from the past but what they had in common now was their belief in a Jewish victory. Discussions among this rather extraordinary group could be found in progress at Kafr Shmaryahu any evening after the sun went down, and one of the places where they gathered was the roadhouse.

The roadhouse is a bistro/cafe with a dance floor and porticos that lead out to a terrace. It has a tan stucco exterior and you can hear the sound of the surf from the outside tables. One night we arrive in a single jeep and we take drinks from the bar out to the terrace. Sid Antin winds up the gramophone near the wall and looks through a pile of records. All of the records are old and Sid Cohen wants 'Beyond the Blue Horizon', but Antin can't find it and he puts something else on. At the tables they talk about operations, about when the fighting will start again, about the aircraft, about the politics of the war. The complexities of the policies, both domestic and external, involving Israel at this stage is a subject regularly debated and an absolute master in this category is Ezer. They talk about politics now but Ezer ignores the issue for the moment. Reclining in a wicker chair and holding a glass of cognac he pulls at the light, sparse beard on his chin. He smiles at a thought which has occurred to him and tells everyone to shut up about political bonds. He says the strongest bond in the Squadron is the collective desire to survive the Messerschmitts.

At eight o'clock in the morning the entire Squadron is assembled at Natanya. The Prime Minister isn't due until ten and we sit near the trees and try to stay out of the sun. There is one plane up on a patrol but everyone else is waiting for Ben-Gurion. Nothing has changed. No one is dressed differently except Moddy, who has added a wide, webbed British service belt to his regular attire. None of the aircraft are lined up in show formation and they remain scattered about the airfield at the dispersal points. Most of the groundcrew have their shirts off as usual. The guards from the army camp are lounging near the revetments. Everyone is perspiring by the time the two Rapides come in from Sde Dov and taxi over to the eastern border. Ben-Gurion, with his prominent array of cotton-like hair gets out of the first one, accompanied by his wife who is holding a purse with exceptionally long straps on it. They are officially greeted by Moddy and, of those in the surrounding group, many are taking photographs. Moddy and the escort show the party to a jeep and they go on a short tour of the perimeter. When they return the pilots are introduced. There is shouting and jostling and laughter and we all feel suddenly honored shaking the hand of the illustrious leader about whom we had heard so much. Everyone is milling about when a shufti kite appears high overhead, a tiny speck against the wisps of cirrus clouds that are streaked across the deep blue above. The patrol aircraft had landed before the Rapides came in and everyone just looks upward and watches the intruder plane.

B Flight is on standby and Sid Cohen looks over at Moddy to see what he is going to do. Ben-Gurion, wearing dark slacks and a white summer shirt, is also looking at the sky, shading his eyes with his hand. Abruptly, Moddy tells Sid to scramble four planes. Sid points to me and grabs Giddy by the arm and shouts to Bill Pomerantz. We start running to the nearby readiness jeep and jump in. Sid floors the throttle pedal when the motor starts. We head for the revetments. The rotund Pomerantz smiles sceptically as we watch the shufti kite fast disappearing to the north. Everyone knows it is futile to scramble and when we get to the standby Messerschmitts, Moddy cancels it. A red flare arches up from behind the Ops tent and falls to earth out on the field, where it burns and sputters for a moment. The gesture for the Prime Minister has been made. An hour later Ben-Gurion leaves Natanya and the Rapides lift off slowly in the midday sun.

The strip at Herzliya is nearly ready by the middle of August but we are still at Natanya. George Lichter and Red Flint come in from Czechoslovakia and a few days afterward Flint wrecks one of the machines while landing. Moddy sends him down to Sde Dov. The veteran Lou Lenart is tired of fighting the Messerschmitts and he goes to a desk job at the Yarkon. The ungracious Desert Hawks continue to take their toll of the pilots as, in turn, Stan Andrews is sent to Ramat David to fly the Beaufighter they have procured somewhere. Lichter is going back to a European assignment in a week and he stays temporarily in the tent with us. There are no more Messerschmitts coming in from Czechoslovakia but Lichter says they are trying to make a deal for Spitfires. We all smile but Lichter looks unelated. He says the Czechs want a hell of a lot of money for them. Before he leaves Israel, Lichter puts on an admirable display of aerobatics in the clear morning air at Natanya.

On a weekend when a section of each Flight is off duty we go down to the beach. We take the jeep and Sid Antin goes across the lane to the farm corral and borrows the white horse, Gebor, and rides him bareback down the hill. At the beach some of the Communications girls from camp are there on the sand and Sid Antin gallops Gebor past them to the tide swirls and the hooves throw water high in the air. We wear our khaki shorts and we go into the surf. It is cool and everyone shouts. When we come out of the water Giddy lies down on the sand next to Leni. All of the girls are pretty and Leni is the smallest and she and Ruth have dark hair. The one with red hair is Miriam and she is married. Her husband is with the army in the Galil. I lay down on the warm sand too. To the north I can see the empty beach stretching into the distance beneath the bluffs of the plateau. We stay there most of the day and late in the afternoon someone in a Messerschmitt comes low along the surf line. The propeller is barely missing the tops of the waves.

The Spitfire Brigade is activated during the second week of the month and it is decided that only those who have experience on the type will be assigned to it. The names are written on the blackboard at the Ops tent and mine is on it, along with Sid Cohen, Moddy, Maury Mann and Arni Ruch. The photo reconnaissance missions begin with Moddy taking the first sortie in the Jewish shufti kite. It is mid-morning and I go with Sid Cohen over to the Spitfire revetment where Moddy is talking with Dave Croll. We look underneath the aircraft and see where the camera is lined up with the opening. We walk around in front and Moddy and Croll have a map spread out under the wing and Croll is indicating an area with a pencil. He is a bespectacled American Jew, young and conscientious about his job. He makes the trip into the Yarkon with the films each time the missions are completed. Moddy folds the map a certain way and climbs into the cockpit of the Spitfire. When he starts the engine it fires smoothly and we all stand back from the blast of the propeller wash. The cockpit canopy has been removed like they were on the Spitfires in the Western Desert and the Star of David emblem on the fuselage of this machine is so large it laps over the top. Moddy taxies out, stops near the boundary and turns the Spitfire around. After a moment he nods over to us and opens the throttle.

The following day I go on one of the reconnaissance flights. I sit in the cockpit for a while before the mission and my thoughts return automatically to 1943, the last Spitfire I had flown and the plains of North Africa. Croll jumps up on the wing, bends over the seat and explains the camera operation. It is an uncomplicated procedure with a switch box on the right-hand side of the cockpit and when the switch is on a small green light flashes for each exposed frame in the camera. The section to be photographed is circled in pencil on the map attached to a clipboard beneath the instrument panel. The circle surrounds an obscure sector on the edge of the salient eight miles west of the Jordan River. Croll gets down from the wing. It is almost noon and the smell of exhaust fumes and hot oil is heavy in the air. I look over at the mechanics standing to one side and resembling, for all the world, the crew of a pirate ship. I think of the labor in the sun that was necessary to resurrect the Egyptian machine for service with the Israeli Air Force. I look at them and the others in the far revetments, sweating over the Messerschmitts, and I am reminded of the unsung heroes in this war. I start the engine.

Croll wants the run at 8,000 feet and when I get to the target vicinity there are some billows of white clouds at the same altitude. The Spitfire handles well and I drop down 500 feet to clear the base of the clouds and begin the camera run from west to east. There is nothing visible on the terrain below to suggest that there is anything of importance along the course. Some of the fields in the area are green from irrigation and there are dissecting roads and junctions at various angles. To the left, in Israeli territory, Nazareth seems complacent in the sun. Below there is no movement. There is little concern for enemy fighters on these sorties but I look around at intervals during the run. It is necessary to fly relatively steady while the camera is operating and, as the seconds tick by, one becomes curiously aware that one is intruding on someone's property. I finish the first segment and turn onto the reciprocal course and use up the film coming back across and then turn south-west toward Natanya. When I land at the strip the Spitfire floats lightly in the ground thermals before the wheels touch the dust.

We soon find that the reconnaissance missions cause the Arabs to complain each time about truce violations and it amuses us because both sides are engaged in the practice. The Israelis, in turn, report the shufti kite incursions and the UN observers take note of the complaints.

The resulting success of the Spitfire Brigade during the remainder of August so impressed Military Intelligence that Headquarters requested additional PR aircraft from the fighters and two of the Messerschmitts were subsequently modified to carry cameras. By September most of the pilots in 101 Squadron were periodically engaged in these flights and the Yarkon became ever more ambitious in ordering missions which strayed far into enemy territory. The energetic Croll does not always divulge what they are looking for when he gives the map reference and course for the runs, but the day after the northern mission he shows me prints of the photographs and say they discovered a recently reinforced enemy artillery position.

It is late August and I walk with Sid Cohen to the tent at Kafr Shmaryahu. The afternoon is waning and we are off duty for the day. The side flaps of the tent are rolled up but the air inside is warm and we remove our shirts and lie down on the cots. Sid takes his high-top desert shoes off and we get under the nets to escape the harassment of the flies and we talk about the war. This war. Sid discards his normally casual manner for a moment. He says that if he survives up here and if, in the end, the Jews are guaranteed their national homeland, he is going back to university in Johannesburg and complete his degree in medicine. He leans on his elbows beneath the transparent, curtain-like net and looks out to where the sun is bright on the white walls of the pension buildings. He says that the Jews need a decisive military victory, not just a moral one. Then, maybe, there will be hope for some kind of peace in the future. After a pause, he gets up from the cot and goes outside to the faucet for a drink of water. When he comes back he sits on the edge of his bed and says that the UN mediation isn't going to really solve it. He says that Bernadotte is weakening toward Arab demands and the only way the Jews are going to get what they want is to fight for it. I listen and what he says is something that we all already know. He picks up a piece of paper and a pencil from the top of an ammunition box at the foot of the cot and, using the surface of the box to write on, he makes out the flight schedule for the next day.

Sometimes at night a party developed in Falk's garden. On one of these occasions a plank has been placed atop two empty fuel drums, and bottles of beer and cognac and seltzer are placed on the plank and everyone serves themselves in the middle of the yard. Moddy, who doesn't drink much and usually stays in Herzliya after dark, comes over for a while and by ten o'clock everyone but he is drunk. There is a full moon and we all sit beside the porch. Down the slope, moonlight is shining on the sea. Voices gain in volume when an argument starts over whether the Americans are the better pilots in the Squadron. Moddy watches with a mechanical smile. Someone starts telling the story about the time they had the party at the Yarden Hotel in Ben Yehuda Street to celebrate Rubenfeld's deliverance from the hands of the farmers of Kafr

Vitkin. Moddy didn't drink much that night either but the others who
were present did and, although their quarters were in the Yarden at that
time, everyone got to bed late. In the morning Ezer missed the jeep to
Aqir and the only other transportation we could find after he woke up
was Moddy's motor bike. He leapt on this machine and was roaring past
the junction at Beit Dagan when he hit a mortar shell hole and went over
the handle bars. He missed a week of the war and even more regretfully
missed the Dakota incident which occurred while his wrist was being put
in a cast at Tel Aviv's Hadassah Hospital.

There is laughter and the talking gets louder. A discussion is on about
what would have happened if Marcus hadn't been shot. Colonel Marcus,
an American Jew and an expert military strategist, was killed in
Jerusalem in early June. An excellent officer, he was a graduate of West
Point and he had compiled a distinguished record in the US Army in
World War II. He had resigned his commission in the States to serve in
Israel and he had originally arrived in Palestine in the first months of
1948, under the name of Stone. A skilled organizer, Marcus was not only
an asset to the army command of the time, he was also involved in
arranging the Messerschmitt deal in Czechoslovakia in March. Great
hopes were pinned on his leadership abilities by the Israelis and he was
considered one of the most valued of the foreign volunteers. Fate had
ended all the plans that night in Jerusalem. The original version was that
Marcus was killed by a sniper bullet near the ramparts of the Old City in
the darkness before dawn, but the official revised account, which was
released a few days later, stated that Marcus was shot by a Jewish sentry
who mistook him for an enemy in the dark.

Moddy finishes his drink under the acacia tree and, waving a hand,
goes out to where his jeep is parked beside the hedge. The headlights
flash fleetingly across the yard as he leaves. When he is gone everyone
exhorts Ezer to do his dance. Some of the pilots had been throwing beer
at each other and everybody is wet. Ezer takes off his saturated khakis
and in only his underwear begins cavorting and whirling through the
garden in the moonlight, the gyrations of his tall, lanky figure
accompanied by shouts and laughter.

At the end of August the operations are finally moved to Herzliya.
Everything is packed up and brought out of Natanya and the aircraft are
flown to the other strip. When Giddy and I bring out two of the
Messerschmitts it is nearly deserted at Natanya. Papers and debris blow
across the space where the revetments had been. We take off and bank
back around and the hot wind trails the dust over the empty field. We
pass above Khalid behind Natanya and see the lorries turning onto the
south road.

The landing area at the Herzliya camp has been completed except for
furrows of soil along the boundaries. We come in low over the orange
groves and land from the south and bump down to the end of the dirt

strip to where the hill rises up to Kafr Shmaryahu. The dispersal section is near the trees at the southern border and to the west side of the perimeter. The Squadron administration has been operating at Herzliya since July and, after we park the Messerschmitts at the grove revetments, we leave our gear and walk along the dusty trail that goes across 50 yards of cracked, dry ground to where the stone block huts are grouped. The mess hall is the largest of these buildings and it sits on a slight rise opposite the Squadron orderly huts. We go in and have the noon meal of lentil stew. There is an alternate meal of lesser substance for the orthodox who question the origin of the meat in the stew. Everyone on the base eats here at midday and we see Leni and Ruth at one of the board tables in the rear of the hall. Leni comes over and talks with Giddy while we eat. When Ruth passes the table on her way out Leni goes with her. We finish the meal and take the tin plates up to the kitchen section and go back outside. Some Palestinian Arab prisoners of war are working on the road that passes by the huts and an army guard, with a Mauser rifle slung on his shoulder, is standing to the right of those who are laboring with shovels. The guard is in his teens and is talking with a grey-haired, middle-aged Arab. The guard smiles when he sees us and we go over. He nods toward the Arab and says, first in Hebrew and then in English, that the Arab's name is Abbas and that he is the chief of the labor gang. Abbas is brown and sinewy and his clothes are covered with dust. He has a winning manner about him and he speaks English well. He says he was born ten miles from Herzliya and has many Jewish friends. We offer him a cigarette and he smiles and lights it. He watches us carefully when we walk down the road to the Ops tent on the fringe of the grove.

CHAPTER VI

HERZLIYA

That afternoon at the base camp strip I fly the northern shufti kite patrol. The control tower is still under construction but the ground radio is more sophisticated than that which we had at Natanya, and I call in over the R/T as Blue One. I am in 115 and they had to wind it twice before it started. The crew has sweated and cursed. It is imperative to get into the air quickly to avoid overheating the engine but Rudy Augarten, who is taking the patrol south of the salient, has just gone down the field and I can't see anything until the dust clears. I hear Rudy on the R/T and he says Red One is airborne and after a minute the dust drifts away from the strip and I start forward. Every time I take off in the Messerschmitts the same three words from a war verse enter my mind – 'Forward and farewell'. The wind sock near the tower shows a slight breeze from the north-west and the aircraft runs its usual length on the ground before it departs into the air. The hill at the boundary seems deceptively close when I pass above Kafr Shmaryahu. I look down and I see Gebor in the farmyard below.

The sky is absolutely clear. The tachometer is fluctuating as I climb but I have learned not to worry about anything on the Messerschmitts unless it is a total malfunction. I level off north of Caesarea at 16,500 feet. I look at the altimeter for a minute and climb again until it reads 18,000 feet. I feel altogether uncomfortable and the height without oxygen gives rise to a certain amount of anxiety, but I remain at 18,000 feet and patrol in a crossing pattern toward Haifa. I stay up sun as much as possible and on one of the inland turns I can see Red One banking away south of Tulkarm. When I am going into the sun's radiance for the third time I glimpse a dot high to the left. Below, Haifa is off the starboard wing and I turn sharply outward. The maneuver brings the Messerschmitt about at a flight angle to the dot which has rapidly enlarged. It is a Mosquito and it is either oblivious or contemptuous of my presence. The course it is following is directly across the path of the Messerschmitt and 5,000 feet above. The dark underside of the shufti kite doesn't reflect much light in the bright air and it is moving at a fast pace on a heading that will take it out to sea beyond Haifa. I can do nothing but watch and, as the aircraft passes overhead, I pull the Messerschmitt up vertically and peer intently through the windscreen. The airspeed drops dramatically and, as I try to see if there are any markings on the twin-engine machine, the Messerschmitt stalls and falls away to one side. The earth does a half-turn under the nose and the altimeter needle spins down to 12,000 feet. I look back at the vanishing shufti kite. I didn't see any markings on it at all.

Kalman Turin is the adjutant at 101 Squadron and he also serves as the Squadron Intelligence Officer. Thin and quiet, he had served in a ground capacity with the RAF as a Palestine volunteer and had come over from Sde Dov when 101 was formed. Efficient and well thought of, he takes my report after I land back at Herzliya. In the Ops tent we sit in camp chairs and Kalman scribbles on a pad but we still don't know any more about the shufti kites then we did before.

When I come out of the tent Sid Cohen is going by in a jeep with Croll. They stop and I ride out to the Spitfire dispersal point with them. Sid is going on a PR flight to Gaza and as he puts on his gear I tell him about the shufti kite episode. He laughs and goes over and looks at the map which Croll seems eternally to have in his hand. A Messerschmitt is taking off and we can't hear anything for a minute. Sid wipes his mouth with his forearm. When he gets up on the wing of the Spitfire, Croll extends a revolver in a fabric holster toward him. He tells Croll he doesn't want it. He says they are too bulky to wear in the cockpit and that they are dangerous to be carrying if you are captured. Croll agrees but says it is an order from Headquarters that the reconnaissance pilots must wear a sidearm. Sid still doesn't want it. Croll looks at the ground beside the wing for a moment. He says it's not necessarily for use against the enemy. He says it's for Sid to use on himself if he is captured by irregulars. The statement amuses Sid. He takes the gun and straps it on and climbs into the cockpit.

With the arrival of September the status along the fronts remained unchanged and the UN progress in the mediations seemed hopelessly bogged down. At Herzliya most of the information comes to us by rumor or from the *Palestine Post* or by English-language radio broadcasts from Tel Aviv or Beirut or Cairo. When anything is reported in Hebrew or Arab we get Ezer or Sandy Jacobs to translate it. The waiting continues and the Messerschmitts remain a paradox. The accidents haven't taken any lives yet but when everyone gathered in the evening outside the porch at Kafr Shmaryahu and the talk came around to the machines as it always did, the unspoken thought in everyone's mind was who would be the first permanent victim.

At the beginning of the new month an order comes down requiring the pilots to serve a night as Duty Officer as the rotation dictated. By the end of the first week I have the assignment and when I arrive at the

Command hut it is almost dark and the light is on in the office. Kalman is inside with sergeant of the guard Avrom Levi, whose regular Squadron assignment is as an armorer on Messerschmitt 120. Levi smiles and tips a finger to his frayed beret when I come into the room. Kalman is leaving and I go over to Moddy's desk and put the gun belt on. In the holster is a British Webley .38 caliber pistol. I look at Levi. A Palestinian Jew, he is husky and has a black moustache, and eyelids that perpetually droop so that he appears constantly unconcerned. He was with Irgun at one time and his early training with the Jewish Brigade is evident in his speech and bearing. We walk outside to where the duty jeep is parked and we can see Miriam at the switchboard behind the doorless entrance of the Communications shack. Levi says something to her in Hebrew. We get in the jeep and Levi moves his pistol holster around so that it rests on his lap when he is driving. The guards at the planes are inspected every two hours throughout the night. Levi turns on the jeep lights and we make the first tour. From the passenger seat I look into the darkness ahead and I can barely distinguish the dispersal areas out on the field. We drive down past the grove revetments and the mechanic guard is standing near the last one on the line. His rifle is propped against an oil drum. Levi stops and they speak in Hebrew for a moment, then both the guard and Levi light cigarettes and we start off again. We go out around the western perimeter and the hooded headlights of the jeep faintly pick out the form of a Messerschmitt. We pull to a stop beside the camouflage net connectors. The sentry comes around from behind the aircraft and hails us. Levi says something and then pushes the vehicle into gear and we go back to the administration section.

The administration area is deserted except for those on duty and the only lights are the dim lamps inside the Communications and Command huts. These all-night duty sessions soon acquire the stigma of becoming boring as the hours wear on and, even though we have the company of the telephone girls, the lack of excitement, along with the necessity of remaining awake, makes the morning seem far away. Avrom Levi had a remedy for all this. He goes across to the mess hall and gets an empty fruit jar from behind the kitchen and we drive into Herzliya and get it filled with cognac at a cafe. The place is crowded with soldiers and girls and the old man at the counter fills the jar from a barrel in the back. We drink a glass of the cognac at the counter before we leave. On the road into camp the cognac sloshes around in the jar and we take another drink and it spills on the front of our shirts.

The inspection rounds become increasingly unmilitary. Levi stands up behind the steering wheel of the jeep and shouts 'shalom' as we speed by the sentry posts. On the ten o'clock tour, Levi cuts away at the east boundary and drives into the hillside fields on the upper edge of Kafr Shmaryahu, where the land girls are employed in night irrigation. We park on an incline and Levi jokes with the girls and they laugh and throw dirt clods at us. When we leave we go through the sprinklers and over the pipes and when we get back down to the strip, Levi plows into the dirt furrow without seeing it. The jeep is flung violently upward and Levi is catapulted out of the driver's seat and disappears into the darkness. The jeep continues on for another 20 yards, barely missing one of the empty fuel drum markers that are spaced along the furrow, and then it swerves to the right and jerks to a stop, the motor choking into silence. With the initial impact I had grabbed the side of the windshield frame and hung on as the suddenly driverless vehicle skidded along on its own course. After the jeep stops, I look around for Levi and he comes running up and jumps back into the seat and starts the motor again without a word. We surge forward and bounce across the end of the strip. Levi is plastered with dirt and his shirt is torn and his knees are bleeding below the cuff of his tropical shorts. His gun holster is around on the back of his belt. He laughs.

When we get to the Command hut and park the jeep, Miriam comes out of Communications and looks at us. We go inside the hut and Levi gets the fruit jar from the floor behind the desk. The quart container is almost empty. We take another drink and then Miriam runs in from next door and says we have to go to Tel Aviv. Someone had telephoned from a bistro in town and said one of the groundcrew from 101 Squadron was causing a lot of trouble in the cafe and we better come in and pick him up before the MPs did. Levi finishes the contents of the jar and puts it down. He points to Moddy's desk where the Duty Officer's arm band is lying. I hadn't worn it all evening but now I go over and put it on. It is black with two Hebrew letters in red and I put it on upside down. Levi is on his way out to the jeep and, at the doorway, he turns around and goes back and gets the fruit jar. He says we'll get some more cognac in Tel Aviv.

We travel the road to Tel Aviv at high speed and when we arrive at the suburbs we encounter a number of other vehicles. Levi turns the jeep in and out between them and at one corner we go over a curb and then jolt back out onto the pavement. We hear shouts coming from the lorry behind us. The bistro is on a side street near Ben Yehuda and when we get there we can't find a place to park so Levi parks the jeep on the sidewalk. There is a big crowd and we get out of the jeep and walk past the outside tables and into the packed interior of the bistro. Levi has the fruit jar in his hand. We go up to the bar and he requests that the jar be filled with cognac. The proprietor has his shirt sleeves rolled up above the elbow and he takes the fruit jar and looks without comment at the upside-down armband and the stained clothes and bloody knees. He points to a table near the entrance. The only one in the bistro who isn't making any noise is the one he is pointing at. It is Reuben, an engine mechanic on Messerschmitt 115. He has had too much to drink and he rests his head on the table while those with him sing and laugh. The

proprietor suggests we take Reuben with us while he's quiet. Levi orders
two cognacs at the bar and pays the proprietor and we drink and watch
the tables. Two soldiers come up beside us and insist that we have a drink
with them. They are drunk also. Both of them have red faces and they
are Gentiles and, as soon as they speak, we know they are British. A
piano starts playing at the far end of the room. The soldiers say they are
Irish. They were with a tank regiment in the British Army and they
deserted with an armored car and are now with a battalion of the
Alexandroni Brigade at Latrun. They buy us a drink and begin to sing.
Levi finishes the drink in one swallow and sings with them. The piano
stops and we walk over to the table and Levi tells Reuben it's time to go.
The others help Reuben to his feet. We get him outside and into the back
seat of the jeep and then Levi places the fruit jar carefully on the floor of
the front seat. The Irish soldiers follow us out, carrying their drinks.
When we bump onto the street in the jeep they are singing again and the
refrain slowly fades away behind us – 'Whether on the gallows high or
on the battle fields we die; no matter, if for Erin fair we fall'.

The day dawns hot and the fruit jar is empty. Our eyes are red as we
sit in the hut and watch the flies land on the walls. There are people
moving outside and the sound of the Messerschmitt engines running up
is loud on the perimeter. Sergeant of the guard Avrom Levi yawns and
gets up from a chair in the corner and tips a finger to his beret. The night
is over.

By the second week in September the modified Messerschmitts had
become active on the PR sorties. On a day when there is a stiff breeze
and small white clouds drift against a dazzling blue sky, the pilots gather
before the map which is spread on the flat plywood table in the Ops tent.
Three reconnaissance missions are planned simultaneously. I get a
parachute from the rear of the tent and go over and look at the map. The
others are already studying it and Croll shows me the course on the
Jerusalem run. He taps the section where the Trans-Jordan lines cut the
city in half and says to make the run in the Spitfire at 12,000 feet. The
two Messerschmitt pilots collect their flying gear from a wooden rack
beside the table. Leon Frankel is assigned the mission to Jericho in
Trans-Jordan and Sandy is taking the low-level flight among the hills to
Nablus in the middle of the salient. Sid Cohen comes in through the tent
flap and there is a lot of joking about Nablus because of the large
numbers of Arab homosexuals reputed to reside there. Sid tells Sandy to
avoid a forced-landing at any costs and everyone laughs except Sandy.
Sid drives us around to the revetments in the jeep and he says he got a
lot of anti-aircraft fire on the morning mission to Rafah at the Sinai
border. I jump off the jeep when we get to the Spitfire and the crew
sergeant, Shimon, is standing by the four-bladed propeller. He motions
that the aircraft is ready to go. The machine is painted the same colors as
the Messerschmitts and it is assigned the number 130. When I get into

the cockpit the pistol that Croll gave me at the Ops tent is jammed under the parachute straps. I extricate it and put it to the side of the seat.

I pass over the large Arab town of Ramallah and approach Jerusalem from the north and the city is etched beneath the wings in intricate detail. The mission is entirely peaceful and I see Frankel's Messerschmitt, tiny to the east, heading across the Jordan for Jericho. I contemplate the magnitude of the history below and I am unable to reconcile the past with now. I think of our discussions at Kafr Shmaryahu and all of us here in the Holy Land fighting a war so the Jews can have a homeland for the first time in 2,000 years. We never talk about religion. I look below again. All I can see are the military targets.

A Flight and the Spitfire Brigade are preparing to leave quarters for the airfield one morning and some of the off-duty pilots are sitting in the chairs under the acacia tree. A moderate wind is blowing and the leaves and the flanks of the hedges are fluttering with it. Everyone around the tree is talking. They are talking about who is going to shoot Bill Pomerantz's dog. The pudgy Pomerantz, who is from Miami, is dressed in a colorful sport shirt and knee-length shorts and he is sitting on one of the beach chairs, holding a small dog on his lap. The dog has been ill for two days and now, plainly, it is dying. Bubbles of foam come from the nostrils as it looks up glassy-eyed at Pomerantz. Everyone agrees that is should be put out of its misery but Bill won't do it and no one else will volunteer.

Bill brushes flies away from the dog's mouth and looks from face to face around the circle of those beneath the tree. He skips past Sandy because Sandy doesn't like the animal and impudently refers to it as a wog dog. Bill's expression is almost comically sad and his gaze comes around to Giddy. Giddy shakes his head and says it's Bill's dog and that he should shoot it. Bill shakes his head and speaks to Red Finkel in Yiddish. Red declines in English. The dog tries to move and its legs twitch and it kicks Bill in the crotch. There is laughter but then everyone is silent and there is only the sound of the wind in the leaves. Chris Magee comes out of a room behind the porch. He has the red handkerchief around his head and an automatic pistol is in the belt of his flight suit. Bill gets up from the chair and carries the dog over to where Magee is standing near the porch. No one says anything and we can see Bill gesturing and finally Magee nods and they walk around the corner of the building to the maize field. In a moment Bill comes back without the dog and stops near the tent and then we hear a noise like a tree branch breaking and Magee reappears with the gun still in his hand. He motions over his shoulder with his thumb and Bill goes slowly out to the field again.

The photographic-reconnaissance missions in mid-September began to encounter increasing anti-aircraft resistance and in some cases the hostile barrages were disconcertingly accurate. Both Maury Mann and

Arni Ruch received shell splinters through the tails of 130 and Sid Cohen was followed out to sea by some of the bursts at Gaza.

The Egyptian-held coastal town of Majdal is on the main supply route to the enemy forces which are camped at Isdud and, because of its strategic position, it was considered worthy of frequent aerial observation by Military Intelligence. It now lies passive and white next to the deep blue of the sea as I turn on to the final camera run. It is a half hour past midday and at 10,000 feet the eight miles from Majdal north to Isdud seem no distance at all. I look down through the sundrenched air and line the Spitfire along the sliver of connecting road and switch on the camera.

Five darkly-blooming flowers appear magically off the port wingtip. Although they are at the same altitude, the shell bursts are not alarmingly close but their mere presence is unnerving and I try to concentrate on keeping the nose of the aircraft on a straight course. More anti-aircraft bursts begin to unfold ahead and then again, off the left wing, another pattern of shells arrives and I can see the flash of the explosion in the center of the last one that came up. Beneath the drifting smoke puffs a trail of Bofors tracers arches skyward and they are bright as they curve up with deadly grace against the dark background of the sea. I have an intense impulse to maneuver the aircraft evasively but I restrain the urge and finish the run. The film ends and I open the throttle and, a thousand feet below, I see the dispersing layer of grey haze left by the lighter pom-pom shells. In three minutes I am over Israeli territory.

From the open cockpit of the Spitfire the view is unrestricted but the wind rushes over the top of the windscreen with force. On the right side of the cowling two of the engine panel fastenings have sprung loose, and the air is beginning to get under the section in a dangerous manner. I reduce speed but the panel has a good chance of tearing away and when I am opposite Tel Aviv I spiral the machine down from the seaward side and land on the runway that parallels the shore at Sde Dov. There is a 90 degree crosswind coming in along the beach but I manage to drop down before the danger marker and, at the dirt near the end of the strip, I turn and taxi back toward the Operations shack.

Some of the groundcrew around the utility planes come over when I shut the engine off on the sunbaked southern border of the field and they are smiling because they don't see the fighters down here. The strips are too short for the Messerschmitts. I leave the parachute and helmet on the seat and get out on the wing. The cowling metal is hot when I reach forward and snap the panel buttons back into place with a five-mil piece. The groundcrew are still smiling and inspecting the Spitfire and I get down from the wing and walk over to the Ops shack.

I don't see Mischa Keren, but Kurtz and Al Schwimmer are standing out in front of the building. They are laughing and Schwimmer holds out his hand. I am glad to see him and Schwimmer says they just came in from Ramat David in the Lockheed Lodestar which is sitting out on the grass apron. He says he now has Israeli citizenship and he tells a funny story about his hurried departure from the States. He has on sweaty khakis and he puts his hands in his pockets and laughs. Some of the Sde Dov pilots have joined us and while we are talking one of the Norseman reconnaissance planes taxies by and blows sand over everyone. Schwimmer and Kurtz walk back to the Spitfire with me and I tell them about the mission to Majdal. Kurtz whistles when I mention the volume of the anti-aircraft fire and Schwimmer just keeps smiling. They say they are going into Tel Aviv and when I get into the cockpit Schwimmer waves and they go back over to Operations. The crosswind is stronger when I take off for Herzliya.

If anyone played a singularly key part in the inauguration of the Air Force in the new Israel of 1948, it was the smiling Al Schwimmer. His ingenuity and energy were behind almost every aircraft that was ferried from the States in the first months. The transports, the bombers and, because of the transports, the fighters. Schwimmer not only procured the aircraft, he gathered many of the volunteers who served during that year and he put everything he had on the line. Because of the laws of the times he eventually had to lose everything privately but, when it mattered the most, he won his personal war for Israel.

The summer was coming to an end and incident piled upon incident. On one of the September days Bernadotte is assassinated at Jerusalem. We hear the news on the radio at Falk's when we return from afternoon duty. The Jews had assassinated him and everyone knew right away that it was the extremist faction. Stern Gang was the most frequently mentioned name during the evening. Haganah deplored the act and at Kafr Shmaryahu that night we wonder about the motivation behind this violent termination of the UN Mediator. Perhaps the rumors we had heard about concessions were true but, still, the assassination was totally unexpected and the ramifications were unlimited. Bernadotte had been in the open rear seat of his official car and was proceeding to a scheduled conference when the car was stopped by several vehicles in the Jewish section. Three people, one of whom was a girl, ran over to where the Mediator was sitting and someone placed a Sten gun automatic on Bernadotte's chest and pulled the trigger. One news reporter who was witness to the event seemed fascinated by the fact that the ribbons on Bernadotte's uniform were shredded by the blast and bits of them floated off on the breeze. At Kafr Shmaryahu everyone talks about the assassination and someone says that the Arabs will have a lot of fuel for their propaganda machine tomorrow.

B Flight has the afternoon duty and Giddy is due out on a patrol. I walk with him to the revetment of Messerschmitt 119. The armorer has been checking one of the cannon ammunition drums on the machine and he goes from the cannon to the side plate on the fuselage and looks at the feeder belt on the port machine-gun. He nods and steps down from the wing. Giddy gets ready and 30 yards up the line Cyril Horowitz starts the engine on 117 and pulls away from the camouflage net. Lichtman climbs into the cockpit of 119 and a Belgian mechanic prepares to turn the inertia crank. The one everyone calls 'The Belgian' is short and wide and is the only crewman in the Squadron who is strong enough to work the handle alone. Coming from five years in a German forced labor camp, his face is prematurely old and now it shows strain as he pulls down on the crank. The muscles of his naked upper torso expand. Above the whining of the inertia we can hear Cyril open the throttle to take off. We can't see him because the corner of the revetment obstructs the view of the southern end of the strip, but as soon as the engine sound reaches a certain pitch there is the rending report of an impact and the engine becomes abruptly silent. The Belgian stops winding and Giddy jumps from the cockpit and everyone runs out in front of the revetment. Cyril has taken off into a jeep.

Some of the other pilots and groundcrew are already there when we get across the field to where the Messerschmitt is merged with a maintenance vehicle. What had occurred is obvious. Cyril had fallen victim to the torque and had allowed the aircraft to swing off at a quarter angle. It had hit the jeep on a frontal course at the west perimeter. The two mechanics in the jeep had leapt out when they saw the Messerschmitt bearing down on them and now they are standing nervously behind the wreckage. The plane and the vehicle had traveled along together after the collision and the undercarriage of the Messerschmitt had folded. The debris is way off the strip and the earth is plowed up for 50 yards. Cyril is over at the ambulance. He has a cut across the top of his nose and blood has run down onto his handlebar moustache. He is dazed and wants to know what happened. Under the circumstances no one finds it necessary to tell him. The ambulance is marked with a red Star of David and Cyril is helped into the back. They leave for the infirmary at the far side of the mess hall. I look over at the Messerschmitt. The long-suffering Harry Axelrod is standing near the tilted wing and staring without emotion at the smashed propeller spinner.

During September the Squadron acquired two additional aircraft. They are in totally different categories because one is a P-51 Mustang fighter and the other is a little Seabee amphibian. The story behind the P-51 was interesting in the fact that it had arrived in Israel in a crate marked as farm implements, and had actually cleared US Customs as such. It had eventually made its way into Haifa harbor aboard a run-down Greek freighter and after being transferred to the docks it was immediately sent down to Herzliya, where it was re-assembled. When it was airworthy again, Giddy, who was partial to P-51s to the point of fanaticism, was designated to test it. It flew well on its first flight and the only problem deterring it from full operational status at the time was a complete absence of spare parts. Notwithstanding this problem, he managed to fly the aircraft frequently during the month.

The Seabee became, almost immediately, the plaything of Ezer. Although Moddy and a few of the others flew the ugly little underpowered craft occasionally, Ezer flew it whenever he wasn't engaged in operations and he was constantly luring others to take a ride in it. It was to provide one of those tales that became more exaggerated with time. When the Squadron had been relieved one afternoon, Ezer started up the Seabee and began to look around for passengers. By the time the engine was warmed up he had convinced Red Finkel, Maury Mann and Bill Pomerantz to accompany him on a local flight. They all climbed into the four-place machine and when the Seabee took off it barely cleared the hill at Kafr Shmaryahu, and then disappeared from view behind the slope to the north-west. Those who were watching stared at the empty sky and we didn't know what happened until Ezer brought the plane back an hour later.

They had gone down to buzz the beach. The Communications girls were there waving from the sand. Ezer decided to land in the water behind the breakers. Everything went well until they got on the surface of the sea. One of the wing floats was damaged when they hit a large swell and the pull of the surf started to carry the small plane toward the shore. Ezer applied the rudder until they were headed into the wind and opened the throttle to take off. With the shortage of power in the engine, and with the heavy-bodied Maury and Bill in the rear seats, the amphibian hummed along over the waves but refused to lift into the air. Ezer closed the throttle. He thought their dilemma was extremely funny and rested his head on the control column and shook with laughter. Next to him Red looked out the side window and his only reaction was a quiet smile. The others laughed but neither was really amused because they suspected what the ultimate solution to the problem was going to be. Ezer tried three more runs but they remained steadfastly on the water. Someone was going to have to get out. Red couldn't swim and both Maury and Bill were poor swimmers so they flipped a coin. Maury lost. He didn't like it and he threw the ten-mil piece disgustedly out of the window. He began to take off his shoes. Ezer maneuvered the Seabee parallel to the shore line but he had to stay at least 200 yards out. Maury conceded that he was going to get wet so he took off his shirt and trousers as well. The amphibian was rising and dropping on the swells and he waited until they were on the crest of one and plunged out. He ripped the seat off his underwear on the door handle as he left.

At the base camp the Seabee swings around near the Ops tent and Ezer, Red and Bill get out. They say it still took a two-mile run to get airborne after Maury departed. Everybody is laughing. They send a jeep down to the beach to pick up the swimmer. The sun has set and the surf is deserted and in the western glow before dark they can see the solitary figure lying on his back in the sand with his hands behind his head, gazing upward at the descending night.

Soon the high winds of the autumn equinox begin blowing. They come in from the east and on some days the aircraft have to be tied down and we spend our time in the tents. There is a moaning sound overhead and the flying sand punishes the canvas outside. During lulls, when there is only a fierce breeze, we are in the air again. The unforgiving Messerschmitts demand more skill than ever.

CHAPTER VII

THE INTERLUDE ACTIONS

It is a morning that is hardly suitable for flying the Desert Hawks but I taxi to the south perimeter and, when I turn upfield, the wind is so strong that I continue around in a complete circle. When I finally line up with the strip I can see that a dust layer has ascended to 3,000 feet above Kafr Shmaryahu. I am ready to open the throttle when I see Giddy running toward me from the Ops tent. I let the engine idle. It is back firing as Giddy comes around behind the port aileron and gets up on the step panel next to the cockpit. The wind tugs furiously at his clothes. I open the canopy. Giddy is shouting but I still have to remove the helmet to hear what he is saying. He bends his head forward into the cockpit and says that the red Rapide has been reported over Safad again. Giddy doesn't have to explain what he means. For a week we have known that a red Rapide has been periodically violating Israeli airspace and it is always in the same area of the Galil. I nod and close the canopy.

When I get in the air it is bumpy and I climb north along the edge of the salient. I can see where the Alexandroni Brigade has positions along the border and at 6,000 feet I pass Kafr Yona which had been shelled in the May fighting. Beyond, the Natanya auxiliary base lies windswept in the sun. At 12,000 feet I am above Nazareth and the wind keeps blowing me westward. I correct for the drift and turn toward the Galil. For a half hour I circle the vicinity of Safad but I don't see anything so I climb higher and return to the Israel corridor between the salient and the sea to look for shufti kites.

Two days later Giddy encountered the red Rapide. He was making a last turn above Safad before returning to Herzliya. The area below was not unfamiliar to him because he had been coming to the same place for the past three days. As he began the final sweep he saw the two-winged transport plane cutting across the airspace east of Safad and some five miles behind the Israeli front-line outposts. The foreign aircraft was undeniably red in color and at 5,000 feet it was slightly below the Messerschmitt. The Rapide apparently didn't see the Israeli aircraft and it continued south, halfway between Safad and the Syrian border and heading toward Lake Tiberius. Giddy immediately rolled downward and passed beyond the slower moving machine and took a position between it and the settlement of Mishmar Ha'Yarden, which was the Jewish town directly on the frontier. It can be stated early of this incident that Giddy employed proper procedure in accordance with an Air Command order, in the attempt to persuade the unidentified aircraft to land before more extreme measures were applied. The transport ignored the presence of the fighter momentarily and then it changed direction suddenly and headed east. It passed beneath Giddy, who had to maneuver sharply to stay to the port quarter. The Rapide proceeded on the revised course toward the sanctuary of the Arab lines beyond the Jordan River. Giddy edged in toward the other craft and, lowering the undercarriage on the Messerschmitt, he signaled to the pilot of the Rapide that he wished him to land in Israeli territory. Giddy had the intention at this point of escorting the transport down to the base at Ramat David. The Rapide pilot was apparently not similarly inclined and the aircraft again cut under the Messerschmitt.

By now Giddy was becoming angry because he was having difficulty handling the fighter at the slower speed, and he could clearly see that they were nearing the Syrian border. He moved in close again and he observed Arabic script on the fuselage of the red Rapide and what he termed 'bearded, turbaned faces gawking from the cabin windows'. He had to extend the flaps partially to avoid overshooting the other plane and he motioned toward the ground again. The Rapide drifted outward and this time Giddy fired a burst from his machine-guns across the flight path of the disobedient aircraft. The glowing tracer bullets left a brief trail and succeeded in forcing the transport into a dive toward the river.

There wasn't any more time left. The red Rapide would be clear in 30 seconds. The nose of the Messerschmitt followed the descending craft. They are down to 2,000 feet and the sections of the fields near the river are below them. The form of the transport moves into the gunsight of the Messerschmitt, looming nearer as the higher speed of the fighter quickly closes the distance between the two aircraft. Giddy fires directly at the red Rapide. The cannons pump out three rounds and then they jam and the bright color keeps turning away in front of him. He fires the machine-guns and the rivet-like tracers fly outward again. The red Rapide goes down.

At Herzliya we gather around the returning Messerschmitt and its appearance seems properly sinister. We were waiting for it because the base tower had called Operations and reported the interception of the red Rapide. Giddy is excited and he stands beside the fuselage and his voice is high-pitched when be talks. Everyone is listening to him and Moddy and Ezer are smiling. The Rapide had gone into a spiral after the burst of machine-gun fire had smashed into the starboard engine and set the fuel tank alight. The fabric on the machine became quickly enveloped in flames but the height and momentum of the falling aircraft carried it across the river where it struck the ground near some Iraqi positions. This fact was going to result in charges being hurled but for now Giddy takes a drink from a canteen and says no one in the Rapide could have survived the crash.

The day passes. Intelligence at the Yarkon listens for reaction from Arab sources and foreign news reports are monitored but as the afternoon progresses there is no mention of the incident. We still don't know the identity of the red Rapide. The day ends and we go back to Kafr Shmaryahu and after a meal we go down to the roadhouse. Nothing is discussed except the affair of the morning and at the roadhouse we drink and wait for the nine o'clock English-language news relayed from Beirut. The wireless-radio behind the bar is sending forth the exotic sound of Arabic music which suddenly subsides when the news broadcast is presented. The first item is about the downed transport.

Neither Giddy nor anyone else was prepared for the version that now unfolded over the air waves. Everyone unconsciously leans forward at the tables as the English voice recites. The Arabs are charging Israel with an atrocity. They are claiming that an unarmed civilian transport plane which was en route from Beirut to Amman was intercepted over Syrian territory and shot down without warning by an Israeli fighter. There are murmurs at the tables and the voice on the radio continues. It says that the British pilot of the Arab Airways' Rapide survived the crash with minor injuries as did two others who were aboard. Another four passengers were killed, including two well known British foreign correspondents* and two minor Arab potentates. Everyone looks at Giddy. He is incredulous. He gets up from the table and says he doesn't understand how anyone could have survived the crash. It is apparent that the Arabs are coming out with a story that is the opposite to the Israeli report of the incident. It doesn't surprise anyone and no one believes it. Sid Cohen laughs and says that's what they're expected to say. More details are given by the radio commentator. The pilot of the Rapide claims that everyone on board would have survived but that the four who were killed jumped out of the plane before it got to the ground. Giddy stares at the floor and shakes his head from side to side. The furore was stemming from the Arab assertion that the Messerschmitt came into Arab airspace and from the fact that two allegedly neutral British newspapermen were killed. The quiet Hebrew accent of Moddy's voice is heard and he comes over and puts his hand on Giddy's shoulder. He tells him not to worry. He says the Arabs are making propaganda. The news broadcast has moved to another subject and someone turns it off and the room is suddenly filled with loud talk. Ezer can be heard above

---

* The two British correspondents were John Nixon of the BBC and David Woodford of *The Daily Telegraph*.

the others. He says that the British correspondents were definitely not neutral. They were on the Stern Gang 'list'.

Reactions to the red Rapide incident hadn't died away when the shufti kite episode occurred and this mission was to retain a certain aura of mystery. Wayne Peake [a newly arrived American volunteer] in this instance was on patrol without oxygen at the remarkable height of 21,000 feet. He somehow managed to proceed on the flight at this altitude without passing out and, when he was above Cape Carmel with the sun directly overhead, he saw a Mosquito approaching at high speed. The shufti kite was 2,000 feet below and Peake had to react quickly. He completed a maneuver which brought the Messerschmitt [in fact Peake was flying the newly acquired P-51, *not* a Messerschmitt] just about behind the Mosquito but at a considerable range. He shoved the throttle all the way forward. The intruder aircraft reacted also and Peake could see the twin streaks of dark mist coming from its exhausts, suggesting that maximum power had been applied. A chase began that coursed across Haifa and over the harbor and out to sea. Peake soon realised that the Messerschmitt [*sic*] was not gaining on the shufti kite and that he was in danger of dropping out of range entirely.

To follow the Air Command procedure with this unidentified aircraft would be preposterous and Peake adjusted the gunsight setting and peered through the reflector. The Mosquito had no visible markings and was of a light color on the upper surfaces. As it became framed in the sight at a three-quarter angle, Peake fired an extreme deflection burst. It gave no evidence of having found its mark and one of the cannons jammed, causing the Messerschmitt [*sic*] to swerve to the left. Peake cursed and pulled farther to port of the other machine. He tried another deflection shot with the one cannon and both machine-guns. The tracers appeared to be on a strange trajectory and were curving away from the Mosquito. Peake put pressure on the starboard rudder control. Suddenly the port engine cowl of the leading aircraft revealed the tell-tale flashes of bullet strikes and a thin stream of pale smoke erupted from the exhausts. It continued on a level plane for a few seconds and then it threw its left propeller and the cowling disintegrated and bits of metal trailed behind like so many silver butterflies. It then went into a steep, rolling dive which Peake had difficulty imitating. Down below the shufti kite began to break up, continuing its uncontrolled dive until it plunged into the sea 12 miles off the Ladder of Tyre in Lebanese waters.

Silence from the other side not only greeted this action, it persisted. Intelligence interrogated Peake and as much information as possible was obtained. No recognizable insignia had been observed on the other aircraft. No parachutes were seen ejecting from the falling Mosquito but the glare from both sun and sea were strong and there could have been parachutes. No return fire had been noticed. For obvious reasons no one wanted to claim ownership of the shufti kite and so there was silence.

There were some ground witnesses in Acre who saw the encounter from afar but they were unable to supply pertinent details. Whispers that the victim was British were barely audible for the rest of the month*.

After all the agonizing, oxygenless patrols, the Squadron was elated that a shufti kite had finally been brought down but this novelty also passed as October neared. More and more armed clashes were developing on the fronts in spite of the ceasefire. The UN peacekeeping force was inadequate and unrealistic and the negotiations continued to be unproductive. Guarded reaction had hailed the arrival of the new UN Mediator, Dr Ralph Bunche, who had replaced the late Count Bernadotte at the end of September, but Bunche's task of arranging a peace acceptable to all the combatants appeared, at best, monumental. The situation was volatile.

The month had brought other developments in 101 Squadron. Chris Magee returned to the States and Cyril Horowitz was taken off flying duty and assigned to a job with Headquarters fighter operations at the Yarkon. A strong rumor was circulating that the Spitfire purchase had been concluded in Czechoslovakia – and I had to crash-land one of the Messerschmitts.

The wind had been blowing hard during the previous night but that morning it was comparatively calm and we got the patrols off. Sid Antin gives me a ride in the jeep and I get out at the dispersal area of Messerschmitt 121. It is another shufti kite mission. At 14,000 feet the supercharger cuts in and I feel the added power surge in the engine and the manifold pressure increases. I fly far to the north. Passing above Acre I proceed over Nihariya and the sky is deserted when, after an hour, I turn toward the east. Tiberius hovers ahead and I lose track of time in the high solitude. I have a headache from the altitude, and from the drinking at Kafr Shmaryahu the previous night, and when I bank southward again I remember to check the fuel reading. The litre content is low. I look at the clock on the instrument panel. It is past eleven and I have been out for over an hour and a half. I turn for Herzliya.

On the downwind leg at the base strip the red warning light is indicating ten minutes of fuel left. Plenty of time. I call the tower and turn onto the base segment and lower the undercarriage. I can feel the shudder as it extends and I am pulling on the flap wheel when I see that the undercarriage light is still red. I close the throttle and the warning horn sounds ominously. I check the gear indicator on the instrument panel. It shows the starboard leg locked in the down position and the port leg stuck at the half-extended mark. I return the handle to 'up'. Nothing happens. I put it down again. Nothing. Hydraulic failure. I look beneath and I am over the groves and coming into the final approach.

* Wayne Peake had in fact shot down an RAF Mosquito PR34 of 13 Squadron flying from Fayid in the Canal Zone, in which Flg Off Eric Reynolds and Nav 2 Angus Love were killed.

The strip is directly ahead and I open the throttle and go around. I pass low over Herzliya and I resort to flinging the aircraft from side to side in the hope of forcing the errant leg to lock down. When this fails I try the dangerous centrifugal force remedy and execute a tight vertical turn above the center of town.

In the streets below everyone is looking skyward. This maneuver is also met with negative results and I start to regain altitude when the power cuts off and the propeller slows to windmill speed. The fuel has run out. I switch on the emergency fuel pump and the engine coughs to life again but it is clear that time has run out. The emergency system might provide another minute of flying but it is doubtful that I can obtain the proper height to use my parachute, so the decision becomes fundamentally simple. I must get into the strip and land with one undercarriage leg down and one not down. My mind races and yet I seem to be unreasonably calm and my consciousness had been spared apprehension because everything has happened too quickly. The realization of what could lie ahead is mercifully prohibited from entering my thoughts. I turn onto the approach again and the strip is still waiting. I see the ambulance and the fire truck crossing the boundary. The jeeps are trailing them to the eastern perimeter. On the road between the mess hall and the Ops tent a crowd has gathered and many of the groundcrew are standing in front of the revetments on the south path. The Messerschmitt is descending fast and the voice from the tower has ceased calling. There is silence in the earphones of the helmet. I try to imagine that I am performing a normal landing. The trees at the end of the grove rush past and the strip rises closer. The aircraft drops onto the dusty surface.

When the Messerschmitt touches the ground it rolls for a distance on the extended wheel and then the opposite wing drops and contacts the earth. Things take place in rapid sequence. The most fortunate event in the series is the collapsing of the down gear leg which immediately causes the machine to flop onto its belly. Simultaneously with this occurrence, the propeller shatters into flying shards of wood and chunks of dirt and parts of the plane's underside begins to follow in the wake of the still fast-moving and potentially lethal aircraft.

I sit in the cockpit and grip the now useless control stick and I have no thoughts at all. It is like waiting for a story to end. The aircraft itself will write the final paragraph. It is on its own and I have nothing more to do with its progress or direction. I am merely a passenger now and its whim will dictate how the chapter will close.

With the initial impact I am jarred forward but the harness holds taut and now I travel oddly near the ground, down the middle of the strip. I look through the center of the windscreen but I concentrate on nothing. Slowly the machine veers to the right and its speed still seems exceptionally high. Its change of course puts it on a direct line with the fire truck and all at once this mandatory acquiescence to the aircraft's preferences injects me with an overwhelming feeling of helplessness. The marker drums on the east boundary race up and suddenly the fire truck becomes an insurmountable obstacle. All motion becomes like the stop-action frames of a camera. The two occupants of the vehicle sit tensely on the high, old-fashioned seat above the red-painted hood and in the first frame we stare at one another in disbelief. The next frame shows two figures leaping wildly through the air. The nose of the Messerschmitt plows into the dirt furrow and the machine is propelled upward onto its spinner where it hangs, tail straight up, for several suspenseful seconds. Then it falls, with a certain curious dignity, back onto its belly. It has stopped five feet away from the fire truck.

Moddy, Ezer, Sid Cohen and Harry Axelrod are the first ones to reach the side of the cockpit. I open the canopy and the dust is stifling and when I get out it seems strange to be able to step directly onto the ground.

* * * * *

A week before September ended Moddy, Arni and Sid Cohen are summoned to the Yarkon and advised that they will be travelling to Czechoslovakia. The Spitfires had been purchased. Five of the ex-RAF machines at Budejovice had been procured and there were indications that even more were being sought from the Czechs. Now their delivery to Israel depended in part on the 101 pilots. At Zatec, Sam Pomeranz had fitted the five aircraft with external auxiliary fuel tanks and he had devised a modification to the internal fuel system to enable the planes to have an increased range of eight hours in the air. Technically they could make the long flight to Israel non-stop. Pomeranz would also be one of the pilots on the journey. The fifth participant in this ferrying operation was the industrious Boris Senior.

Flying the much desired Spitfires from Czechoslovakia to Israel was not necessarily a difficult or dangerous project. Taken first to the Czech base at Kanovice in the extreme southern section of the country, the planes would be fuelled to capacity and begin the flight from there in the company of a C-54, which would act as a mother ship and navigate the course for the Spitfires. They would generally travel the Velveta route and pass beyond Titograd to the Adriatic and then, skirting Greek territory, make their way eastward and then south past Crete and Cyprus to Ramat David. All would go well until they were opposite the island of Rhodes.

Maury and I are to remain at Herzliya with the Spitfire Brigade. The night following the announcement of the deal, the three Europe-bound pilots are ready to leave. At Kafr Shmaryahu we see them off and there are drinks and laughter and only Moddy is serious. Boris comes in from Tel Aviv and then the four get into a jeep and head for Lydda. It is a week before we hear anything more.

Maury becomes acting CO during this period and the quiet Rudy Augarten takes over the recently appointed post of Operations Officer. Rudy has the task of supervising the Flights and, on the last evening of the month, we are sitting in Falk's garden after dinner when he comes in from the base camp with the next day's flying schedule. He also has a request from Headquarters for a special mission. They want a single-plane sortie to the Egyptian airfield at El Arish to be flown at first light in the morning. Rudy reads from a paper he is holding and everyone around the tree becomes still. It is nearly dark and the lights from inside the screen porch are casting a yellow glow on the hedges. Rudy finishes reading what is in the paper. Operations wants a low-level flight over El Arish at dawn with the PR Spitfire. The pilot is to make only one pass and he is to try to retain everything he sees while finding out how awake they are down there. No camera will be used on the mission and the fact that there is a prevailing ceasefire demands that precaution and discretion be utilized during the operation. The resurrected Egyptian Spitfire was being employed on the sortie because it has a good chance of getting in and out of the enemy area without creating undue alarm in advance. The Egyptians generally trusted Spitfires, but even a long-range glimpse of a Desert Hawk had by know become a reason for profound consternation in the Arab strongholds. Rudy repeats the last sentence of the notation – one pass over El Arish and out. Everyone knows that Maury and I are the only Spitfire pilots left in 101 and Rudy looks at me without further comment. It is a volunteer mission. Maury is in the latrine, so I tell Rudy I'll take the assignment.

The duty jeep comes round before daybreak the next morning. With Sid Cohen and Arni in Czechoslovakia, I am alone in the tent and when Rudy arrives at the entrance I am already awake. The jackals had howled persistently during the night and I had awakened and listened to them for an hour. Now it is time to go. Rudy waits while I get dressed in the dark and then we walk to the kitchen near the porch and drink some of the tea which is always left on top of the stove. We go out to the jeep and the garden shrubs are obscure when we pass through. We get in the jeep and take the rutted road down to the base camp. We are both sleepy and we don't talk. When we arrive at the Spitfire dispersal, the groundcrew is preparing to run the engine up. In the east a streak of light is now visible. Shimon is in the cockpit and in a few moments he throttles the engine back and the half-light permits one to see the blue flame that flickers hypnotically from the exhaust stacks. Shimon gets out of the cockpit and I take the parachute from the edge of the wing and climb up and get in. After I fasten the safety belt Rudy steps up beside the windscreen. He has to speak above the idling engine and he wants to know if I will need illumination from the lights of the jeep at the north end of the strip to orient the aircraft on the take-off. I pull the helmet on and look over my shoulder. The sky is growing paler by the minute. I shake my head. Rudy gets down and walks back to the jeep and I ease the throttle forward and turn upfield.

The day is fast arriving when I pass over Petah Tiqva. I haven't risen higher than 2,000 feet and after I turn down the coast beyond Jaffa I drop close above the waves of the sea. I stay three miles out and parallel the contours of the shore line. A ship which I assume to be an Israeli corvette is making its way southward off Jaffa. I watch it for a moment and then it falls behind and I dismiss it and begin to think of other things. I wonder about the ground defenses at El Arish and I wonder how alert they will be at this early hour. I don't worry about their fighters because on the missions I have thus far flown in Israel the challenges by enemy aircraft have been non-existent. The coastal flats around Majdal approach and recede and Gaza looms ahead. The sun is beginning to show above the ring of the eastern hills and the emerging rays cause tiny glints of light to hit the crests of the rolling swells beneath. Ashore all appears motionless and now the port wing points at Gaza.

Presently the coastline bends seaward and I pass the border of the Sinai. An odd outcropping of land juts into the sea beyond the town of El Arish and when it is in front of the Spitfire I bank sharply in and cross over the beach. The desolation of the desert spreads before the spinning propeller and the climbing sun causes shadows to creep outward in long patterns from the ridges and rocks on the arid sand dunes of the landscape. I turn north. The town and the airfield are separated by a short distance that is filled with makeshift dwellings and tents and I pull the Spitfire up to 200 feet and get a broader view. The line I am on is bringing me across the base over the south-east runway and the fact that this very machine took off from here to attack Tel Aviv in May borders on comedy.

I look alternately to the right and to the left. The fighter dispersal points, the hardstands, gun emplacements, the hangars, the REAF Dakotas scattered about and, on the eastern edge of the field under camouflage, is one of the recently acquired Fiat fighters we had heard about [it was in fact a Macchi MC205V]. I dip the starboard wing of the Spitfire but I see nothing resembling a mass buildup of aircraft. On the contrary, they seem to have moved aircraft out of the base. Below, a lorry is moving down a side road, the dust billowing upward behind it in the morning light. It is the first sign of movement I have seen. The runway ends and I pass the north border of the base and there are more tents and houses and then they fall away behind as I continue toward the sea. As I re-cross the beach I look back and a feint line of shell tracers makes an erratic pattern in the air above the base. I smile at the instrument panel. They are much too late.

The sun is higher on the return flight and it is bright in my eyes when I look at the shore. When I am nearing Majdal I see the corvette ahead, plowing through the swells on a south-westerly course. It is five miles off the coast and there is suddenly something imperceptively strange about its presence. Impulsively I turn the Spitfire outward and in a few minutes I come around behind the ship. I am low on the water and, as the vessel grows in the windscreen, I can see it rolling and pitching in the sea troughs. I am trying to identify the ensign flag which is flying at the stern when a volley of Bofors rounds rushes past the starboard wing like orange-colored tennis balls. The ship is Egyptian. I instantly turn away and, as the Spitfire's wing drops vertically near the surface, I see the flash and white smoke of a high-caliber anti-aircraft gun which is firing from the after deck. I get out of range.

The suddenness of the unfriendly salvo had surprised me and it has also instilled in me a certain amount of fear which had given way to a desire for retaliation when I was a good distance off. I release the safety of the gun control button on the stick and then I hesitate. I have thoughts of being involved in a truce violation. I remember the orders and turn for Herzliya.

It was upon landing from this mission that the sight in my right eye diminished drastically. I knew it was a recurrence of a condition caused by a war wound and the effect was usually of short duration. By the next day the vision had improved and I never mentioned anything about it.

CHAPTER VIII

DEATH OF A HERO

Three days into October we are alerted that the Spitfires from Czechoslovakia are due at Ramat David during the afternoon. An escort flight is organized and we draw cards to see who will fly it. Sandy and I get the sortie. Information from the Yarkon says the Spitfires are scheduled to cross the harbor at Haifa at four o'clock and we make our plans to intercept them and escort them the rest of the way to Ramat David.

We take two Messerschmitts and depart Herzliya at three-thirty. The Spitfires were to be flying in at 5,000 feet so we proceed toward Haifa at 6,000 feet. Near Natanya we pass the Lodestar flying up the coast and whoever is in the co-pilot's seat is smiling and waving. South of Cape Carmel we turn away from the land and go out to sea and then cut north again to the harbor. There is a haze which is aggravated by the afternoon sun but we still have fair visibility. Sandy is doggedly hanging close to my port wing and we circle an area of 20 miles of the water. We can see no other machines. We keep watching to the north and an hour passes and there is nothing else visible in the air. The circling is becoming monotonous. We are unable to contact Ramat David on the radio and we can barely hear Herzliya. They tell us to continue to search. More circling and looking toward the north. Emptiness. After another 15 minutes of the criss-cross pattern above the harbor we receive a garbled message to return to base. The wind has changed direction when we get back and we have to approach over Kafr Shmaryahu. We come into the strip high and when we get on the ground we both roll down to the grove revetments before we can stop.

Almost everyone is at the Ops tent and we hear the news. Three of the Spitfires are at Ramat David. Sid Cohen, Sam Pomeranz and Arni Ruch. They had crossed the coast north of Haifa at three-thirty but Ramat David hadn't notified Herzliya until later. Moddy and Boris had force-landed on the Greek island of Rhodes. Their reserve fuel tanks had malfunctioned and now the Spitfires were interned by the Greeks. So were Moddy and Boris.

The other three Spitfires are remaining temporarily at Ramat David to be refitted and Sid Cohen and Arni fly back to Herzliya that evening in a utility plane. When they arrive we all gather at the Command hut and they tell us about the flight down from Czechoslovakia. Sid says there were no problems until the fuel system failures west of Rhodes. He says Moddy didn't say much on the R/T at the time but that Boris was joking over the radio as they were preparing to land on the island. The other aircraft, including the C-54, had circled until the two were down on the Greek runway but they couldn't tarry and had to leave them behind. Sid and Arni are laughing although everyone feels Moddy's absence. They say that Yigael Yadin, the personable Chief of Staff of the Haganah forces, and even Ben-Gurion himself, are already negotiating to get the Greeks to release the pilots and the aircraft. Sid thinks it is an amusing coincidence that the UN Mediator, Dr Bunche, displaying understandable caution, had decided to set up his headquarters on the island of Rhodes.

On the eve of the Yom Kippur holidays the base at Herzliya is visited by a certain US Senator. He is accompanied on a tour of the airfield by Yigael Yadin and some aides and, though the ransoming of Moddy from the Greeks is on everyone's mind, nothing is said at the time. We stand by the aircraft and the visitors pass in casual review and everything is formal as usual. I look at the Desert Hawks. I couldn't have known it at that moment but I had taken my last flight in them.

The next day the holidays begin and it is a clear October evening when the party starts at Kafr Shmaryahu. Bottles are produced and there is a lot of drinking at Falk's and then we all go down to the base camp mess hall for a special meal. Tables have been arranged outside and they reach all the way over to the roadway. There is music and dancing and laughter in the air. After the food has been served at the long tables, the pilots begin to drift away into the coming night and some find their way back up to Kafr Shmaryahu. From there everyone is planning to go into Tel Aviv. Red Finkel has somehow engaged a taxi which has come over from Herzliya and he gets into the back seat with one of the new girls from camp. Four more of us crowd into the back with them and we all sit crammed together on the ride into town.

There are parties all over Tel Aviv and some of 101 are at the Park Hotel bar. It is nine o'clock and I am drinking at a table with Sid Cohen and Ezer. Dov Ben Zvi, Yacov and Lev are with us. Music is coming from somewhere near the terrace. The austere Ben Zvi* is transportation officer at Herzliya and Yacov and Lev are riggers on the Messerschmitts. Called Jake, Yacov is another who had served in the Mandate forces and he has a cynical sense of humor toward life. Lev is young but his face

---

* Dov Ben Zvi was the name adopted by British-born Baron Wiseberg, a former Royal Navy Fleet Air Arm fighter pilot who had flown with 101 Squadron early in the war.

reveals the hard lines of silently endured tragedy that one saw on many of the faces in this land. His brother had been with Irgun and was hung by the British the same week that Irgun had abducted and hung two British Army sergeants.

We drink and then Ben Zvi leaves. Sid and Ezer go up to the bar where they are joined by Giddy and Lou Lenart and some of the Yarkon people. Jake and Lev are going to a bistro off Allenby and I get up and go with them. Outside in the semi-blackout there are three street fights in progress and all of them involve foreign volunteers. We stop and calmly watch the nearest one. A South African has a bloody nose and is struggling to rise from the curbside. He uses outrageous language which is apparently directed toward his adversary, a large soldier who is standing in the middle of the street. The sidewalks are jammed with people and many are urging on one or the other of the combatants. I look out at the soldier in the road. He is standing on the same spot where the body had lain in June.

The bistro is full and after an hour of drinking at the bar, Jake and Lev go somewhere else and I go over to a table and sit with Sol Rosen, Esther and Rachel. Rosen is a likeable American volunteer who is attached to the Yarkon motor pool and Esther and Rachel are army girls. They work at Headquarters also. Both girls are attractive and dark and Esther has grey eyes. They smile when I pull up a chair. Another hour of drinks and laughter and then we go up to Ben Yehuda and patronize the Yarden bar until after midnight. The girls have to go back to their quarters in the suburb of Montefiore and we wait with them in front of the Yarden until they get a ride in a jeep that is already full of people. We laugh and shake hands and then the jeep speeds down the street. Sol and I go back into the bar and drink until it closes.

It is early afternoon when I wake up on the couch in Sol's flat behind Shahar Street. I am alone in the room and I have a headache from the cognac and a pain over my right eye that aspirin doesn't touch. The flat is small. I go to the basin and wash and try to brush the wrinkles from my khakis. Sunlight is coming through the partly-closed blinds on the single window and I look out at the small garden below for a moment. I remember that I should be back at Herzliya but Sid Cohen had taken over as acting CO from Maury Mann and I don't worry about it for now. I leave the flat and go down the dim narrow stairs to the bright street and, when I am halfway down the block, I see Sol coming from the direction of the Yarkon. He is smiling and looks fresh and when he comes up to me on the walkway he says he is off duty for the day. He had been down at the motor pool since sunrise and now he laughs when I look at him. He has a pleasant face and a rather large nose and when he talks he has an entertaining personality. He says the girls are off duty too and they want us to join them for food and drink. We walk over a few streets and go way up to the far end of Allenby and meet Rachel and Esther at a sidewalk cafe. We sit in the shade of the trees that shelter the open section and we eat some pickled fish and drink beer. The holiday spirit continues. A party develops in a bistro across the street and we go over. We don't see anyone from the Squadron all day. When we are leaving the cafe at dusk, Dov Ben Zvi drives past. We shout at him but he maneuvers the jeep fiercely down the middle of Allenby and doesn't look to either side. We laugh.

Night falls and we are at the Gallim Yam. We had walked down along the sea wall and we could barely hear the breakers because there was so much noise on the beach road. At the Gallim Yam we have a table in the center of the open area and everyone around us is crowded together. Sol is saying something funny and the girls are laughing. They are sabras and they don't always understand Sol's humor but they laugh anyway. The evening is mild and the sea smell is good and everyone is in high spirits. Three tables away someone spills a drink on a girl's dress and a fight starts. Two volunteers lunge across the congested space and one of them falls onto Esther's lap. The volunteer grabs Esther's skirt to steady himself and she ejects him onto the floor and then everyone in the vicinity becomes engaged in the dispute. Chairs crash downward. The MPs arrive.

The Military Police section at the Yarkon takes up the entire west side of the basement area and when Sol and I and five others from the Gallim Yam arrive under escort the place is crowded. The main orderly room is busy and contains both those who are assigned there and those who have been arrested. In an adjoining room are more people behind bars in a large cell. The most interesting fact that one noticed upon entering was that everyone was arguing. Hebrew and English are being shouted at the same time and we laugh and sit down on some orange crates along the wall of the orderly room. We have lost our animosity toward the other volunteers who were brought in with us and Sol touches his swollen lip. We wait. One of the sabra MPs says we are all charged with disorderly conduct. I look at the floor and have a great desire to go back to the Gallim Yam. A half hour goes by while we watch the activity and then a Provost Marshal comes over to where we are sitting and hands us back our Service identification cards. The Provost Marshal has thinning hair and two front teeth missing from both rows. He says the disorderly conduct charges have been dropped and that all but two of us can go. He smiles and points to me and another volunteer and says we have been reported absent from our units and that we will have to remain in custody and see the military court. I have had too many drinks to be surprised and I sit back down on the orange crate and tell Sol to call Sid Cohen for me.

The military detention barracks in Jaffa had seen similar use with the British during the Mandate and, when the lorry arrives there from the Yarkon, it is three o'clock in the morning. One of the MPs helps me down from the back of the truck and we follow the others to the narrow barbed-wire gate which is the entrance. The drink is wearing off and the mounting annoyance that I am beginning to feel is only surpassed by a craving for sleep. There is an army guard at the gate and he swings it open and we pass through into the compound. There are five others in the group and we stop near the sentry post while the MPs talk with the guard. I don't know anyone who is with me although most of them are foreign volunteers. It is dark but the dirty, whitewashed walls which surround the large courtyard are quite visible as are the two low buildings which form a semi-rectangle about the open space. A light is showing from a room in an extension of one of the buildings that is nearest the gate. We soon learn that this is the Commandant's office.

Morning comes and I have slept for two hours. There is movement around me and I hear voices. I am lying on a pallet in a room of one of the low buildings. There are many more pallets and I am reminded momentarily of the long ago hostel in Haifa. I sit up. The flies are here also. I look around. The walls are bare and white and the two windows in the room are screenless. The entrance has no door. People are sitting and standing in numerous poses, dressed and undressed. Someone stops on the narrow aisle in front of the pallet. I look at the desert shoes for a second and then I look up at the face. It is Jake. He sits at the end of the pallet and laughs when I tell him what happened. He says he has been here since the first night in Tel Aviv. He is charged with assaulting an army major. He laughs again and shrugs. He says he didn't know that the chap was a major because he wasn't displaying any rank.

Outside they are serving breakfast from a table under the red-tiled overhanging roof that creates a corridor along the edge of the buildings. We stand in line and take the tea, bread and hard boiled eggs. I give mine to Jake. I keep the tea and sip from the tin cup and we go over and sit against the north wall. It is too early for the sun to reach into the courtyard and a certain coolness in the air is a sign that it is autumn. Jake looks up at the strands of barbed-wire on the top of the wall and smiles. He says that there is word that the upper echelon at Headquarters has ordered a harder line on military offenders. They think the foreign volunteers are particularly undisciplined. He throws the remainder of his tea on the ground and we laugh. I expect to be out of here by evening time.

Slender and tough, Jake has a philosophical attitude which I am well advised to initiate as the day passes. I hear nothing from the Squadron. The irritation at being in the detention compound is tempered by the fact that many of the occupants are straight out of the pages of a novel and there is a camaraderie here which makes it seem as though one is a member of a family. I walk through the yard with Jake after the meal and we talk with some of the others.

The Egyptian. Suave, even in dirty khakis, the one called the Egyptian is a Jew who was born in Cairo and he was in the Givati

Brigade. He had lost the middle finger of his right hand and he liked to say he had been wounded, but everyone laughs and says he had the finger amputated after he was stung by a scorpion. He has smooth, black hair which he slicks back. He is charged with confiscating a jeep in Tel Aviv.

The Mascot. Happy natured and pathetically trusting, the Mascot is fourteen years old. His entire family had died in the death camps of eastern Europe and how he escaped to the West no one really knew because he was fond of exaggerating. It was known that he had been adopted by a unit of US infantry and he had lived with the troops for three years and spoke English with an American accent. No one was sure how he got to Israel but he was apprehended when he tried to join the Palmach and sent to the barracks in Jaffa until it could be decided what to do with him.

Asher Ginsberg. Muscular, balding, keeping his thoughts to himself and always giving half his food to the Mascot. He was said to have been with the Stern Gang and the reason for his presence at the Jaffa barracks was obscure. No one asked any questions.

Stahl. A skinny German Jew, Stahl had miraculously escaped the death camps also but he was forever cheerful and he had an inexhaustable supply of Yiddish jokes which he recited at every opportunity.

The Italian. Small and fair-haired, the Italian spoke only his native tongue and was thus faced with a considerable conversation barrier at the compound. What little had been learned about him was almost ludicrous. He had been a fighter pilot with Mussolini's air force in World War II and had served against many of us when he was stationed in the Western Desert and Cyrenaica. He had journeyed to Israel by some devious and uncertain route without any official papers and, not only did he fail to join the Israeli Air Force, he was actually suspected as a spy initially. He had been picked up by the Military Police, penniless and singing operatic arias on a street corner in Tel Aviv. He has no charges against him but is waiting at Jaffa for a disposition on whether he will even remain in Israel. The Italian is a Christian and he has a good singing voice and in the evenings he sometimes stands at the entrance to the barrack room and entertains us with his talent.

Stahl, who is here for pilfering supplies from an army unit other than his own, points to a figure sitting alone near the wall of the south barracks. The figure wears a yarmulke and he is young and is the one everybody refers to as the Rabbi. He is in reality a fanatical religious student and now, in the midst of the holy days, he does nothing but seek solitude for the rituals that he performs with seemingly endless fervor. He has been remanded to custody for allowing his prayer practices to interfere with his military duty. The day of Yom Kippur is a half week away.

The next day I walk down to the gate with Jake. It is mid-morning and beyond the walls of the compound the sun is shining on the buildings of Jaffa. Most of them are deserted, the vacant windows staring silently at other vacant windows in a place of ghosts. Some of the facilities, like the detention barracks, are being utilized by the Israelis but for now the departure of its inhabitants from this Palestinian Arab city has left it with an aura of surrealism. We pass the Commandant's hut and he is standing on the steps. He is short and wears glasses and is good humored and sympathetic toward those who are temporarily under his control. He served with the Mandate Postal Service and he always answers questions by saying 'wait and see'. We walk on and stop at the gate and Dov comes over. Dov is the tall, blond sabra guard who has the sentry duty at the gate during the day. He also brings us the news from the outside. He speaks in Hebrew to Jake and searches in his shirt pocket for something. He has difficulty finding the article and gives Jake his Mauser while he continues searching with both hands.

By the third day at Jaffa I am beginning to believe that the Squadron doesn't know where I am. I have still heard nothing. I am lying on the pallet in the barracks room in the afternoon and others are also lying about when Jake comes through the entrance. He has heard something at the gate. He has heard that the truce has been broken. The war has started again.

It is five more days before I am exonerated of the absent without leave charge by a military board at the Yarkon. They were to be days of decision and of unqualified military successes for Israel. The Givati and Negev Brigades had launched an all-out push against the Egyptians at Isdud and actions were initiated to secure the Jerusalem sector and the roads along the disputed areas in the Tel Aviv-Jerusalem corridor. The salient and Galil fronts were comparatively quiet. 101 Squadron was to carry the bulk of the air support role in the offensive and the new Spitfires were to see their first operations. Moddy and Boris had been returned from Rhodes, unfortunately without the needed aircraft. Moddy was back at Herzliya. The last act had begun.

On the second night of the renewed fighting there is an air raid alert and we all go out into the yard of the compound and watch. Anti-aircraft tracers are sailing into the night sky from both the Jaffa and Tel Aviv areas and, between lulls in the firing, we can faintly hear the sound of engines in the air. We don't hear any bombs falling nor do we feel the earth shake from any hits. After a while there is silence and all-clear sirens wail. We go back to the barracks. In the morning Dov tells us that it was an Egyptian Dakota that was approaching Tel Aviv. Then it had turned around and decided to drop its bombs south of Rehovot. Dov has steel-rimmed glasses and he takes them off and cleans them. He says 50 chickens were killed on a kibbutz.

At the Jaffa detention barracks, Yom Kippur dawns quietly. The fasting goes on and we wait for news of the actions and I sense a strong impatience at being away from the Squadron. It is mid-October. More news of the air operations has filtered in to us. A C-46, escorted by four Messerschmitts, had bombed Gaza and Majdal the previous day and the three new Spitfires struck the base at El Arish. The Egyptians were withdrawing from Isdud. It was joyous and gratifying news but still it was difficult to curb my restlessness. That night after the end of the fast I am down by the gate with Jake and a few of the others. An army jeep has stopped outside the entrance and the two soldiers in it are talking through the wire to the night sentry. The Hebrew words are spoken loudly and Jake listens. Others go up to the wire but Jake takes my arm and we walk over toward the north wall. Jake looks at me. He says Moddy was killed at Herzliya.

In the days that followed, various versions of the crash that killed Moddy were heard but perhaps the account of Ezer, who flew as Moddy's wingman on that last mission, can throw the most light on the events leading up to the fatal accident. With the Egyptian retreat from Isdud starting to resemble a rout, Air Command had ordered the fighters to keep continual pressure on the southward-fleeing forces during the daylight hours. Sorties were flown out of Herzliya all day on Yom Kippur and, as evening approached, Moddy decided personally to take one more flight and he selected Ezer to go with him. The Messerschmitts available at that moment were 114 and the rebuilt 121. Moddy wanted 114, ostensibly because it was considered the best-rigged of all the Messerschmitts but also because the one-legged, nearly disastrous crash-landing of 121 was still fresh in his memory. Undaunted, the agreeable Ezer hopped into 121 and Moddy led out. They look off and stayed low, flying down the coast and turning in across the flats north of Majdal. Both machines were carrying bombs which they dropped on targets along the road out of Isdud. They then began to strafe the road with their guns and Ezer proceeded all the way down to Majdal. The weather was clear but they lost visual contact and, when he was out of ammunition, Ezer turned for home. His inter-plane R/T reception was faulty so he didn't bother with it and continued north. He still couldn't spot Moddy's aircraft. It was Saturday night and he made a detour to fly over the rooftop of his uncle's home in Rehovot as an impulsive triumphant gesture. As soon as he neared Herzliya he saw the tower of black smoke in the evening air and somehow he instinctively knew that Moddy had been killed. Ezer came around into the strip and landed. He had no trouble with 121.

Number 114 had crashed in an open field just south of Herzliya. The machine was destroyed and Moddy was killed instantly. There was no indication that the aircraft has been hit by return fire on the mission. One of the groundcrew at the scene has best described the real reason for the tragedy with a succinct observation. Hydraulic failure. When the undercarriage refused to lock down, Moddy had applied the centrifugal force solution. He was at 2,500 feet when the Messerschmitt went into a power spin. It was over. All Israel lamented the loss of Moddy Alon because he was a national hero – and a hero he had died on Yom Kippur. Strangely, he was the only accidental airborne fatality claimed by the Desert Hawks.

The morning sun rises brightly over the Jaffa compound but the searing heat of summer is gone. We wash our clothes at the yard trough and by the time they are dry the lorry from Yarkon is outside the barbed-wire gate. I say goodbye to the detention barracks. The Commandant hands me the order from Headquarters which dissolves the charge and returns me to duty. Jake walks with me to the barrier and Dov swings it open. I feel a certain sadness at leaving those whom I had met at Jaffa. Jake smiles when I get into the lorry and he lifts his hand in a salute. Before the week ends he will be sent to a punishment garrison at Acre.

I report to the Yarkon and prepare to go back to the Squadron. Much has changed in the time I have been away. Sid Cohen is now CO of 101 and when I see Cyril Horowitz in one of the hallways at Headquarters he says there are some new pilots at Herzliya. The Czechs have sold a whole squadron of their well-preserved Spitfire 9s to Israel and four Gentile volunteers are settled at Kafr Shmaryahu. Cyril says that the days of the Messerschmitts are numbered.

The death of Moddy seemed to have drawn the curtain on the early era. In wartime, weeks endure as months and the distant days of June and the dusty summer and the time of the Squadron pioneers were fading rapidly into the past. By November the unloved Desert Hawks were to be withdrawn from service in favor of the popular and now abundant Spitfires. It was sometimes said, by those who thought about it, that it was odd that Moddy and the Messerschmitts had passed on together. But others said, or maybe thought, that this was altogether appropriate. Their destinies had seemed intertwined since the first weeks of the conflict. The Messerschmitts had been there when it was essential that they be there and so had Moddy Alon been there. Together they had fought and defeated the enemy and now their service to Israel had ended.

CHAPTER IX

WINTER OF VICTORY

I never returned to Herzliya. That afternoon, at the Yarkon, the vision in my right eye fails again as I am walking to the motor pool to get a ride to the Squadron. This time it cannot be concealed. An orderly helps me to the Yarkon infirmary and Cyril is called down. After an examination by the Flight Surgeon I am sent out to Hadassah. There is another examination at the military hospital and the eye is bandaged to keep out the light. I am grounded and placed on detachment duty with Headquarters fighter operations which, in fact, meant that my flying days with the Israeli Air Force were over. Hadassah is out near the Yarkon River and I remain at the hospital two weeks. The chief surgeon is curious about the original head wound that caused the affliction but nothing is attempted clinically on the eye except for the daily inspection and a change of bandage each morning. The sight is returning at a slower rate and, at the end of the second week, it is decided to send me up to Haifa to a specialist. Some of the wounded from the southern fighting are coming into the hospital at intervals but they are all army and there is no one I recognize.

Leave has been cancelled at Herzliya and I don't see anyone from the Squadron either but, during my last day at Hadassah, Sol Rosen comes out to visit me and he has Esther and Rachel with him. We go outside where there are benches beneath a row of eucalyptus trees and we sit in the shade of the leaves and talk. We laugh about everything at first and then Sol is serious. He says that Stan Andrews was shot down by ground fire near Majdal. His remains were found in the wreckage of the Beaufighter by a Palmach patrol. Sol lights a cigarette. He says that Sam Pomeranz was also killed when he flew one of the recently acquired Spitfires into the side of a mountain in Yugoslavia during a storm. The girls are looking past the trees toward the river. Esther says that she used to come out here when she was ten years old and they would visit the British War Memorial and sometimes they would walk down the river bank to the beach and spend the whole day on the sand, collecting sea shells.

I leave for Haifa the next morning. During the day I go to the Yarkon and Sid Cohen brings the rest of my kit in from Herzliya. We have only a little time because he has a meeting with Aharon Remez. Sid is wearing one of the new peaked caps that have been lately issued but otherwise his appearance hasn't changed. He smiles and grasps my hand and neither of us say much. We stand next to the kit inside the main entrance of the Yarkon. Someone passing bumps Sid's shoulder but he ignores it. He says we don't have time for a drink. Maybe in the next war. We both smile and then he turns and goes into the crowd at the stairway.

It is dusk when we board the Rapide hospital plane at Sde Dov. Some of us wear sweaters because now the night breeze from the sea is chilly. I look down toward Tel Aviv and in the fading light I see the shadow-like form of the LST for the last time.

At Hadar hak Karmel I am eventually released by Haganah and returned to the States. There was, however, one more chapter to be written by 101 Squadron in Israel's War of Independence.

The assaults by Israeli forces, especially against the Egyptians, continued into the winter of 1948. The long period of containment had ended for the Jews and now the enemy was being pushed back to the Sinai. The offensive achievements of the Givati and Negev Brigades had led them to the very gates of El Arish. The situation that had prevailed in May had been reversed and, historically, it was the first Israeli thrust into the Sinai. The proceeding battles had cleared Isdud and Majdal and Gaza, as well as inland Negev positions, of enemy concentrations. As a result, the forward bases which had been evacuated in the earlier months were again put into service. 101 Squadron moved down to Hatzor, which had been shelled periodically for six months by the Egyptians in Isdud, and began operations aimed at harassing the Arab rearguard on the Sinai border. The B-17s, still operating from Ramat David, had participated in some destructive raids during this southward push and had particularly bestowed havoc on targets in what was known as the Faluja Pocket or 'bend', east of Majdal, and at Gaza where many of the Egyptian supplies were destroyed. Enemy air opposition during this time had been negligible to the point of being invisible but their anti-aircraft defenses were another matter, and could at times be deadly. The Israeli Air Force in general had been greatly strengthened by now with additional aircraft and personnel and, during the months of November and December, they roamed freely above the sands of the Sinai.

By late December only the disorganized Egyptian army, and the countless wretched Arab refugees who followed in its wake, lay between the Israelis and the Suez Canal. At this point, the British, who still maintained a sizeable force in the Canal Zone, acted under the nine-year-old Anglo-Egyptian Treaty and presented the Israel Government with an ultimatum ordering them to halt their advance into the Sinai. This was followed by a similar order from the UN and, at the same time, the

United States applied certain political pressures in an effort to persuade the Jewish leaders to comply with the ultimatum. Facing this awesome combination of diplomatic and military power, the Israelis stopped their pursuit of the Egyptians and withdrew to the Sinai border. To the credit of Dr Bunche, the UN Mediator who had been laboring diligently if unsuccessfully since October to enforce another ceasefire and settle the war peacefully, an armistice agreement was now accepted by all the belligerents which would become effective during the first week of the new year. It was to be an armistice, not another of the endless ceasefires that had stretched across the summer months, and it was to mean, in effect, an end of what would become known in Israel as the War of Independence. It was to produce a mixture of joy and frustration for the Israelis.

The original Partition boundaries were now unmistakeably secure for the Jews but many claims and counter claims that had been at issue for so long were left unresolved. Jerusalem; Samaria and Judea in the salient West Bank, places with untold religious significance for the Jews. The creation of the Gaza Strip which would point straight at Tel Aviv. The Golan Heights, where the Syrians would continue to look down on the Jewish farm settlements. The Israeli military had grave forebodings but the Armistice meant a beginning. The new State had survived its birth and now it would have time to grow strong. The Armistice became a fact on 7 January 1949.

At Hatzor, 101 Squadron welcomed the overcast winter dawn of 7 January by despatching Spitfire patrols to Abu Ageila in the Sinai where one of the largest of the Egyptian forces had halted. The armistice was not officially in force until two o'clock in the afternoon. It was meanwhile developing across the desolate expanse of the southern desert that the British, apparently to verify compliance with the earlier ultimatum, were sending out their own RAF patrols and some of these aircraft began to violate what the Jews considered Israeli airspace. An unavoidable collision course was set.

The opening clash occurred at mid-morning when six [in fact, four] Canal-based Spitfires of the RAF's 208 Squadron flew over Israeli territory in the vicinity of the El Auga-Beersheba road and then turned west and continued in the direction of the Rafah border area. Mistaking them for Egyptian aircraft, Israeli ground gunners fired at them without result. Over Rafah one of the British planes was then hit by a barrage from the Egyptians who mistook them for Israeli fighters and the pilot of the stricken machine parachuted out. Simultaneously, the remainder of the RAF flight was pounced upon from above by Spitfires of 101 Squadron. In the ensuing, and undoubtedly confusing, fight between the opposing Spitfire forces, two more [in fact, all three] of the British aircraft were shot down, one of which crash-landed behind the Egyptian front. The Israeli Spitfires in this instance were piloted by foreign volunteers and their report of the action when they landed back at Hatzor, while providing excitement for the rest of the Squadron members, was met with apprehension and anxiety at Headquarters. A retaliation by the British at this stage was a thought not to be pondered. The bizarre chain of events continued.

Sid Cohen was in Tel Aviv for a staff meeting and it left 101 under the joint control of Rudy Augarten, who was now Deputy Commander, and the new Operations Officer, Ezer Weizman. Ezer was extremely anxious to get into the air because, although he had seen more combat operations than most during 1948, an aerial victory had been denied him. The time was approaching noon. By 1230, Ezer and Sandy were aloft and though they toured the Abu Ageila-El Arish area for an hour, accompanied by two of the volunteers, they saw no other aircraft. As soon as his aircraft has been refuelled, Ezer wanted to go out again but Headquarters was on the Ops telephone, urging caution. While conceding that it was essential to defend Israeli airspace, they hinted that it would be unwise 'to twist the lion's tail too hard'. Two o'clock arrived and the armistice was now in effect. The last airborne flight landed and made their report. An Egyptian Fiat fighter [in fact, a Macchi MC205V] which had strayed northward had been downed by a volunteer pilot. In frustration, Ezer ran to the telephone and contacted control at Headquarters and somehow convinced them to authorize another sortie over El Arish to, as Ezer termed it, 'put on a final show of air strength'.

The British were continuing to send forth aircraft from the Canal area in an attempt to ascertain the fate of their missing fighters and this was probably the mission in which they were engaged when eight [in fact, four] of the RAF Spitfires [plus 15 RAF Tempests] encountered Ezer's flight of four over the Sinai border at 45 minutes past two o'clock. The weather was not considered good. It was cold and generally bleak and there were cloud formations across the entire front. In the cockpit of the Israeli Spitfire, which was minus the canopy, Ezer sat bundled in a heavy jacket and he wore fur-lined gloves, but he was still cold and occasionally he shivered inadvertently. The Sinai boundary was 10,000 feet below when he saw the British machines flying north-west into Israeli airspace. When they passed beneath the Israeli aircraft, he did not hesitate. He rolled the Spitfire over and went straight down through the other formation. Because of this brash maneuver, one of the foreign volunteers managed immediately to bring down the startled Englishman [a Tempest] who was flying at the tail end of the first British section. This machine fell near Rafah and while Ezer regained some of his lost height, the other planes became scattered across the sky. Disdaining the fact that he now found himself alone with two of the unfriendly Britishers, Ezer advanced the throttle on his Spitfire and singled out one of the adversaries. The other plane turned quickly and Ezer saw the cloud layers whirl around and become upside down. The British Spitfire [in fact, it was a Tempest] was diving away and Ezer, staring through the gunsight, fired his cannon. To his surprise, spurts of vapor began to emerge from the engine of the machine in front of him and the aircraft began to fall earthward like a leaf in the wind. It grew smaller and smaller and then disappeared into a cloud. It was later reported [incorrectly] that this plane had to force-land on the base at El Arish. Ezer had his triumph in the air. He had righteously defended Israeli airspace and won. The fact that his opponent had been an RAF Spitfire [*sic*] and that the war had been officially over for an hour didn't seem to dismay him in the least. The largest victory party in the brief history of the Squadron was held that night at the Park Hotel in Tel Aviv. Ezer Weizman was master of ceremonies.

The subsequent reactions of the British to that day were at once ominous and threatening but, by the following week, Israel had been absolved by a UN investigation of the incidents of provoking the events. The British pilots who had been interned by the Israelis during the affair were returned to the RAF and the repercussions diminished and died.

There were, undoubtedly, many in the State of Israel who found significance and irony in this skirmish with the British Empire on the last day of the War of Independence. No Israeli planes had been downed in the actions. During operations 101 Squadron had accounted for 22 Arab or otherwise hostile aircraft. Not a single fighter machine was lost to the enemy in aerial combat.

The foreign volunteers drifted away one by one. In the spring of that new year [1949] the contingents of Israeli air cadets who had been training abroad would return to expand the ranks. They were young and of the future and they would see a different era. The job that the combat veterans had come to do was finished and now they drifted away. Israel would be grateful and record their deeds but now they were leaving and Israel must turn to the present and self reliance. The volunteers left as they had arrived, unheralded. There were no military bands, no medals, no uniforms, no rank. Their accomplishments wouldn't be praised or even mentioned in the annals of modern warfare. Some had died, most had survived, but the ultimate nobility lay in having served. They served in a period of desperate need at the re-birth of an ancient nation which had been waiting to be born again for twenty centuries. A homeland for the Jews. Time was to confirm that they served in a moment of history the world would never forget. Like the Desert Hawks, they served when none other was there to serve in their place. They were volunteers.

APPENDIX I

$$\overline{IIN42/a4l}$$

- 105

INTELLIGENCE AND PERSONAL COMBAT REPORT.

P/O. L.S. NOMIS (AMERICAN).

Date.	(A)	11/1/42.
Squadron.	(B)	71 (Eagle) Squadron.
Type of our aircraft.	(C)	Spitfire V3.
Time attack was delivered.	(D)	About 0950 hours.
Place of attack or target.	(E)	About 50 miles East of Lowestoft.
Weather.	(F)	10/10ths cloud at 11,000 feet.
Our casualties Aircraft.	(G)	Nil.
Personnel.	(H)	Nil.
Enemy casualties in air combat.	(J)	1 JU88 damaged by P/O. Nomis (American).
Enemy casualties - ground or sea targets.	(K)	N/A.

General Report.

Two Spitfires VB, Red section, 71 (Eagle) Squadron were airborne Martlesham Heath 0910 hours, 11/1/42, with orders to scramble base at 8,000 feet. Several Vectors were given by the Controller (F/Lt. Cooper) and the section became separated in cloud. After receiving several Vectors from the Controller Red 11 P/O. L.S.Nomis (American) (Spitfire VB) found himself well out to sea and turned for home flying at 12,000 feet. He saw a JU88 break through 10/10ths. cloud at 11,000 feet about 600 yards away to the starboard. He immediately attacked it from the beam to the starboard quarter firing two 2½ seconds bursts with his machine guns, opening at 300 yards and closing at 50 yards. Pieces fell off the starboard wing of the JU88. P/O Nomis then directed his fire towards the cockpit of the JU88 and saw some of his bullets hitting the hood. Almost immediately the enemy aircraft dived into cloud cover and was not seen again. The JU88 is claimed as damaged. The combat took place about 50 miles East of Lowestoft.

Two Spitfires landed Martlesham by 1010 hours.

Our casualties.   Nil.

Enemy casualties. One JU88 damaged by P/O. Nomis (American).

L.S. Nomis
Pilot Officer,
No. 71 (Eagle) Squadron, RAF.

Roland Robinson
Flying Officer,
Intelligence   Officer,
No. 71 (Eagle) Squadron, Royal Air Force

Secret.

Personal Combat Report. *Pat-2* *Personal.*
P/O. L.S. Nomis (American). *Pat 3* *W/C Tactics* *Form "F".*
SP20

Date.   (A)   17/4/42.   *II N 42/d 13/4.*
Unit.   (B)   71 (Eagle) Squadron.   - **106**
Type and mark of our aircraft.   (C)   Spitfire VB.
Place of attack.   (D)   About 8 miles East of Felixstowe.
Time attack was delivered.   (E)   About 0715 hours.
Weather.   (F)   Clear.
Our casualties (aircraft).   (G)   Nil.
Our casualties.   (H)   Nil.
Enemy casualties in air combat.   (J)   1 Ju 88 destroyed. (Shared with
                                                     P/O. J.J. Lynch (American).
Enemy casualties ~~on gun~~ targets   (K)   Nil.

General Report.

I took off with P/O. Lynch with orders to patrol convoy off Felixstowe.
After being on patrol for about ten minutes we heard some mention of a bogie on the R/T
and we proceeded out to sea to see if we could find anything. After about 15 minutes
I observed an aircraft coming up very fast to our port beam at our same altitude, which
was nought feet. This proved to be a Ju 88. P/O. Lynch and myself were flying fairly
close line abreast and we saw the 88 at about the same time he saw us. The 88 made a
hard right turn upon seeing us and we made a hard left turn to attack. The 88 levelled
off and made off at top speed, altering his course about 45 degrees to either side every
so often. P/O. Lynch and myself were coming up astern of the 88, he Lynch being slightly
ahead and above as he was nearest to the 88 when we turned. I saw P/O. Lynch fire a
burst which was slightly out of range as it hit in the water behind the 88's tail.
I then fired one burst from directly astern, and this too hit behind the tail.
I decided not to fire again until I was closer up. During this time I was closing up
both on P/O. Lynch and the 88, and when I was about 50 yards behind P/O. Lynch and below
he being about 200 yards behind the 88, I saw black smoke coming out of Lynch's engine.
This increased in volume as I was watching and he suddenly pulled up and away to port,
saying on the R/T that he had been hit. That was the last I saw of him as all my attention was on the 88. All this time I was closing on the 88, making quarter attacks from
astern and beam and changing my position all the time from port to astern to starboard
as I was receiving fairly accurate return fire from the top rear gunner. I observed
strikes on the wings, fusilage and tail of the 88 and on my next to last attack the
gunner did not fire, that is, stopped firing and did not fire at all on my last attack
during which I ran out of ammunition.

My last three attacks were with machine guns alone as I had used up all
my cannons. My last attack was from abeam and above at a fairly steep angle and I
observed strikes in the fusilage and starboard wing. I closed to about 50 yards and
broke away to the left and above upon running out of ammunition.

I then turned my aircraft around in time to see the 88 emit a billow of
                                                          (an explosion and)
black smoke and plunge into the sea. Upon climbing my plane to observe the spot
I could see a great disturbance and wake on the water but no sign of the aircraft or
occupants. I then reported this on the R/T and turned for home on a reciprocal until
I got a direct vector from the controller.

L.S. Nomis
Pilot Officer,
No. 71 (Eagle) Squadron,
Martlesham Heath.

APPENDIX II

DELIVERY SCHEDULE
OF AVIA S-199s FROM CZECHOSLOVAKIA TO ISRAEL

Balak	Delivery	Aircraft	Date of Arrival	Comments
5	C-54	NC58021	20/5/48	
7	C-46		21/5/48	
9	C-54	NC58021	22/5/48	
11	C-46	RX-136	24/5/48	Crashed on arrival, Avia destroyed.
12	C-46		25/5/48	
13	C-46		25/5/48	
16	C-46		30/5/48	
18	C-54		30/5/48	
19	C-46		31/5/48	
20	C-46		31/5/48	
51	C-46	RX-133	1/7/48	
52	C-46	RX-138	?1/7/48	
55	C-46	RX-133	?4/7/48	
54	C-46	RX-134	7/7/48	Delayed in Yugoslavia for four days.
58	C-46	RX-135	9/7/48	
60	C-46	RX-138	13/7/48	
62	C-54	NC58021	14/7/48	
63	C-54		?15/7/48	
65	C-46	RX-134	11/48	Emergency landing at Rome airport 18/7/48; departure delayed until November 1948
66	C-46	RX-135	?17/7/48	
67	C-46	RX-130	19/7/48	
68	C-54	NC56011	18/7/48	
70	C-46	RX-138	20/7/48	
76	C-54		24/7/48	
79	C-54	RX-121	28/7/48	

APPENDIX III

RECORD OF LEO NOMIS' KNOWN S-199 FLIGHTS IN ISRAEL

IDF/AF archival records, from which the following basic details were extracted, suggest that Leo Nomis flew a total of 10.50 hours on the S-199 while in Israel, but this is clearly incorrect.

Date	Aircraft No	Times	Comments
6/8/48	108	1535-1615	Training flight
7/8/48	120	1501-1551	Training flight
8/8/48	108	1203-1245	Training flight
9/8/48	121	1540-1617	Operational patrol; intercepted UN Dakota carrying Count Bernadotte.
13/8/48	115	1715-1758	Operational patrol, searching for reconnaissance aircraft. Sighted RAF Mosquito but unable to intercept.
16/8/48	114	1302-1330	Operational patrol
20/8/48	115	1220-1323	Operational patrol
24/8/48	114	1245-1355	Operational patrol; returned early due to engine malfunction.
5/9/48	121	1140-1310	Operational patrol; damaged in landing accident on return to Herzliya.*
7/9/48	122	1125-1246	Operational patrol
11/9/48	118	1150-1209	Operational patrol; returned early due to engine malfunction.

* During the course of this patrol Leo sighted an RAF photographic-reconnaissance Mosquito from 13 Squadron, at which he fired, believing the shufti kite to have been an Iraqi aircraft:

'I came close enough to fire a burst at long range. The Mosquito then entered a long bank of clouds and contact was lost. After I reported to the IO we talked for a while about confirming something in the matter of time and place, which was north of Acre. We determined that the Mosquito had probable Iraqi markings. By the end of the month nothing further had arisen so I more or less forgot about it.'

Five flights are apparently not officially recorded in IDF/AF records shown above; these are recorded in Leo's manuscript as:

1/8/48	114		First flight with 101 Squadron; duration of at least 1.15 hours (morning).
1/8/48	114		Second flight, of about 1 hour duration (afternoon).
8/8/48	113		Test flight, duration 30 minutes. On return to Natanya ground-looped without damage to aircraft.
21/9/48	?		Operational flight, searching for intruding Dragon Rapide.
3/10/48	?	1530-1645	To provide escort for Spitfires being flown to Israel from Czechoslovakia; failed to rendezvous.

In addition, Leo clocked 4.45 hours on the S-199 during the conversion course in Czechoslovakia; he also carried out three operational flights in the PR Spitfire (130) while in Israel.

APPENDIX IV

INDIVIDUAL HISTORIES OF ISRAEL's S-199s

101   Shot down by ground fire either 29/5/48 (Eddie Cohen killed) or 30/5/48 (Milton Rubenfeld baled out).

102   Shot down by ground fire either 29/5/48 (Eddie Cohen killed) or 30/5/48 (Milton Rubenfeld baled out).

103   With Maintenance Unit in late July 1948; no other details known.

104   With Maintenance Unit in late July 1948; no other details known.

105   Sustained damage by ground fire 10/6/48 (flown by Moddy Alon); with Maintenance Unit late July, no other details known.

106   Damaged in take-off accident at Herzliya June 1948 (flown by Giddy Lichtman). With Maintenance Unit late July 1948; to Maintenance Unit November 1948 for salvage.

107   Shot down by Syrian Harvard 10/7/48 (Leslie Block killed).

108   First S-199 to receive 101 Squadron badge on port engine cowling. Accident 21/8/48; accident 30/10/48, to Maintenance Unit. Repaired and renumbered 1906; transferred to Tel-Nof 1950.

109   With Maintenance Unit late July 1948; subsequently written-off.

110   Lost in action 9/7/48 (Bob Vickman killed).

111   With Maintenance Unit late July 1948, probably written-off.

112   With Maintenance Unit late July 1948, probably written-off.

113   Delivered to 101 Squadron 19/7/48; ground-looped by Leo Nomis 9/8/48 undamaged. Written-off in belly-landing accident 16/10/48 (flown by Leon Frankel).

114   Delivered to 101 Squadron 19/7/48. Leo Nomis' first Avia flight in Israel 1/8/48; Crashed near Herzliya 16/10/48 (Moddy Alon killed).

115   Delivered to 101 Squadron 20/7/48. Written-off in landing accident

at Herzliya 9/9/48 (flown by Sandy Jacobs).

116   With Maintenance Unit late July 1948; believe damaged in landing accident at Herzliya in August 1948 (flown by Cyril Horowitz). With MU in November 1948.

117   Damaged in landing accident 20/8/48 (flown by Mitchell Flint); damaged in belly-landing at Tel-Nof 17/10/48 (flown by Giddy Lichtman). To Maintenance Unit, repaired and renumbered 1901.

118   Shot down Arab Airways Dragon Rapide 23/9/48 (flown by Giddy Lichtman). Renumbered 1902 and transferred to Tel-Nof in 1950.

119   Delivered to 101 Squadron 20/7/48. Modified as PR aircraft; written-off in landing accident at Herzliya 8/10/48 (flown by Bill Pomerantz).

120   Ground-looped 14/9/48 Sflown by Bill Pomerantz). Repaired and renumbered 1903; transferred to Tel-Nof in 1950.

121   Landing accident at Herzliya 5/9/48 (flown by Leo Nomis). Shot down REAF Spitfire 16/10/48 (flown by Rudy Augarten). Renumbered 1904 and transferred to Tel-Nof in 1950.

122   Written-off in take-off accident at Herzliya 16/9/48 (flown by Cyril Horowitz).

123   Renumbered 1905. Damaged when undercarriage accidently retracted on the ground 18/2/49; repaired and transferred to Tel-Nof in 1950.

124   Delayed at Rome Airport on board C-46 RX-134 18/7/48 until November 1948. Renumbered 1907 and written-off in take-off accident 15/12/48 (flown by Wayne Peake).

NB: Unidentified Avia damaged in landing accident at Herzliya 1/8/48.

For the record: On the eve of Operation Yoav, which commenced on 15 October 1948, 101 Squadron had on strength eight operational Avia S-199s: 108, 113, 114, 117, 118, 120, 121, 123.

Research would suggest that the Avias were credited with shooting down two REAF Dakotas (by Moddy Alon); three REAF Spitfires (one each by Moddy Alon, Giddy Lichtman and Rudy Augarten); one Syrian Harvard (by Maurice Mann); and one Arab Airways Dragon Rapide (by Giddy Lichtman).

DRAMATIS PERSONNAE

Alon, Mordecai (Moddy) 33, 34, 43,
  57, 58, 61-64, 69, 70, 74, 75, 77-
  81, 85, 86, 92, 95, 96, 100, 104,
  105, 110-112
Andrews, Stan 63, 73, 78, 113
Antin, Sid 62, 69, 76-78, 98
Augarten, Rudy 63, 83, 101, 116
Avriel, Ehud 47
Axelrod, Harry 74, 91, 100

Bar Lev, Chaim 67
Ben-Gurion, David 20, 39, 71, 76,
  77, 105
Ben Zvi, Dov 105-107
Berger 24, 25, 34
Bernadotte, Count Folke (UN) 43,
  73, 80, 90, 98
Bernstein, Meyer 26-29, 31, 32, 34-
  38, 43, 44, 59
Beurling, Plt Off George (RAF) 14,
  16, 27
Bieberman 23-36, 38-40, 43, 60
Bilek, Captain (Czech AF) 48-53,
  56, 57
Brereton, General (USAAF) 18
Bunche, Dr Ralph (UN) 98, 105,
  115

Churchill, Grp Capt Walter (RAF)
  12, 13
Cohen, Eddie 58, 62
Cohen, Sid 61-66, 68, 69, 74, 76-78,
  80, 84, 87, 89, 96, 100, 101

104-107, 112, 114, 116
Croll, Dave 72, 78-80, 84, 87, 88

Duke, Flt Lt Neville (RAF) 16

Falk 74, 80, 90, 101, 105
Finkel, Aaron (Red) 62, 69, 88, 92,
  105
Flint, Mitchell (Red) 47, 48, 52, 53,
  56, 78
Frankel, Leon 63, 76, 87, 88
Freeman, Al 60, 61

Ginsberg, Asher 109
Goodman 24, 25, 34
Grant, Wg Cdr Stan (RAF) 15

Hlodek, Colonel (Czech AF) 48
Horowitz, Cyril 63, 91, 98, 112, 113

Ish-Shalom, Freddie 70

Jacobs, Alexander (Sandy) 62, 66-68,
  84, 87, 88, 104, 116

Keren, Mischa 40-42, 89
Kurtz, Ray 54, 55, 89, 90

Lenart, Lou 63, 64, 78, 106
Levi, Avrom 85-87
Lewis, Sam 34
Lichter, George 47, 48, 51-53, 56,
  78

Lichtman, Gideon (Giddy) 62, 64-68, 70, 71, 73, 77, 78, 81, 82, 88, 90, 91, 94-96, 106
Love, Nav2 Angus (RAF) 98
Lynch, Plt Off John (RAF) 10, 11

Magee, Chris 63, 88, 98
Mann, Maurice (Maury) 63, 68, 69, 78, 88, 92, 100, 101, 106
Marcus, Colonel 81

Nixon, John (BBC) 96
Nomis, Leo (father) 7

Peake, Wayne 97, 98
Peterson, Sqn Ldr Chesley (RAF) 9
Pomerantz, Bill 63, 77, 88, 92
Pomeranz, Sam 57, 100, 104, 113

Remez, Aharon 42, 43, 64, 74, 114
Reynolds, Flg Off Eric (RAF) 98
Roscoe, Plt Off Art (RCAF) 11, 13
Rosen, Sol 106, 107, 113
Rubenfeld, Milton 58, 80

Ruch, Arnold (Arni) 63, 65, 74, 78, 89, 100, 101, 104, 105

Sarah 26-30, 32, 59, 60
Senior, Boris 42, 62, 100, 104, 105, 110
Schwimmer, Al 23, 24, 26, 34, 46, 53, 57, 59, 89, 90
Stahl 109
Stein 26
Stern, Avraham 20

Tolkowski, Dan 64
Turin, Kalman 84, 85

Vickman, Bob 57, 61

Weizman, Ezer 43, 58, 63-67, 70, 71, 74-78, 81, 84, 92, 95, 100, 105, 106, 111, 116, 117
Weizmann, Chaim 63
Woodford, David (*The Daily Telegraph*) 96

Yadin, Yagael 105

Readers who have enjoyed Leo Nomis' *The Desert Hawks* are invited to read Brian Cull's *Spitfires over Israel* for further in-depth information and background to the story of his personal experiences during this conflict, which became known to Israelis as the War of Independence.

Brian Cull has written the following titles for Grub Street of London, publishers of this book.

Air War for Yugoslavia, Greece and Crete, 1940-41 with Christopher Shores and Nicola Malizia

Malta: The Hurricane Years, 1940-41 with Christopher Shores and Nicola Malizia

Malta: The Spitfire Year, 1942 with Christopher Shores and Nicola Malizia

Bloody Shambles, Volume 1 (the fall of Singapore and Dutch East Indies, 1941-42) with Christopher Shores and Yasuho Izawa

Bloody Shambles, Volume 2 with Christopher Shores and Yasuho Izawa

Twelve Days in May (Hurricane Squadrons in France, May 1940) with Bruce Lander and Heinrich Weiss

Wings over Suez (the Suez Conflict of 1956 and sequel to *Spitfires over Israel*) with David Nicolle and Shlomo Aloni

249 at War (a history of 249 Squadron, the RAF's top-scoring fighter squadron of World War II)

Amongst forthcoming titles is the eagerly-awaited two-volume study of British and Commonwealth participation in the Korean airwar of 1950-1953.

A "Constitutional" Voyage
Round the World: 1870 & 1871

Pencillings
by the Way

1870 & 1871.

CHRONICLES OF A

"Constitutional"

ROUND THE WORLD

By

T. E. BEAUMONT.

A "Constitutional" Voyage
Round the World: 1870 & 1871

Pencillings by the Way

by Thomas E. Beaumont

Edited by Geoffrey A. Godden FRSA

BARRIE & JENKINS
LONDON

First published 1971 by
Barrie & Jenkins Ltd.
2 Clement's Inn, London WC2

ISBN 0.214.65311.0

Printed and Bound
by W & J Mackay & Co Ltd, Chatham
in 11/12pt 'Monotype' Bell Roman

Contents

Editor's Foreword ix

Introduction xiii

Chapter 1 *The preparations, the voyage down the English* 1
Channel and the passage onwards to Madeira.
Christmas at sea. The Doldrums and the "Dead
Horse" ceremony. Crossing the Line.

Chapter 2 *March 1871, the approach to Australia,* 39
Melbourne after three months at sea. The Races
and by steamer to Sydney. Sydney Harbour
and the gunnery practice. Botany Bay and a
fishing excursion.

Chapter 3 *April 1871. On board the "Wonga Wonga"* 56
bound for Auckland. On once again to
Honolulu, the state education. H.M.S.
"Zealous", exchange rates. Passage on the
"Ajax" for San Francisco.

Chapter 4 *San Francisco, a Chinese theatre and the Skating* 69
Club. Trip to Yosemite and the Gold Fields
before returning to San Francisco.

Chapter 5 *May 25th 1871. Departure from San Francisco.* 88
Salt Lake City and the Mormons. The Rocky
Mountains and Nebraska. Chicago, Detroit
and Niagara.

Chapter 6 *June 5th 1871. Into Canada. Toronto and by* 106
mail-boat to Montreal, Saratoga and down
the Hudson to New York. The city and
Central Park. Return home on the Cunard ship
"Russia", arriving at Liverpool, nearly
seven months after leaving for Australia.

Illustrations

Frontispiece: Photograph of title page from Diary

Between pages 50 and 51

The opening pages of the Diary
View of Grantham in 1860
Flinders Street, Melbourne, about 1872
Melbourne race course, 1865
Collins Street, Melbourne
Roman Catholic cathedral, Melbourne
Queen Street Wharf, Auckland
Engraving of a Chinese theatre at San Francisco
The Bridal Veil Fall
Inspiration Point looking down Yosemite Valley
Engraving of Central Pacific train
Inspection car approaching the Great Salt Lake
Mormon Tabernacle, Salt Lake City

Between pages 82 and 83

Sherman Hotel, Chicago
Suspension Bridge, Niagara
Niagara Falls from Prospect Point
Goat Island
The Thousand Islands
Engraving of Central Park, New York
Running the Lachine Rapids
Broadway, New York
Cunard S.S. "Russia"
The Adelphi Hotel, Liverpool
A page from the Diary

Editor's Foreword

The following pages were written between December 4th 1870 and July 1st 1871. They describe the "Chronicles of a Constitutional round the World", as undertaken by Thomas Beaumont of Grantham, in Lincolnshire. Having been advised by his physician "That the only means of restoring me permanently to my former good health lay in my taking a long sea voyage", Thomas Beaumont undertook this trip to Australia, returning via New Zealand, Honolulu and North America. More importantly, he wrote a daily record of his travels and adventures which he modestly called "Pencillings by the Way". Our diarist was obviously an educated man, with keen powers of observation, and a welcome sense of humour. He must also have been a man of some substance, for he was able to occupy the "whole" of the largest cabin in the ship, although he was not above trying "for several days to induce the owners to lower the price . . .". He also often remarked on the cost of living—the high cost of meals in the refreshment rooms, at which the train stopped three times a day, on the journey across America, and of the half-a-dollar charge at Niagara. Similar little extra charges of course, still irritate the present-day traveller.

I purchased this hand-written diary early in 1970, mainly to preserve an original and well-written document from the fate that befalls so many similar diaries. At first my view was that the period that it portrays, 1870–1871, was too recent to arouse much interest, but on re-reading the account I became fascinated with the changes that world travel had undergone in the past hundred years.

The first part of this diary is concerned with the sea trip to

Australia, with Christmas at sea, of storms and the doldrums. The trip would suit few modern travellers, . . . "the average speed during the last twenty-four hours is only four miles per hour and we are [after nearly two months at sea] over 6000 miles from Melbourne". Those who prefer air travel must surely marvel to read "we are once more becalmed . . . and I spent the day in rowing about and shooting birds . . .", or that the passengers were woken by a "chorus of crowing cocks and cackling hens, bleating sheep and grunting pigs, besides lots of ducks and geese . . .", for this was before the days of refrigeration and livestock was carried aboard to be killed and eaten as required. However, life aboard was not without its pleasures—"at six o'clock this morning I was awake and went up on deck, where one of the sailors gave me a jolly and refreshing bath by pouring three buckets of water over me"!

The account then continues to give a most interesting contemporary word-picture of Melbourne and Sydney, of Auckland in New Zealand and of the passage to San Francisco, via Honolulu. To many present-day readers the most interesting part of this journey will be found in Chapters 4 and 5, which are concerned with a nine-weeks trip across the United States of America—where perhaps more than elsewhere, the passage of a mere hundred years has left its mark. Reading such passages as, "In a few miles we shall be out of the Indian district. Up to now we have been passing through a country infested with them; the only way they are kept in check is by the United States Troops", does bring past history to our notice with a jolt.

In addition to the historical and geographical details contained in this diary, the writer gives a typically Victorian and British view of the world and its inhabitants. Some of these views are so dated and unjust, that I at first considered editing-out some of the more derogatory statements, but on reflection it seemed that the value of such a document as this is to learn of the person's reaction to places and people and that the present-day reader is entitled to read the bad as well as the good, to have the complete picture. I trust that the present-day reader will accept the fact that these are the opinions of a long since departed Victorian and that they do not in any measure reflect the views of the editor or of the publishers. The following account therefore represents the complete diary as written between December 1870 and July 1871. However, some points of explanation have been added within square brackets or in the form of footnotes. Some of these notes also underline the differences in travel or cost that have occurred over the past hundred years. The original narrative has been divided into convenient chapters and an index has been added so that present-day readers can readily trace a particular event or place.

Contemporary photographs and engravings have been added to the original material to give the present-day reader a visual, as well as a verbal picture of some of the places visited by the diarist. The scenes of Victorian Melbourne are taken from photographs in the collection of the State Library of Victoria and have been kindly supplied by the Principal Librarian, Mr. T. A. Kealy. The photograph of Auckland in the 1870's has been supplied by Mr. R. Duthie, the City Librarian, Public Library, Auckland. The 1860 engraving of the diarist's home town of Grantham has been supplied by Mr. D. E. Hayward, the Borough Librarian, Grantham Public Library and I am most grateful to these Librarians for their ready response to my requests for these contemporary views.

The illustrations depicting North American scenes have been taken from two main sources, firstly the Victorian photographic views have been copied from the once popular double-imaged Stereoscopic cards which give a wonderful three-dimensional effect when seen through the special Stereoscopic viewer. The engraved views have been copied from the Victorian books— "*American Pictures, drawn with Pen and Pencil*" by the Revd. Samuel Manning and "*Canadian Pictures, drawn with Pen and Pencil*" by the Marquis of Lorne, both published by the Religious Tract Society in the 1870's and 1880's. Two engravings in this book had previously appeared in the weekly journal *Leisure Hour* in February and September 1871, so that these engravings are almost exactly contemporary with the narrative told in the following pages. The contemporary engraving of S.S. *Russia* has been supplied by The Cunard Steam-Ship Company Ltd.

Introduction

"Some minds improve by travel, others, rather
Resemble Copper Wire or Brass
Which gets the narrower by going farther".
Tom Hood

In the following remarks which literally speaking are "Pencil-lings by the way", and which are my first attempt at keeping a Diary, I wish at the outset to dispel the notion my friends may perhaps entertain, that I am anxious to write my Autobiography. My wish for doing so arises from the feeling I hold very strongly that an Autobiography as a rule originates in an over-estimate, which the Writer sets, either upon his own powers of description, or of his usefulness to his fellow man. At the same time as some of my friends may not have the opportunity and, I sincerely trust, may never have similar reason for visiting places which in the course of a few months I expect to visit, I have at their request, though contrary to my own previous intention and wishes, agreed from time to time to jot down short Memoranda of incidents in my journey as they occur, and I trust that my simple endeavours to record facts from first impressions, may be a sufficient apology for any want of classification of ideas, or for the crudeness with which they are certain to be portrayed.

Greens Ship
"The Superb" "at sea"—
8th December 1870.

Chapter 1

Having partially recovered from a severe attack of spitting of blood which since the middle of last October had prostrated and entirely incapacitated me for all kinds of business, Dr. Wilks the eminent Physician whom I was advised to consult in London, gave his decided opinion that the only means of restoring me permanently to my former good health, lay in my taking a long Sea Voyage. Accordingly I decided to visit Australia and at once took measures to insure as far as possible the Doctor's predictions being verified.

After personally inspecting several Ships which were advertised to sail about the beginning and end of December and taking the advice of an old friend in the Shipping line I proceeded to inspect "the Superb" one of Green's Ships then lying in the East India Docks at Blackwall [London]. She was the largest Ship then in Dock being about 1700 Tons Register and of which Captain E. Jones was the Commander.*

After trying in vain for several days to induce the Owners to lower the price they originally asked for a whole Cabin, I had eventually to pay them £77. 10.† for the whole of Cabin No. 15. This price is half as much again as a half Cabin.

This Cabin is I believe the largest and the nicest in the Ship being 10ft × 10ft–2in. It has two windows opening directly on to the Main Deck. My small outfit and bedding I procured at

---

* The *Superb* was built in London in 1866 by the owners, R. & M. Green, and had an overall length of two hundred and thirty feet. She does not appear in Lloyd's Registers after 1902.
† The P. & O. liner *Oronsay* left England on 21st December 1970, a hundred years after our diarist; the best double cabin, or suite, with bathroom and toilet, cost slightly over a thousand pounds.

Messrs. Silver's [S. W. Silver & Co.] in Cornhill whom I paid in all about £30.

This is too large a sum generally but I purchased several articles of dress which I had really during my illness run short of.

The Ship was to sail on Tuesday 5th December, accordingly I left Grantham for Town on Monday morning the 4th December and after making my final preparations I slept for the night at the Crown Hotel in a cold damp Attic, which owing to it being Smithfield Show was the only bed I could find disengaged. I left Town on Tuesday 5th December by Fenchurch Street Station for Gravesend where I took a small boat and went on board the Ship. My luggage had been previously placed on board Ship. I may here remark that at this time the weather in England was wretched in the extreme; hail, snow, rain, and damp fog prevailed.

Owing to various causes which I could never satisfactorily ascertain "the Superb" did not sail till the next day. I therefore decided to stay on board that night and arrange my Cabin furniture. The Steward at first, as is generally the case, was unusually busy and I therefore took my first lesson in bed-making, a process by no means easy to one unaccustomed to being a Ship's Steward—however after the third trial, during which I was wary enough to keep my swing lamp constantly burning, I succeeded in obtaining a tolerable night's rest.

Somewhere about 7 oClock on Wednesday morning (7th December) I was awoke by the excitement caused by the Captain's coming on board and at the same hour a powerful Steam Tug with two Funnels called "the Scotia" came alongside. At a few minutes after 8 oClock the Steam Tug was connected with the Ship, our moorings were slipped, and we started on our way down the Thames with a fine fresh North West Wind. During the way down, the Sailors were busily engaged setting several of the sails and after we had arrived some few miles beyond the Nore, about 12 oClock our Sails were set and we parted company with the Tug.

The Ship continued, in charge of the Pilot, to sail with a fair wind and the day being remarkably fine, we had a very pleasant view of Shoeburyness, Tilbury Fort, Margate, Ramsgate and many other places along the Coast. During the night the breeze continued fresh and fair and in the morning we were agreeably surprized when we were informed that in the night we had safely passed the Isle of Wight and were then off Torquay. This pretty place was very visible from the Ship and the outline of the Coast was remarkably picturesque and interesting. I could clearly distinguish the houses in Torquay with my Glass.

THURSDAY 8th DECEMBER, 1870

This day at Noon the Pilot left us, in a small boat, which picked him up and landed him at the Start Point.* We sent our final letters by the Pilot, just to tell our friends that we were going along merrily and all was well so far. Unfortunately for us the wind went down and we made way very slowly. At night, however, it freshened again and we ran out of the English Channel and found ourselves midway between the Lizard and Ushant Isle, being now in what is commonly called the Chops of the Channel at mid-day. "The Ethiopian" a large ship and about whose sailing powers great things had been reported, had two hours start of us from Gravesend, and at this time, owing to the favorable breeze, we had overhauled her and kept her well in sight. Again the wind failed us during the day and we lay with our sails idly flapping the Mast. Towards 4 oClock in the Afternoon it began to freshen and at the same time it veered round dead against us, so that we had to sail slowly within a few points of the wind's eye during the night. We had twenty-two Saloon Passengers on board many of whom had already become invisible from Sea sickness. This night was rather rough and our numbers at Breakfast were visibly diminished.

SATURDAY 10th DECEMBER

The fresh breeze increased towards the middle of the day and at last became a regular Gale—so much so that we had to shorten sail and we ran for many miles under easy sail right North West, or out of our course, which was South West. For the remainder of this day the good Ship rolled horridly—every thing was made tight and Ship-shape and "the Fiddles" or long Green Baize bags filled with Peas and three in number were placed length-wise on our Dinner Table. The Company at dinner was

---

* Near Salcombe, Devonshire. The pilot had apparently guided the vessel not only out of the river Thames, but also along most of the English Channel.

extremely "limited" and consisted of only six Passengers, one being a Lady who throughout bravely bore up against the fashionable complaint. I am thankful to say I was not at all Sea sick. During Dinner time the Ship rolled most marvellously and a large Gravy Spoon Steeplechased out of one of the dishes in truly sporting style on to the floor heedless of fiddles and all other obstructions, and to complete the old adage the dish very quickly "ran after the Spoon". At Tea Time the rolling continued and Crockery was sent flying about in all directions. Two Teapots and the Steward's Servant who was carrying them were precipitated headlong into Cabin No. 13, the next door to mine. Very many ludicrous scenes occurred—in fact food generally appeared suddenly to become animated and to possess the strongest desire to resist all attempts to reach its proper destination : two boiled fowls especially became reanimated and actually "flew" from their dish whenever they liked. Altogether comfort was temporarily banished from the Ship and I dreaded the idea of having to go to my bunk to sleep, from the probability which stared me in the face, that I was pretty certain to be rolled out "nolens volens" on the floor. This catastrophe I happily escaped by sleeping "with one eye open" during the night.

We again ran along before the Gale though we went some distance out of our course.

SUNDAY 11th DECEMBER 1870

From enquiry it appeared that we had made very little progress (if any) during the night, which was very rough—yet the morning which dawned upon us was fair and fine and successful efforts were made by several of the invalids to come on deck. At 11 oClock Prayers were read by the Captain, and one of the Passengers, who is a Clergyman, read the proper lessons and preached a short extempore Sermon from a text selected from the 1st lesson. The whole Service occupied some 45 minutes after which the remainder of the day was spent in sitting on deck and trying to teach the various invalids to find their "Sea legs".

MONDAY 12th DECEMBER

Nothing unusual occurred during the day except the appearance of several Porpoises which leapt out the Sea continually. The day was very fine—the wind however, being "dead ahead", we made but slow progress towards our destination—the whole distance run during the last twenty-four hours was 186 miles. At night it rained very heavily.

TUESDAY 13th DECEMBER

This day began tolerably calm but towards Evening it blew a heavy Gale so much so that as soon as we went to bed the Ship lurched terribly; first left, then right; and this it did four or five times consecutively—this was repeated at frequent intervals during the night, and any articles in the Cabin or Saloon, which were not fastened, simply dashed themselves to destruction. It is needless to say that sleep was out of the question, and very many Passengers, like myself, never closed their eyes.

WEDNESDAY 14th DECEMBER

"After the storm comes a calm" and so it was on this occasion and we did not yet even reach the Latitude of Cape Finisterre. Today we saw several Gannets or "Solan Geese". They are large White Birds with Black tips to their Wings and resemble in flight large Gulls rather than our Wild Geese. We ran today 86 miles only—head winds prevailed.

THURSDAY 15th DECEMBER

Winds are light and contrary—today Porpoises were in great numbers—20 and 30 were leaping out of the water at the same instant.

NB. Porpoises being seen is a sign of head winds as they always swim "head to wind". We also saw several small Whales spurting out Water, in *one* volume at a time, resembling a round shot hitting the water, and not in two spouts, like they have it in the "picture books", which are wrong in this particular—this is a very pleasant day on deck—all the passengers are out and the weather is very perceptibly warmer—the Sky, especially in early morning, is very fine, more beautiful than it is on land, by reason of its displaying itself along the whole horizon.

Today we ran only 65 miles—head winds.

5

FRIDAY 16th DECEMBER

Nothing unusual occurred today, except that the patience of every one was sorely tried by the wind being still South West. This was as I have before said dead against us and, though on one tack we made some South, yet on the other tack we made West with some North, which really did nothing for us, and our position was only thirty six miles different from what it was yesterday. This was beginning sorely to try our patience—nine days out of Dock and we had not yet even reached Cape Finisterre. The weather was very squally; the wind being against us, and thus we do not make any progress. Towards afternoon about 4 oClock the wind veered round a little, and in the Evening became North East and freshened up at night. This revived our drooping spirits somewhat and the Thermometer of our tempers which had been at "boiling point" came down to "temperate". We set our "Royals" today.

SUNDAY 18th DECEMBER

We had Service again today at 11 and a short Sermon—at Noon our Lat: was 39.50. Long: 12.52. dist: run 174—in the evening we had singing on Deck—the day was delightfully fine and we had a good favorable breeze.

MONDAY 19th DECEMBER

A first rate steady breeze "right aft" today—the black board marked Lat: 37.30. Lon: 15.41. dist: run 226 miles.

TUESDAY 20th DECEMBER

Fair winds continue and our distance run was 228 miles. We are now about 100 miles due North of Madeira; it is probable we shall, if the wind continues fair, pass it during the night.

WEDNESDAY 21st DECEMBER—SHORTEST DAY

Warm and mild. We awoke about 7.30 a.m. found Madeira about five miles distant on our Starboard quarter; the Island was enveloped in a Strong mist through which we caught glimpses

6

of most lovely scenery. It is evidently of volcanic origin. The Cliffs are high and the Country resembles North Wales, though much more bold, picturesque, and rugged. The North extremity reminds one of The Great Ormes Head [near Llandudno, Wales]. The Clouds hung about heavily, and produced wonderful effects, by displaying the high Mountain peaks above them. We were all but becalmed for several hours—afterwards we slowly drew along and until 2 oClock we had constant peeps of the wildest and most romantic scenery, ever varying at each mile or so we travelled. The South West end of the Islands was most remarkable for a long serrated ridge of rocks running for several miles and terminating very similarly to "The Needles".

The variations of colour and of light and shade were grand—several detached rocks rose from the sea in front of the other rocks and through one of these was a natural Arch—the vegetation appeared to be similar to our Moors though more variegated.

Several of the passengers attempted to sketch the remarkable ridge of rocks but their efforts proved failures owing to the moving of the point of sight—a very picturesque Lighthouse terminates the headland or ridge of rocks, and after passing the Lighthouse and displaying as usual our Ship's flags, which the lazy Portuguese were too idle to notice, we had a most wonderful sight of the other side of the Island, which is the one, usually seen by Ships outward bound—altogether we spent several most delightful hours and were thankful for the relief afforded to our otherwise monotonous Voyage. We had a good view of the Town of Funchal which is on the opposite side of the Island to the one we passed along.

While passing Funchal which is the main Island just described, on which the Town of the same name is situate, and which is Madeira proper, we passed on our Port quarter another Island called Porto Santo; and again after passing the Lighthouse we ran close by another Island of the Group called Desertas. This latter island commences with a tall head rock pointed like a Needle, then there is a flat headed rock resembling a large bride cake—this is followed by two bolder and more precipitous rocks which together form "The Desertas"—the whole of these latter occupy some four or five miles in length, and are entirely devoid of all kinds of Vegetation, as far as I could discover through a powerful Glass.

The formation of the Madeiras is evidently Volcanic. Grey Granite being mixed with bright Red Prophyry; which makes a very pretty contrast and the face of the rock resembles closely, though it excels, the brightest patch of Moorland on the 12th of August.

The Sun in the middle of the day begins to grow quite hot. Our distance was 114 miles which proves the accuracy of our last surmise, that Madeira was 100 miles away last night. The Sailors saw a large Sun fish today—we also saw two birds, which had black wings and backs, and white underneath, and in their flight resembled Kingfishers and our common Swallows, though they were larger than either. These the Sailors call "Urias" (qy spelling). This Evening we set all Sky sails and "Stunsails" (studding sails) and after Dinner we danced on Deck. Two of the Passengers formed a "Comb" band. During a Waltz a young Lady was cannoned against by my Partner and me and was deposited in the lap of our Parson. Altogether we passed a pleasant though somewhat noisy Evening.

THURSDAY 22nd DECEMBER

Owing to the lightness of the breeze during the night, Madeira was still just visible at daybreak, though the outline had quite faded away by 8 oClock. This was the day of the Eclipse. It was distinctly visible from Deck, yet to us it was by no means annular; three quarters being only hidden at the time of the greatest contact. Preparations were made during the Afternoon for a Christmas Tree, each Passenger contributing something. I was retained to cut out with a Penknife several wooden dolls, which afterwards were gorgeously dressed out in Lace over Scarlet Skirts and large Panniers, their heads were elaborately ornamented with very fine Chignons. The stem of the Tree was made of deal through which wires were run for branches—to the branches leaves were tied; the latter were cut out and painted by various Passengers—we ran about 146 miles.

FRIDAY 23rd DECEMBER

Today we had more doll carving and very hot weather. Pea jackets were superseded by lighter clothes and Straw and light hats were rigged out with Puggaries and everyone appeared to feel the heat. At Noon the black board shewed Lat: 29.20. Lon: 19.41. dist: 176.

Whist as usual in the Evening—the first rubber at five in my Cabin and afterwards a rubber with the Captain in the Saloon.

SATURDAY 24th DECEMBER

Today the awning has been put up taking the heat away from the Poop. This is a great luxury. The Christmas Tree grows and bears every kind of fruit—Candied Plums as well as fresh ripe Oranges. One cannot imagine it is Christmas eve. After dinner about 5 oClock we receive a special invitation to the Childrens' party. Accordingly we repair to the Saloon where we find about fifteen small Children First and Second Class Passengers sitting down to a gorgeous Meat Tea with Tarts, *"Tantadlins", Toffy and all kinds of good things. The prolific Tree stands at the head of the Table. My large doll has been dressed in white silk train trimmed with chocolate ribbon—white satin cloak edged with Swansdown—She has blue eyes, pink cheeks, and a most approved golden chignon made of Oakum. On the Tree are my two smaller dolls which might represent the bridesmaids of their elder sister. Strings of Nuts, Almonds, Figs, Raisins, and other delicacies, strung on Red Worsted, make the Tree very pretty—all this is illuminated with fifty or sixty wax candle-ends, each about two inches long, which are stuck on the Tree or, rather, on the sharp points of the wire branches, by first warming the branches in the flame of the candle and then running the hot branch into the Candle-end. After the Tree had been dismantled in due form, and the small children had had enough "Goodies" given them to ensure our Doctor having his hands full for some time to come, we again went on Deck. Some of the Middies [midshipmen] however waylaid two or three of us, and invited us into their Cabin, and as on these occasions and at such seasons, it is perhaps not well to go empty-handed, we took a good stock of Grog with us. This was passed round quickly and Songs and a general "free and easy" life prevailed, till about 8 oClock. The Steward then put a stop to the further harmony of the "Midshipman Easy" style by announcing that Snap Dragon was all ready in the Saloon. This part of the Evening's amusement passed off capitally and then we had Songs

Author's footnote: * open tarts with preserve in the centre—a vulgar word.

9

from the Captain and others, most of which were highly appropriate to the festive occasion.

I forgot to mention that several of us took to and treated the Sailors in the Forecastle with eighteen bottles of Bass (a pint per man) and in exchange we heard more "Songs of Ocean" and applauded several good Hornpipes and the true style of Sailor "breakdown" Dances.

To return to the Saloon, during the Captain's Songs we routed out a Fiddling Waiter whom we pressed into our service, and about 9 oClock we all went on Deck, and danced Quadrilles, Waltzes, Etc. till half past ten.

We had five Ladies on board who danced (including our Captain's Wife who danced capitally). This was a very novel and alfresco way of spending Christmas Eve and at the same time a most enjoyable one. The night was very calm and the slight rolling of the Ship made it greater fun in guiding your Partner amidst the coils of ropes, and steering clear of the railing of the Deck. Dancing was very hot work, even in the open air, so to cool ourselves we kept up "piping" before going to bed. We could not but "laugh in our sleeves" at the sympathy and pity which probably was at that time being lavished upon us, "miserable creatures" by our kind and well meaning friends at home. I forgot to mention our dances included Sir Roger de Coverley in which sexes mixed indiscriminately and the dancing wound up with a game at Leap Frog in which there were several good tumbles on the Deck, especially one in which one of the Officers knocked me over and then tried to plough up the hard Deck with his nose. I need not say his efforts were unsuccessful and caused him damage by removing from his face some of the upper Cuticle of his nose. Dist: run was 120 miles.

SUNDAY 25th DECEMBER

At 6 oClock this morning I was awoke and went up on Deck, where one of the Sailors gave me a jolly and refreshing bath, by pouring three buckets of water over me as I stood for the purpose.

The water was quite warm and I enjoyed my bath immensely. Miss W—— one of the Passengers thoughtfully brought some Holly and Mistletoe with her which made the hot day look more like "Christmas at home". At Breakfast on our Plates we also found some Christmas Cards which an invisible Postman had left for us—these caused us some very fair chaff and fun. We had Service on deck as it was a particularly fine day. In the afternoon we signalled an English Brigantine which we expect was bound for the West most probably for Brazil. We had several Geese for Dinner also plum pudding which was spiritually burned in the orthodox fashion. The male portion of the Saloon Passengers treated the Officers and Ladies to Champagne and Dinner Wine and a *goodly quantity* was consumed both at Dinner and afterwards.

A very pleasant Evening was spent on Deck but the fact of its being Sunday rather put a stop to Christmas gaiety. Altogether I was agreeably pleased at the merry time we had had and the After-dinner speeches agreed in making out that it was one of the pleasantest and most merry Christmases the Speakers had spent. Lat: 25.47. Lon: 21.23. Dist: 150 miles.

MONDAY 26th

This was another splendid day and we had a favorable breeze. In the Evening the Middies had an "Evening party" after Dinner in their small cabin which was frightfully hot. I find it impossible to read during such hot weather. We are now fairly in the North East trade winds and if they will only continue for a week we shall probably reach the Line.

We danced in the Evening. We are fairly in the Tropics which commence about Lat: 23.30. Lat: 23.19. Lon: 22.1. Dist: 175 miles.

TUESDAY 27th

Today as well as yesterday we saw several flying fish; they average about six inches long and resemble English Dace or Mackerel with two long transparent Wings or Fins just behind their Gills. They fly out of the water sometimes singly, at other times, in Shoals. Some are silvery, others have black backs and Copper coloured wings—these latter are the larger kind and are quite six inches long—they appear to have scarcely any power of flapping after they have fairly left the water, though they will skim on for twenty yards or more, and the slightest touch of the water enables them to continue their flight. They can flap their

11

wings for about two seconds after they leave the water; after that, they sail along and fall into the Sea as soon as their wings become at all dry.

It is reported that a Grampus or other large fish chases them, and they fly out before him from fright—this they also do from being frightened at the Ship—they are very plentiful and shoals leap out every minute. I hear they are very good to eat especially those of the West Indies. Lat: 43.48. Lon: 10.8. Dist: 280 miles.

WEDNESDAY 28th

This morning we are just off the first of the Cape Verde Islands called "Sal". We then pass "Boovista" which is large—though we are twenty miles to the Eastward, we can make out with our Glasses that it is extremely barren and sandy—there are no houses visible but it is inhabited by "Blacks" of some sort or other, who probably live in holes or sand pits—we are in sight of it for two or three hours and come to the conclusion that no Englishman would be able to live at such a sandy desert place.

Being inside this Group we do not see any more of the Islands. The Westward track would have taken us close past St. Vincent which is the Coaling Station for Steamers. This is very probably the last land we shall see till we arrive at Melbourne. This evening one of the Officers hurt his back seriously from a fall he had while playing at Leap Frog. At first rumour reported that he had broken it or some of his ribs, eventually it was found that he had very seriously sprained his back and that he would probably be well again in the course of a few days. Lat: 16.6. Lon: 22.22. Dist: 274 miles.

THURSDAY 29th

I really have very little to report of this day. We have a favorable breeze and we think that it may last out till we cross the Line—doubtless our "wish is father to the thought"—flying fish are now no longer a novelty and scarcely attract any notice at all. I propose to begin to write a Letter but everything is a trouble as the heat is very great. Lat: 12.16. Lon: 22.24. Dist: 265 miles.

FRIDAY 30th

One of the ideas which suggests itself to you every morning on waking is that you are not on board Ship, but sleeping at a small Country Farmhouse in some snug corner of old England. In the first place the smallness of the Cabin,—its clean white paint and the size of your Port or Window is highly suggestive of a Country Farm Bedroom. When however the combined Chorus of crowing Cocks and cackling Hens, bleating Sheep and grunting Pigs, besides lots of Ducks and Geese, to say nothing of five barking Dogs, greets your ears, I assure you it requires a less imaginative brain than mine to dispel so pleasant and yet so false an illusion. The day is hot but our Ship has lately made such good runs that I dare not any longer delay my much talked of Letter. I therefore write it. Lat: 8.43. Lon: 22.19. Dist: 245 miles.

SATURDAY 31st DECEMBER 1870

During the night we were nearly becalmed and made but little way. We are now fairly in the "Doldrums".

They extend something like 10 degrees North of the Line.

I was awoke by some serious shouting on the part of the Chief Officer and on looking out I found we were just going in for a heavy squall and that the Sailors were busy shortening sail—the squall came on and we again ran with it gaily and were highly delighted once more to see the Deck all on one side, and the Ship gliding along in grand style. During the squall we had plenty of Lightning and as usual *very* heavy rain. Afterwards the wind died away and we proceeded to make but slow progress. We danced in the Evening and sang several Songs. The Sailors and main deck passengers also amused themselves and sang very well. They had also an extra allowance of Grog tonight, and proposed the healths of Captain, Officers, and Passengers. A young main Deck Passenger, who had a grudge against the Middies, foolishly proposed "down with the Midshipmen" for this folly a jolly Tar who stood by reproved him by putting his fist in the Passenger's eye, which rather astonished the Passenger, who lay sprawling on the ground. This summary punishment met with universal satisfaction and approval. Lat: 6.36. Lon: 22.25. Dist: 144 miles.

SUNDAY 1st JANUARY 1871

This was a day of squally rain which at times was very heavy. The Captain treated the Passengers to Wine at Dinner. One of the Officers came under the Captain's displeasure and was sent to his Cabin for talking to a Lady Passenger. Unfortunately the wrong person was punished as is often the case, he being not the person to blame. This night was so terribly hot that I slept on Deck, till 3 oClock in the morning, when it became a little cooler. There was incessant lightning during the evening and throughout the night.

Although it was incessant, yet it was not brilliant owing to the Storm being apparently at a great distance. Lat: 5.43. Lon: 22.16. Dist: 62 miles.

MONDAY 2nd JANUARY

Excepting the excitement of frequently trimming Sails and preparing for occasional squalls there was nothing worthy of special notice on this day—the intensity of the heat is a subject now almost worn threadbare in the Diary. We scarcely move except during Squalls. Lat: 4.35. Lon: 22.15. Dist: 76 miles.

TUESDAY 3rd JANUARY

We discover a Sail about six miles away on our Starboard quarter, i.e. Westward of us—she is, however, going the same way as ourselves, so we do not trouble about her, except there are several jokes made as to her being "The Ethiopian" our old friend which preceded us from Gravesend. Very shortly after Breakfast we discover another Sail over our lee bow. This we soon find to be a homeward bound Ship. All Passengers at once betake themselves to their Letters, hoping we may have a chance of sending them home. Onward comes a very fine ship with every conceivable Sail set which she can muster. The Letter bag is sewn up, and all the Newspapers we have on board are tied in a parcel for the benefit of the homeward bound Ship's Crew. At 12 oClock when the Vessels are about two miles apart, our First Mate lowers one of our Quarter boats with a Crew, and rows to the other Ship and meets her when about a mile away. He and his Crew go aboard her and are very well treated by the Captain, who turns out to be an old friend of one of our Passengers. Captain Anderson then steers his Ship right under our stern so as to save our boat's crew a long row in the heat. We find the Ship is a very handsome and smart China Tea "Clipper" bound for London and called "The Kaisow". We have a first-rate view of her. Our Mate then returns, not empty-handed, but bringing as a present for us, a live Turtle and a Shaddock, which was the last they had on board, and was sent specially by Captain Anderson for our Ladies. We cheer each other and dip our Ensign and away goes the "Kaisow" under all Sail with a fair breeze considering the hot Climate. During the Afternoon we are within signalling distance of our outward bound friend, about four miles away. We find her to be the "Fearnought" thirty six days out from North Shields bound for Aden with Coal. At night we have a wonderful rising of a storm—The Eastern Sky suddenly becomes lighted up with a brilliant colour resembling bright Cochineal. In two minutes or less this fades into the darkest black, so much so that we are in the midst of night in five minutes and we hastily prepare for the expected storm. We find however that it is the tail end of a Storm, the main part of which, has spent itself before it reached us, and it merely helps us with a slight favorable breeze for some twenty minutes and then all is calm again. Its appearance as it rose was really terribly grand, and our feelings were greatly relieved when it passed off so quietly. Lat: 4.10. Lon: 21.40. Dist: 45 miles only.

WEDNESDAY 4th JANUARY

This was the Evening of the "Dead Horse" or exactly *a month* since the Sailors left Dock. The explanation of the term appears to be this. When a Sailor is engaged for the Voyage he receives a month's pay or rather a sort of Promissory Note from the Owners of the Ship, for a month's pay. This document of course is a negotiable one and as a rule the Sailor discounts it at a Public House and spends the money on shore, before he comes on board, hence they say they are working out a "Dead Horse" for the first month of the Voyage. At 7 oClock we saw a Sailor dressed as a Policeman walking up and down the Main Deck keeping guard. Very shortly a Procession was formed and in the centre was a Horse stuffed with Straw and made of Sail Cloth painted.

On the Horse sat a Sailor fantastically dressed, and he and

the Horse were dragged along by the rest of the Sailors, who as usual were singing some appropriate and descriptive song—the whole scene was highly suggestive of a "Triumph of Bacchus". When the Horseman at length arrived before the Quarter Deck he dismounted and having made a short address to the Passengers explanatory of the hardship the Sailors had endured, from having worked a month for nothing, he proceeded to put up the Horse by Auction. The Horse was sold for £2 to one of the Passengers who bid for the whole number. Shortly afterwards the Horse and Man are hoisted overboard, dragged aloft up to the "main-yard arm"—the rider lighted a blue light and then ingeniously cut the Horse from under him with his Knife, and let it drop into the Sea and it floated astern. Of course the rider has tied himself separately from the Horse, and on the latter's falling away, was left hanging at the end of the Yard Arm. The Sailors thenceforth are as they say "earning pay for the work they do".

THURSDAY AND FRIDAY 5th AND 6th JANUARY

Very little can be said to have occurred during these two days—the wind such as it was, was against us and we had to tack in order to make any way. One day the distance run was only twenty-eight miles and we have several days apparently to run before we cross the Line and catch the "South East Trades". However "patience is a virtue" but we have had quite a week of "doldrums" and intense heat. We have seen several Whales and large fish. A fish called the "Skipjack" appears very numerous. It is about the size of a large Bream and continually jumps out of the water. On Thursday we had one of the boats let down for us, and had a good row. Some of the Middies insisted on bathing; a rather dangerous proceeding as two Sharks had been seen that very morning near to the Ship. Of course we kept them close to the boat while they were bathing for fear of accidents. Lat: 3.10. Lon: 22.

SATURDAY 7th JANUARY

As we were going slowly (although with a fresh breeze which was against us) yet we believe that in all probability we should cross the Line on Sunday or Monday at the latest. Accordingly we were told that Neptune's Secretary would probably appear at 7 oClock in the Evening and bring his Official parcel of

Letters on board. Accordingly a man dressed black, with a long beard and "tall hat" appeared on the Forecastle and hailed the Officer of the Watch. He enquired the name of our Ship, her destination and number of days out, etc. To these enquiries due answers were given by the Officer and he was invited up on the Poop. He then delivered a set speech to the Captain and enquired after our welfare generally and left his bundle of despatches from the great King of the Sea. Having received a Glass of Grog he wished us good bye till Monday, and the Captain handed the Letters to the Doctor to distribute. A lighted Tar barrel was shortly afterwards seen floating astern and the supposition was that the Secretary went away to the King's Palace in that Vessel.

SUNDAY 8th JANUARY

We had Prayers on Deck and in the Afternoon a small Whale came to the ship and rubbed his nose on our Rudder. He was a Bottlenose Whale and we saw him for several minutes. I ran for a Gun to shoot him but unfortunately was too late.

MONDAY 9th JANUARY

This morning on getting out of bed signs were visible of pre-parations going on for the "Shaving". There was a Sail raised over two Spars and a Barber's Pole stuck up with a notice "that Shaving was done on the premises". Shortly after 10 oClock sounds of music were heard and presently a Corporal and six Policemen, with the approved style of helmet, marched forth; afterwards came four bears well got up in Sheep skins, who were under the care of a Keeper. They went on all fours and were harnessed to a small Gun carriage, which was draped with a Union Jack forming a kind of hood or bower. In this carriage sat Neptune and his wife and daughter on the Throne and on the top of his Trident was fixed the only fish now "in season", viz. a red herring. After informal procession came his Suite, including his Surgeon and Barber and several others of his Court. Having paraded round the Deck and made enquiries as to whether any of the Passengers had not ever as yet crossed the Line, he promised to treat those of us who had to come to his Shop kindly. The first who did so was the Captain's infant Son who of course received his baptism of soap and a good ducking. The Police then fetched the Doctor. He was dressed in an old Shirt and Trousers and being taken before the King, expressed his willingness to undergo the ordeal. Accordingly he was blindfolded, and led up to a scaffold which had been erected in front of the poop deck; he was then made to sit upon one end of the bath formed by the two spars and the sail. The four bears, I must mention, were unharnessed and turned loose into the bath to attend to the bathers. The Doctor sat facing the passengers and Neptune's Doctor, who stood by, felt his pulse and said "he required some Medicine". Thereupon a large pill was put into his mouth which was made of bread or some thing of that kind and not very palatable. He then had to have a tooth drawn which was effectually done with a very large pair of Pincers in which a horse's tooth had been placed previously. Of course the Patient appreciating the joke appeared to be in great agony and howled at the proper time. Afterwards he was well lathered with a composition, purporting to be "Shaving Soap", but which really contained some not very nice ingredients such as Ammonia, Train Oil, etc. They then asked him several questions and when he foolishly and unguardedly opened his mouth to answer, the lather brush and "soap" were thrust into it—he was then shaved with a large wooden razor and afterwards tipped over to the expectant bears to have his bath. They on the whole treated him very kindly and not too roughly. Very few of the Saloon Passengers went through the ordeal preferring to pay a fine of ten shillings rather than suffer the inconveniences before mentioned.

The Sailors were treated rather more unceremoniously by their companions, yet everything was done in good nature, and created great merriment.

During the afternoon there were all kinds of games; climbing a greasy pole for a ham, diving in flour and water for coins, and several other similar sports. The whole day was kept as a general holiday and the Vessel crossed the Line about 1.30 p.m. amidst the usual jokes and tricks played to Telescopes such as putting hairs in them, drawing lines across, etc. Lat: 0.12 N. Lon: 23.33. Dist: 168 miles.

TUESDAY 10th JANUARY

There is little to record of this day except that we now appear to have caught the Trade Winds but they are very light at present. Lat: 1.11 S. Lon: 25.35. Dist: 168 miles.

WEDNESDAY 11th JANUARY

During the previous day we had sighted and had fairly ran away from a Ship called the "Star of Erin". At Sunrise this morning I was awoke and was very much surprised to find the "Star of Erin" not more than a mile astern of us and gaining rapidly. Our Captain came on Deck, and as there was evidently a desire on the part of the "Star of Erin" to race, we put up every description of canvas which our Officers could devise, and away we raced, though the breeze was much too light for a steady-going Ship like ours, which goes really well only in "a gale of wind". The "Star of Erin" still gained, and at 11 oClock was about two hundred yards astern. During this time we were trying to jockey her by forcing her to "windward". To our great surprise and dismay, she ran "close up" and then apparently without any effort, she ran close up to windward of us and passed us easily. We could not help admiring the way she did it, and after this she continued to run away and was nearly "hull down" at night, greatly ahead of us! It was certainly a very pretty sight the two Ships, running neck and neck for some couple of miles. Of course we expect to pick her up during the night if the wind freshens, but it is very probable we shall not do so. The "Star of Erin" had an immense amount of fancy sails or Muslin flying and I counted no less than thirty-three sails. Of course she could not carry half these in a stiff breeze, while we could carry almost all of ours. Lat: 3.18. Lon: 27.12. Dist: 173 miles.

THURSDAY 12th JANUARY

This morning there is no sign of the "Star of Erin". No doubt the light breeze favoured her as it lasted till 10 oClock last night. We pass a Dutch Ship who appeared very anxious to exchange signals. At the first attempt she carried away her "signal Haulyards" and as we were both in a fresh breeze she could not repair them in time. Lat: 5.58 S. Lon: 29.21. Dist: 236 miles.

FRIDAY 13th JANUARY

I remember the two Anniversaries of yesterday and today and drink the toast in silence having no one around me who would appreciate them. Nothing unusual occurred and the "Trades" are becoming daily more favorable for us. Lat: 9.6. Lon: 31.7. Dist: 268 miles.

SATURDAY 14th JANUARY

One of the objects which strike the eye of any one who travels on the open Sea is the Phosphoric light which illumines the darkness of the night. At first when we sailed we considered the slight rays of sparks left by the wake of the Ship were something rather extraordinary.

This has become exaggerated, and *now*, on several occasions, the small waves had apparently on their crests, balls of fire, sometimes larger than a cricket ball, which burst out and emit, for a second or two, a distinct and palpable light, and frequently on striking the Ship's side, they would brilliantly light up your face as you looked at them. I have seen similar exhibitions in England, but on a very small scale indeed compared to what I have since seen. In the Tropical regions the Skies are of remarkable beauty especially about Sunset. The Seas all around and as far as the distant horizon, is generally in these parts of a deep Indigo colour relieved occasionally by the White crests of the countless small waves.

As a background the Evening Sky presents a light pea green aspect, which is interspersed with very pretty light Maroon or Salmon coloured detached clouds, of the lightest and most airy character.

Thus the contrast between air and water renders the view from a Ship's Deck beyond my powers of description, for beauty, and can only be imagined by those who have sailed for days through the Trade Winds and the Tropics.

We are now sailing along the Coast of South America. We are distant some two hundred and fifty or three hundred miles. The point where we are today is just opposite Bahia or S. Salvador on the Coast of Brazil.* We shall I expect pursue a Southerly course until we can obtain a wind which will carry us to the East just below the Cape of Good Hope. We are getting along capitally and only hope our Trade wind will last us some time. Lat: 12.34. Lon: 32.3. Dist: 245 miles.

* The course down the Atlantic was by no means a direct route, but rather an arch bulging out westwards in the direction of South America.

SUNDAY 15th JANUARY

We have a stunning breeze and the old Ship dips her nose into the Sea and kicks up again finely. The bilious subjects again, like Miss Killmanseg "assume their rich complexions" and ever and anon they retire mysteriously to their Cabins and come out again looking very white and "washed out".

It must not be imagined that this Trade Wind is so extraordinarily favorable for us. It blows South East and we are steering South or South West, hence it is in reality almost against us; yet being a strong and steady breeze we can sail "close hauled" almost against it and still make good way. We had a very long Sermon and Service this morning—I cannot stand so much of it! It becomes very tedious in hot weather. Lat: 16.21. Lon: 31.56. Dist: 260 miles.

MONDAY 16th JANUARY

We are favored still with a good breeze which I am thankful to say keeps us tolerably cool. Were it not for the breeze, we should be very hot indeed, as we are now almost directly under the Sun's rays. We have a very pleasant rubber of Whist almost every Evening on Deck in which the Captain, who plays well, and I, are generally partners. Our table or rather "my" table is made from an old Flour tub, which has been sawn through the middle and we place my rug over the top of it. It has served as our Whist table during the Voyage, and many have been the rubbers played on it in my Cabin, which is generally used for this purpose. Today the Sailors are busy painting the Ship, a process which reminds one unpleasantly of the "cleaning" at home and renders everything in state of discomfort.

One of the pastimes appears to be now to watch the various hen coops, and try and find Eggs—nearly the whole of the fowls are hens and they begin to lay now owing to the hot weather. The cocks crow loudly in the morning and disturb the Passengers and crew, hence they are the first to be executed by the Ship's Butcher:—the fowls themselves are particularly partial to Eggs and unless you look "very lively" the Egg is quickly demolished by its "Mamma". The poor hens have a sorry time of it and very little leisure to sit down—if they do so they are quickly roused up by some Amateur Egg-gatherer who at once insists on their allowing him to search their persons for imaginary Eggs. Lat: 19.44. Lon: 33.00. Dist: 242 miles.

TUESDAY 17th JANUARY

Today the Sun's rays are said to be vertical. We still have something of a breeze—so we are not oppressively hot. The Thermometer marks 85° in the shade. We play in the Evening our usual rubber of Whist and afterwards we have our mock Parliament assembled to settle the various local questions of the day.

We have members representing almost every quarter of the Globe and the discussion ran chiefly on Sanitary matters, having especial reference to one of the Passengers, who is sadly troubled with "hydrophobia".

The business was conducted in a "quasi" formal manner and served to pass an hour or two very pleasantly. Lat: 22.33. Lon: 33.39. Dist: 198 miles.

WEDNESDAY 18th JANUARY

Last Evening the winds were very light and this morning it was a dead calm, reminding one of the words of Edgar A. Poe.

"Our Ship lay like a painted Ship upon a painted Ocean".

During the calm we saw several "Portuguese Men of War". They are a sort of jelly fish, and all that is to be seen is a pink colored bladder, resembling the end of a transparent kidney bean, and about the size of one's fist, which, floating on the surface, supports a large jelly fish with long tentacles—they are said to sting very severely. We also saw two lots of small fish which are said to be Pilots to, and precede a Shark. We did not happen to see the latter. The Pilots are about as large as a Mackarel, and swim generally in fours at a time. A breeze though very trifling springs up at 11 oClock and renders the air somewhat cooler. The heat today is insufferable, the Thermometer being 95° in the Shade—this without a breath of air is too warm to be pleasant. We are now in what is called "The Calms of Capricorn", and wish they were over and we could run towards the East. I fear that we shall not make Melbourne in six weeks from today. I hope we may do so sooner. Lat: 23.42. Lon: 33.35. Dist: 79 miles.

THURSDAY 19th JANUARY

We have run tolerably well during the night and this morning we are steering rather a better course being more Easterly:— this course is in our favor as our Westerly longitude is getting something considerable being 33 degrees. About 6 oClock this Evening the whole surface of the Sky was of the wildest description and we could see squalls all round us and we fully expected we were in for a "dirty night". We had several thunderstorms, the lightning was very vivid in various points of the Sky. After a very heavy shower, the small amount of wind we enjoyed died away, and we had a dead calm from 6 oClock till bedtime. Dancing on deck as usual, but it was too hot for me to join in it.

Dancing on Ship, at first recommends itself for its novelty: after this has worn off and the paces of the small stock of partners have been thoroughly tested, it becomes very tame work. Lat: 25.21. Lon: 33.7. Dist: 114 miles.

FRIDAY 20th JANUARY

We had little or no wind during the night.

We saw a large Whaler who was laid up without any Sails set, patiently watching for Whales. We are now in a district much frequented by Whales as also by Seals. The latter of course are to be found in some of the smaller islands in this neighbourhood. We had very heavy rain this morning. In the evening everything was got ready and we expected to have a very serious squall as the horizon to windward was very black. The Cloud passed pretty well over us and after a vivid flash of lightning and a smart shower the Sea became painfully calm, and we lay motionless for more than six hours. After that the wind such as there was blew from every quarter, and greatly tried the temper of the Sailors who were perpetually trimming sail. Lat: 26.54. Lon: 32.9. Dist: 120 miles.

SATURDAY 21st JANUARY

I have nothing of interest to record today. Lat: 28.35. Lon: 31.16. Dist: 130 miles.

All night and this morning it has been blowing "great guns" and our good Ship has been putting her Nose into it pretty considerably. About 7 oClock we lost our fore top gallant sail which was split up. We had previously stowed our "Skysails" and "Royals" and still we had enough canvass set, to be pleasant.

We had great fun this morning with the Pigs which were styed on the Forecastle. Owing to the seas constantly breaking over, it was deemed necessary to save the Pigs from a watery grave; hence they were ordered to be removed to a vacant Sheep-pen on the main deck. While this was being contemplated the whole herd, from some unexplained cause, got loose and sauntered about the Forecastle. One poor Pig, more venturesome than his fellows, went overboard and doubtless became a prey to the Sharks. The others were gradually chased down by the "Tars" and the unceremoneous treatment the Pigs received at their hands was most laughable. The Bull dog we had on board constituted himself as kind of Gaoler of the new Pigstye—he showed his authority by biting each Pig behind, as it was being lifted into the Stye—this caused a great amusement to those of us who were byestanders. One large wave washed over the Poop and wet several of the Passengers to the skin. Every one today got a Ducking at some time or other. Service was in the Saloon and our Clergyman had a very poor Audience, as the fresh Gale had made several Passengers "feel very queer". One of the Officers was quite laid up and took to his bed through Sea sickness—this will show we had a good Sea running. Whilst we were dining, another Sail, the Main-top-gallant went literally to ribbons, and we had to take it down and bend on a new one. The Sails which split were light Sails, which had been used for going through the Tropics. After dinner we were sitting together on Deck when without any warning a wave came, and wet the whole lot of us. We are now nearly in the Latitude of the Cape of Good Hope though we are over two thousand miles to the Westward of it. It is a great pity so "fine" a breeze should be so "foul" for us, as it is blowing nearly East and the course we are making which is the best we can make under all circumstances is nearly due South. Today we saw for the first time an Albatross. They will soon become no novelties to us and I trust to be able to secure a stock of pipe stems from the bones of their wings. Lat: 32.6. Lon: 30.32. Dist: 246 miles.

MONDAY 23rd JANUARY

A stiff breeze. We have all Sails set and have to steer nearly due South. By noon today we shall be in Latitude South of the Cape of Good Hope which is about 35.15. Melbourne is about 38. No news stirring. The Ship like Bridgnorth Election is all on one side but this is nothing when you are used to it and think you are the nearer the end of your Voyage. Lat: 35.51. Lon: 29.35. Dist: 264 miles.

TUESDAY 24th JANUARY

During the night I awoke and found the Ship going very well indeed under all Sail. Today we saw several Cape Hens. They are large Brown or Copper coloured Birds, somewhat resembling a very large Sea Gull being often five feet across their wings. They have a large black eye with a white colored rim round it; this makes their eye look much larger than it really is—they fly close to the ship and within easy shot—they smell very high and are of no use.

"Mother Carey's Chickens" still follow us. We also have lots of birds which for want of a name we call "Whistle Wassale". They resemble a large Swallow having a light coloured body. They are a species of Tern I think. They are very numerous. The distance marked up today was the greatest we had ever run, in the twenty four hours, being at a rate of fifteen miles an hour. Lat: 38.52. Lon: 25.23. Dist: 312 miles.

WEDNESDAY 25th JANUARY

The weather has become now very much colder—so much so that I have had to put on my Winter clothes again and to sleep under a blanket, a luxury I have never indulged in for the last month or more. We have a goodly stock of curious birds flying in our wake. If they are shot they only fall into the Sea and we are sailing too fast to catch them by hook and line. We have now sailed a distance of 7,688 miles. We are about half way at this time on our journey. Lat: 40.32. Lon: 21.9. Dist: 252 miles.

THURSDAY 26th JANUARY

Again the Wind is foul and we make as much Southing as East. It is becoming very cold and cheerless and we hope for a change of wind or else we shall have to 'bout Ship and then we must sail too much to the North or home again. Lat: 42.16. Lon: 16.8. Dist: 288 miles.

FRIDAY 27th JANUARY

Last night it was very cold and boisterous—all the Evening it · rained heavily and prevented our getting on Deck. This morning it has been blowing hard and the Sea has run very high—cold rain, fog and a strong breeze prevail—several tumbles have taken place on Deck though without serious result. The Butcher was carrying some meat and he tumbled over on the top of it and had to sit there till the Ship righted herself. All Top-gallant sails have been struck except the Main-stop-gallant but the Ship carries her Canvass splendidly.

Rain and a Kind of Sleet the whole day.

By dead reckoning we are Lat: uncertain. Lon: uncertain. Dist: 280 miles.

SATURDAY 28th JANUARY

This morning about 5 oClock I was kindly called by one of the Officers who were on watch to see a very grand sight.

There were two or three Icebergs in sight. I got out at once and went on Deck. There were two large ones on our Port bow and one on the other bow. There were also several detached pieces of Ice floating about. The largest and nearest one I estimated to be a couple of miles from us. It was very visible— the Sun was just rising and lighted it up grandly. It was probably fifty feet high, the top being covered with Snow. I have no opportunity of judging its actual size, but it must have been many hundred yards in circumference. The Ice was beautifully transparent, and the white, shaded with blue and pink, looked very grand. A very small one which passed within fifty yards of us was of beautiful transparent Ice. It is a very uncommon thing to see Ice in outward bound Ships, but we are just in the season to see it, and have been driven by the East winds an unusual distance South. One can hardly fancy its being Summer as it is anything but genial just now. We were glad to have seen the Ice by daylight; it is very difficult to see Ice when it is dark at night. It is so easily mistaken for the crest of a foaming wave and thus you might accidentally run foul of it and go "to the bottom of the deep blue Sea". About 4 oClock this afternoon we again came in with a floe of Ice and saw several bergs—they were not generally so large as the largest this morning, yet the two last of the long file we passed, were very good—one shaped like the Prow of a "Steam Ram" was perfectly white and reminded one of a huge mountain of loaf-sugar. The other evidently of older Ice was transparent as glass, and being low in the water the waves constantly broke in volumes of spray over its rugged walls, leaving the Ice more glittering and transparent than before. It has been very cold during the day, and at night it requires a good deal of wrapping to keep at all warm.

We have to double the Watch tonight on Deck for fear of Ice. Our Potatoes, with one consent, have unfortunately gone rotten, and their remains which to use a mild expression "stunk aloud" have been consigned to the deep.

They have not left a "rack" but a very foul smell "behind" them which I am afraid may last several days.

During the last week we have sailed 1902 miles being an average of $271\frac{5}{7}$ miles a day. I only wish we could keep this up. Lat: 43.47. Lon: 5.43. Dist: 260 miles.

SUNDAY 29th JANUARY

We did not see any Ice during the night and have for some time been very nearly becalmed. During the Afternoon we were sailing very slowly, and as there were several Albatrosses about we set a line out from the Stern. We were at length successful in catching six out of the seven which were flying round—and we also caught a Cape Hen. The Albatross' measured about eleven feet across their wings—when once on Deck they are unable to fly—they have generally white breasts and bodies and dark brown wings—they bite very freely, unless their long hooked beaks are tied with a piece of string. I have the wing bone of one given to me for a Pipe stem—their breasts when cured, make very nice Ladies' Muffs—and their feet make curious Tobacco pouches.

They are very strong and one man could hardly haul a bird

on board. The most curious thing is that they have an extra pinion at the end of their wings which doubles up underneath like a Carpenter's Rule.

There is hardly any breeze this Evening and we are going only about two miles an hour. Lat: 43.28. Lon: 3.6. Dist: 134 miles.

MONDAY 30th JANUARY

This morning we saw two or three Whales which came close to the Ship and were seen frequently. One which we saw was over thirty feet long and rolled out of the water each time he came up—they were smaller than usual yet we had a very good look at them—we yesterday saw several "spouting" in the distance. Today we caught a Mother Carey's Chicken or Stormy Petrel— they are about the size of a Blackbird—brown plumage with white breast and on the lower part of the back above the tails they are also white.

The way they are caught is to tow astern a long piece of Cotton against which they fly and their wings then become entangled in the Cotton and you then easily haul them on board. The Sailors are very averse to such a proceeding, and strongly believe it forbodes a long or dangerous Voyage.

Just before Dinner today we saw in the distance a Ship which had lost her Mizen and Fore top masts. We expected she was bearing up to us for assistance; she however again set sail and went away to the Southward. What his object in so doing was we could not make out. Lat: 42.48. Lon: 1.28 W. Dist: 97 miles.

TUESDAY 31st JANUARY

Most probably today we shall at Noon be in East Longitude. During the Voyage our Watches have been at one period about two hours and a half faster than the Ship's time which of course was the time we had to go by. We have today reached the Longitude, East of Greenwich, and so our time has at some time during the last twenty-four hours been the same as it was at home, and our Watches are found to be correct again. We shall now find as we are making Eastern Longitude that our Watches lose terribly. The broad calculation is that for each Degree of East Longitude travelled over, we gain in time a trifle over four minutes. A rough calculation would shew that the time at Melbourne is about eleven hours faster than in England:— Melbourne being 146″ East Longitude. Today we saw an innumerable shoal of "black fish" or what people call "Porpoises". I am unable to guess at the number as it must have been very great, but in saying there were many thousands I am not wrong. The Sea as far as our eye would reach appeared to be alive with them. The distance run today is in excess of that which we have actually travelled but for the last two days we have gone by "dead reckoning" from the fact that we have not seen the Sun. When we can see it of course the Officers can correctly ascertain our position.

We are right in supposing that we travelled yesterday a greater distance than was put down on the Log Slate viz. 97 miles. The wind is very light but favorable. Lat: 41.58. Lon: 2.47 E. Dist: 232 miles.

WEDNESDAY 1st FEBRUARY

Eight weeks today since we left Gravesend and we are still 15 degrees East of the Cape of Good Hope. This is beginning to look like our making a very long Passage as we now hoped to be running well before the wind. The breeze freshens towards Afternoon. Lat: 41.48. Lon: 5.45. Dist: 154 miles.

THURSDAY 2nd FEBRUARY

We are sailing with a strong breeze right ahead of us yet we are making considerable way. Lat: 41.45. Lon: 10.2. Dist: 220 miles.

FRIDAY 3rd FEBRUARY

This morning the wind suddenly died away about 4 oClock and we are once more becalmed—the Ship as usual keeps up a rolling motion as in the deadest calm there is still the swell of the water. The Captain allowed us a boat and I spent the day in rowing about and shooting birds. We got an Albatross and about thirty Whale birds and "Mutton" birds. Some of them were very pretty and their skins are being preserved by the Sailors for various Passengers. They are not *thoroughly* preserved, and hence I do not choose to make by Cabin smell for the sake of some few skins of birds.

We also took out a boat to make soundings and try the Compass and see which way the Current was setting. It being near the Cape we found rather a strong North West Current. I do so wish it would blow, as my visit to Australia will be curtailed by every day we are becalmed. The Sun was very hot yesterday while we were in the boat and I expect the skin of my nose and Face will peel before long; they were awfully red last night. Lat: 40.39. Lon: 12.30. Dist: 150 miles.

SATURDAY 4th FEBRUARY

My father's birthday—I wish I were dining at home "for a change"; this slow travelling is becoming very monotonous.

The wind or rather the want of it is the general theme of conversation and all hope of our making a good passage is now at an end. Fifty eight days from the Pilot and we have not yet made the Cape.

The average speed during the last twenty four hours is only four miles per hour and we are over six thousand miles from Melbourne. Lat: 41.16. Lon: 14.12. Dist: 98 miles.

SUNDAY 5th FEBRUARY

Calm again till Noon when for about three hours we had a smart breeze.

A Ship was in sight for some time this Evening but too far for us to signal her. Our Ship has been pitching very much from a heavy swell—the waves are very long and when you are on the top of one it appears to be a long way to the bottom of the trough. I am glad we do not roll as well as pitch. The waves are frequently very fine where we are just at present: very nearly due South of the Cape. We are at the present moment merely pitching in the middle of long rolling waves and I am afraid making very little progress. Lat: 40.58. Lon: 15.45. Dist: 84 miles.

MONDAY 6th FEBRUARY

We still have a heavy swell and a foul but strong breeze. I hear that the Sunset was particularly fine this Evening. I was away in one of the Cabins seeing after a friend who was seedy and so missed it. About 9 oClock we saw a Lunar Rainbow. This is the second I have seen in less than six months having never previously seen one. Whist and Dancing on Deck formed the Evening entertainments—the latter was sadly interfered with by the rolling and pitching of the Ship. I expect we were in the Latitude of the Cape about 9 oClock this morning as at noon we found we had pased it. Lat: 40.14. Lon: 19.00. Dist: 175 miles.

TUESDAY 7th FEBRUARY

I had very little sleep last night chiefly owing to the rolling of the Ship, and more especially to the heat—the latter I take it is induced from the various currents of heated and cold water which prevail in the neighbourhood of the Cape. The temperature of the surface of the water varied ten degrees between 8 and 12 oClock today. At the end of every Watch on Ship (that is every four hours), the Officer of the Watch takes certain observations for the benefit of the Board of Trade (Science Department) I believe, at all events the instruments bear the Government Stamp.

These observations consist in the correct reading of the Barometer, and various kinds of Thermometers, etc. finding the specific gravity and temperature of the Sea, and observations on the Clouds, or Physical objects generally. These are carefully noted down in a special book, and probably may prove useful to our Mercantile Marine posterity.

A remarkable phenomenon in these Latitudes seems to be the ever varying colors of the Sea, and the quickness with which it changes such colors—the dark indigo blue and various shades of blue are the prevailing colors but yet there is a peculiar shade of Green (Olive Green I must call it) which for the last several days has been of very frequent occurrence. This is generally of a lighter shade, yet today about 2 oClock the Sea was to all appearance as Green and thick as any stagnant Horse Pond. Today we saw a very fine Whale. I could not guess his length but he was a Monster. We also saw flocks of Whale birds, or as they are properly termed "Blue Petrel". These are small Snipe-like birds, with light blue or french grey feet, and bodies; and they generally frequent the "Whalegrounds". We also saw for the first time this Voyage a Cape Pigeon, a very pretty bird, not unlike our own Pigeon, except that it is nicely barred with black and white. I hope we may be able to catch one as we are trying to do so. They are rather rare, and Voyages are made without seeing any at all, although at other times they may be very plentiful, and no novelties. Lat: 40.48. Lon: 22.20. Dist: 180 miles.

WEDNESDAY 8th FEBRUARY

This morning, very shortly after Breakfast, we saw a very smart squall in the distance which came upon us rather suddenly—so much so that we had to put up our helm and run before it for a few miles—had we not done so we should probably have lost some of our Sails. This squall brought us up a splendid fair South West breeze the only one we have had for a very long time.

Accordingly we ran along with it bravely for a few hours and our drooping spirits revived. The wind, however, all died away in the Evening and we once more are going on our usual "Snail's gallop". Lat: 41.58. Lon: 26.6. Dist: 212 miles.

THURSDAY 9th FEBRUARY

Nothing at all remarkable occurred today except that it rained heavily the whole day and we were becalmed all the morning, though we had still a heavy swell running. Lat: 42.34. Lon: 28.41. Dist: 142 miles.

FRIDAY 10th FEBRUARY

About 6 oClock last Evening a South breeze sprang up at first very gradually but it freshened splendidly and during the night we were running nearly sixteen miles an hour. This continued nearly all the day and allowing for the fact that yesterday we went by "dead reckoning" and were what is called "under logged" (that is the Log book did not state the pace we were going to be so much as we *did* actually go) we were surprised and pleased to find that we had gone 316 miles. The Sea was rather rough at times, but we went very well and every one's temper improved as we "sniffed" in imagination the "fleshpots" of Melbourne. Lat: 41.44. Lon: 34.51. Dist: 316 miles.

SATURDAY 11th FEBRUARY

Another day of calms. We managed to catch four albatross' and this is a proceeding which can only take place when the Ship is going slowly. The number of miles we have already travelled is 10,926 as shown in the Log. If, however, we add 500, the miles between Gravesend and the place where I first began to keep count, the number is 11,426. Lat: 41.40. Lon: 39.5. Dist: 216 miles.

SUNDAY 12th FEBRUARY

We are now in what is usually a very rough part of the Passage, being South of the Mozambique Channel, or as the Sailors call it "The Devil's Funnel". It has this name from the fact of its being generally a very boisterous place, with strong currents, and from the number of Pirates which infest that Sea, especially if a Ship is becalmed, which frequently happens there. We start this day with a nice breeze from the North East and though our Sails are all close hauled yet we hope for better times and are now going well.

This Evening we had a very good view of the Aurora "Australis" which corresponds, as its name implies, with our Northern lights. It was very visible from the Ship. Lat: 42.28. Lon: 41.54. Dist: 156 miles.

MONDAY 13th FEBRUARY

This was a clear fine morning and as the Sun and Moon were both visible at the same time, our Officers were engaged taking sights or "Lunars" so as to correct our Ship's chronometers, some of which they found to be slightly wrong. The weather is now very cold and we require our thickest clothes to keep us anything like warm. Still it is very fine and frosty, but the wind is searching to those who have weak Lungs. We are still going South. Lat: 43.17. Lon: 45.47. Dist: 207 miles.

TUESDAY 14th FEBRUARY

This was a day of Valentines. The first delivery of letters took place during Breakfast and caused plenty of fun. There was also a late delivery about 8.30. It is very cold with light wind. Lat: 43.52. Lon: 49.14. Dist: 175 miles.

WEDNESDAY 15th FEBRUARY

During the whole of the day we were becalmed and lay under the hot Sun without moving. I say "hot Sun" as it really was hot notwithstanding the previous weather had been cold.

We spoke a Ship with whom we were in company all the morning and we also lowered a boat and went on board her. She was the "Mofussilite" bound to Madras. We obtained Newspapers from her up to the 15th December, the day she left London. She had a very good passage to the Line, twenty-seven days, against our thirty-three days. Since the Line she had had about the same weather as we have had. She was about 1,000 Tons Register. We had a boat out nearly all day shooting birds but I could not go as it was too hot to be pleasant. We saw today several Penguins. They are very extraordinary birds which they say will dive even at the *flash* of a Gun, i.e. before the shot gets to them—at all events they are wonderfully quick— they have small flappers and no legs and have a loud cry something like a Cow's lowing and a Frog croaking—it is very peculiar and on a still day is very loud and distinct—they stay a long time under water and if you pursue them in a boat, they jump out of the water and in again, like a fish, any number of times, and can easily run away from you. Lat: 44.7. Lon: 51.18. Dist: 138 miles.

THURSDAY 16th FEBRUARY

This morning there were two Ships in sight one very much to windward of us which refused to signal to us at all—the other was the same which we saw a short time ago and which had lost her fore and mizen topmasts. By slightly varying our course, we found we could run down on her and when we were close enough about noon, we signalled her and found her to be "The Pride of Wales" from Buenos Ayres to Rangoon in ballast. She was consequently very light in the water, and her Captain having very little use for his Topmasts had stowed them away on Deck. We were glad to have solved the problem of her being dismasted as a belief had gained upon us, that it was the "Star of Erin" which had become dismasted in a Gale, and which purposely avoided us on the former occasion when she appeared to steer so eccentric a course. The breeze today began to freshen about noon, and I trust to be able to record a good run tomorrow. Lat: 44.50. Lon: 54.3. Dist: 144 miles.

FRIDAY 17th FEBRUARY

I forgot to mention that last night the Ship being very much on one side I slipped, and came down rather heavily, and two friends who were with me very nearly fell on the top of me. The Decks become very slippery in rainy weather and when there is a good Sea running you are very liable to slip up. All night we had a good breeze and are still going well though it rains heavily and prevents our getting on Deck with any comfort—the rain continued throughout the whole day and so did the breeze which freshened considerably at night. We made the best run today we have yet made and this too with the Sails "close jammed up against the Masts". Our speed was about 13½ miles an hour during the day. Lat: 45.40. Lon: 60.38. Dist: 322 miles.

SATURDAY 18th FEBRUARY

Last night it blew nicely and we had neither Skysails, Royals or Top-gallant sails except the Main Top-gallant. When I went to bed the speed we were going was over 15 knots or 17 miles an hour. I only wish this pace would keep up for a long time and thus put an end to our Voyage. We had some rolling during the night and about 12, or half past, we shipped a heavy Sea, which I think awoke most of us as we lurched heavily just before we did so. I saw a bird today very like one of our Crows, and hear it is master of all the birds including Albatross, Molly-hawks, etc. So sharp is it that when the large birds pounce on a piece of food, this Crow-like bird (whose name I cannot ascertain) makes his large friends drop their prey and they fly away screaming and lamenting their lost meat. We have seen several of them. This Evening probably we were not very far from the island of Kerquelin. This will account for the very extraordinary quantity of birds large and small which followed in the wake of our Ship. There were several hundreds of them, the Albatross being well represented. Lat: 45.15. Lon: 66.54. Dist: 310 miles.

SUNDAY 19th FEBRUARY

A very cold cheerless morning. I stayed in bed for Breakfast. The Sun came out in the Forenoon and unfortunately we then lost our breeze. We are over 4,000 miles away from Melbourne yet. We may do the distance in fourteen or sixteen days if we have wind. Lat: 44.27. Lon: 73.14. Dist: 312 miles.

MONDAY 20th FEBRUARY

I am tired of writing about the wind and the wind appears tired of us, as we have been rolling and bobbing about all day, as well as during the night without making any great progress. I have nothing to record today. Lat: 44.17. Lon: 76.00. Dist: 136 miles.

TUESDAY 21st FEBRUARY

Pancake day—so we eat Pancakes accordingly—this is a queer rainy and foggy cold day. From noon yesterday for the first six hours we supposed we had run about sixty miles. We had a strong breeze afterwards and we hoped to have run the remaining 240 miles to complete our 300. We did not quite do this as our Log shows. Lat: 45.27. Lon: 81.30. Dist: 282 miles.

WEDNESDAY 22nd FEBRUARY

A very cold day owing to the South wind. I was shooting at birds with a Needle Rifle belonging to the Captain but I cannot say I did anything very brilliant with it as the wind was high and the Ship was knocking about. It being very cold I went to bed early and found it the warmest place I had been in all day. Lat: 45.33. Lon: 87.10. Dist: 280 miles.

THURSDAY 23rd FEBRUARY

This was a calm day and we lay some hours without moving. Melbourne which the Knowing ones said was to be sighted on Sunday week is now postponed indefinitely, and we are all in bad tempers at being once more becalmed. To all appearance there is no sign of wind. Eleven weeks today since we left land and our Pilot! Our run today appears pretty good. How we did it I cannot imagine. I expected 180 miles to be the very outside measure. Lat: 45.45. Lon: 91.52. Dist: 230 miles.

FRIDAY 24th FEBRUARY

We were rolled about finely last night and had a smart squall about 3 oClock. We shortened Sail for an hour or two but we soon had it up again in the morning. We are getting on better again and at Noon are just about 2,600 miles from our journey's end.

This is the farthest South we have yet gone. Lat: 46.19. Lon: 97.24. Dist: 268 miles.

SATURDAY 25th FEBRUARY

A very cold day indeed. We had frequent storms of hail and sleet during the night which rattled on the Deck. Our Thermometer registered something like 42° today and the wind comes from the South. I had a "Sea" in my Cabin through the Port this morning but I am glad it did not damage my Clothes very much. We are running well and hope to be at Melbourne in eight days if we can only carry the wind with us. Lat: 46.00. Lon: 103.47. Dist: 310 miles.

SUNDAY 26th FEBRUARY

A memorable day. We ran 361 miles or over fifteen miles an hour for twenty-four hours. The Sea was the grandest we have had yet, and the waves were very large and magnificent—the colour was of intense light and Indigo blue and the crests of the waves of purest white.

In Sea painting, my impression is that the foam on the waves is never painted so pure a white as the original, and this was very evident today. We rolled heavily at times but the pace we were going was sufficient to prevent pitching. Before 8 oClock tonight we shall have Australian ground due North of us. Cape Leeuwin is in Longitude 115°00″, but it is not quite the Westernmost land of Australia (by some 110 miles or more) as a glance at the Map will shew. We are 1720 miles from Cape Otway, which is the land we sight before we come to Melbourne, and the first land we shall probably see. Lat: 45.16. Lon: 111.6. Dist: 361 miles.

MONDAY 27th FEBRUARY

I scarcely slept all last night as the Ship rolled so much by reason of our going before the wind. Our bones were quite sore with turning in bed so much; however we are getting on and still have a nice breeze. We are proposing to have a mild Kind of Concert and we had our first Rehearsal in my Cabin last night. I am afraid it will not be a very musical affair as we have no music on board and "part singing" by ear is not always very correct or good. Lat: 44.32. Lon: 117.34. Dist: 322 miles.

TUESDAY 28th FEBRUARY

A rough night and not much sleep. "Rock me to sleep" may sound very pretty on shore, I doubt however whether the Author of that Song ever tried it with a strong wind "aft" and with all "yards squared". In this opinion I have no hesitation in saying all my fellow passengers concur. Lat: 44.9. Lon: 122.31. Dist. 247 miles.

Chapter 2

This was the Evening of our Concert. There were four performers of whom I was one—this does not say much for the
goodness of the Concert as my friends must allow—the other
three performers were our Conductor a young fellow Passenger
who has a good voice and a fair amount of ear and confidence—
Miss —— who is about eighteen, nice looking, agreeable, with a
fair voice and a quick ear for music—and our Second Mate who
understands music fairly and has a high tenor voice, which came
out well in *Tom Bowline* and similar songs. I must mention that
we have not any music on board, and though we raised four
songs "for appearance sake", and to hide our blushes and con-
fusion, yet the words were all copied out of Poetry-books by
Ladies on slips of Note-paper. We had our final Rehearsal in the
middle of the day and we felt much more confidence in singing
after we had finally arranged the various parts we were to take.
I was deputed to draw up a Play bill which was embellished with
musical emblems and the insignia of Royalty, and the Passengers
were courteously invited to attend at 8 o'clock in the Saloon—
then I had to insert a few jokes such as "Babies in Arms" and
"the Press" were excluded, "Carriages as usual were ordered
for 10 oClock" and it finally wound up with stating that "Music
hath charms" etc. Doubt being cast on the truth of this assertion
in this particular instance, we appealed to the generous audience
in most touching terms to decide in our favour.

As our dress clothes had never seen the light of day during
the Voyage we insisted on a "full dress" concert. We took up

some tables in the Saloon and draped a sort of alcove at one end of it with the Flags of all Nations. Our Programme included "See our Oars", "The Canadian Boat Song", "Hail smiling Morn", "The last Rose of Summer" (trio), "The Hardy Norseman", a couple of rounds, "A boat, etc." and "Man's life's a vapour"—these were the part songs. We also had several solos.

Although it was entirely *Vocal* Music I trust I shall not be accused of "sounding my own *trumpet*" too much when I say that everything went off much better than either we or our audience expected and "The Hardy Norseman", which we had "coached up" with especial care, was worthy even of that Metropolitan Cave of Harmony once the property of the late lamented Mr. Evans.

I must mention that during the First and Second parts of the Programme, two of the Cuddy Servants who were very well got up a la "the original" Chrysty style, gave what was advertised as a "Mohawk Minstrel" entertainment. After the Concert we had the novelty of a Supper ("full dress" of course) and we only lamented that the *"tide"* of Ship's Champagne had "ebbed", several days ago, "n'eer to flow again". We hope to have our Ship tied by the Nose to Melbourne Pier some time next Sunday. Lat: 43.14. Lon: 127.51. Dist: 275 miles.

THURSDAY 2nd MARCH

Were I to go to such lengths in writing my Diary as I did yesterday my paper would hardly hold out. I will merely say then that Lat: 42.5. Lon: 132.19. Dist: 292 miles.

FRIDAY 3rd MARCH

We suppose we shall arrive in Melbourne on Sunday Afternoon. I hope we may. We are today 350 miles from Cape Otway. If we get a foul wind we shall be a long time yet and the wind is now very light, and a tendency to East, our worst quarter. Lat: 40.35. Lon: 137.11. Dist: 227 miles.

SATURDAY 4th MARCH

We have now got a foul wind and have had to make too much Northing.

We found at Noon today that we were not far from land and

at 1.30 we sighted the first land! The points were Cape Bridg-water and Cape Nelson, which are in Portland. I hear this is a very famous place for squatters on account of the richness of the pastures. We coasted along for some time, till we came opposite Percy Island which is a large flat rock, just before you come to Warmambool.

As we had got land right ahead of us and it was impossible any longer to proceed, at 8 oClock all hands were piped on deck and we hoped that if we might make thirty miles of Offing we should (if the wind continued where it was) sight Cape Otway in the morning.

The appearance of the Shore introduced us to the Australian White Sand-drift, which prevails on the Coast, as well as to the Gum trees. Lat: 39.57. Lon: 140.37. Dist: 266 miles.

SUNDAY 5th *MARCH*

I awoke before 6 as I heard them again "bouting Ship" and to my dismay on looking out I saw my old friend Percy island staring me in the face.

The wind had broken away when we were on the return tack and instead of making Otway we arrived at the very same place we left last night. This is trying to your temper. Two Seals followed the Ship for some distance early this morning and I saw them very well. We had a very good view of Warmambool (or "Port Fairy" as it is sometimes called) and could see the Lighthouse and Church and a few small Ships in the Harbour. It was about seven or eight miles away. My first introduction to Australian weather gives me a very favorable impression, as today is simply magnificent, notwithstanding the foul and light wind. No Cape Otway I fear today! the wind is dead East and this is against us especially as it is so very light. In the Afternoon the breeze blew stronger and stronger till it nearly reached a Gale. We shortened sail considerably even taking in Topgal-lants: with all this wind we make little (if any) way—and we are we suppose forty miles from Otway tonight. We have land in sight in plenty on our lee bow. We are running short of lots of comforts—of Cigars there are about three in the whole Ship. My Tobacco store is out and so is every one's. Ship's Tobacco is very strong, and we resort to the process of washing some of the strength out of it, before we can smoke it.

MONDAY 6th MARCH

We are becalmed this morning and a greater part of the night: Cape Otway is just visible about twenty-five miles to windward and we are nearly abreast Cape Moonlight, though to all appearance the Ship is motionless.

If things don't "look up", we may be here for a week yet. After we pass Otway it is fifty-five miles to "Port Philip Heads" and thence forty miles to Melbourne and the passage of the Heads is difficult especially if the wind is not favorable.

Tack! Tack! Tack! and make very little way when you have "tacked". We catch a land breeze this afternoon And slide through the water famously although to little profit. We go to bed disgusted especially after sighting Otway light which is very much to windward of us yet.

TUESDAY 7th MARCH

Still tacking and doing no good as we are suffering from a hot Australian wind which is foul. Some friends of mine are now in my Cabin preparing an address to the Captain—suddenly there is a rush of Passengers, and a shout, and the wind "hauls round fair". Great was the joy; Otway is passed and we bowl away for Melbourne "direct" or at least to Port Philip Heads—the breeze freshens and we again sight land and about three oClock the "Heads" are visible. Everyone is anxious about our Pilot Sweepstakes and bets are made as to which foot he first puts on board. When we are just at the Heads' mouth, below Queen's Cliff out comes a Pilot-boat from the land and after moments of intense anxiety "The Crew" for whom a Ticket in the "Sweep" has been taken are pronounced winners of the £5 sweepstake by only two minutes. The Pilot steps on board and his left foot is on Deck first: this also is a source of profit to some of our speculators, who "in a quiet way" do a little gambling, on any subject, just to wile away time.

We come gaily through the Heads and sight the Quarantine ground and the Doctor's house. Up goes our Ensign to the Maintop and the Doctor comes out in his very nice Skiff and a good crew in uniform. He steps on board and we grudge the delay as we hope to be tied to Melbourne Pier tonight. Suddenly a whisper runs round that a case of Small-pox which we had, last 11th December, and which was pronounced cured last 24th

January, and the Sailor who was the sufferer has "herded" with his mates ever since, has caused the Government Inspector to delay our progress and he has accordingly ordered us to Quarantine. I cannot but think that the Sailors themselves are to blame for this, as they so chaffed and frightened the miserable invalid (telling him that he would be transported etc.) that when the Medical Officer came up to inspect him he came up trembling and asked him "not to hang him". Of course this put the Doctor on the "qui vive" at once.

All our sails so nicely set for going are hauled down, and we are now anchored opposite to a pretty and picturesque hill, covered with Tea-tree scrub and amidst which there is beautiful hospital accommodation for twenty such Ships as ours. When we may get away we do not know. What luck! Yet I think they must be particular as they have to receive Ships from all Nations and Small-pox I hear is frightfully prevalent in the Northern parts of Europe and also at home.

We are to stay here all night and how much longer I do not know. Accordingly we hoist our Yellow flag and make ourselves as happy as we can. Our Pilot felt himself greatly aggrieved as of course he has no more power of getting on shore than we have, and it is a very heavy penalty to leave Ship under the present circumstances.

WEDNESDAY 8th MARCH

I awoke early and found that the Government Doctor had come on board and signed us a "clean bill of health". We were a very long time getting under weigh as the Anchor took a great deal of raising. We had a fair wind and sailed up Hobson's Bay, one of the largest Bays in the world.

There are two channels to sail up and we have to go by the South or longer channel as we draw too much water for the other. The journey up is very picturesque in places. We pass the Masts of the "Hurricane" a large Ship which was wrecked two years ago and which still shew above water.

I now devote my attention to packing. About 2 oClock Melbourne is in sight, and soon we see the Tug which is to take us to our berth alongside Sandridge Pier. The Tug is crowded with people—friends of our passengers: more especially of Mr. E—— who is a Civil Engineer who after an absence of eighteen months is returning to his duties again. The Tug is alongside— there are wonderful greetings amongst the friends. Mrs. E—— is overwhelmed with Bouquets, and a very fine display of fruit, which is handed round for our general benefit—every one appears happy—we have all once again Cigars in our mouths; a great treat this after being so long without! We are presently berthed alongside the Sandridge Pier. This Pier is formed by Piles driven into the Sea and Ships are moored in rows along each side of it. Thus they can discharge their Cargoes directly into the Railway Trucks which run down the middle of the Pier. This is a very convenient arrangement.

A Letter from Annie my Sister is handed to me by Messrs. Green's Agent who came on board in the Tug. My luggage passes the Customs and we take the train to Melbourne. I go to the Port Philip Club Hotel which is close to the Railway Station. I have a Table d'hote dinner at 6 with Salad and *fresh* vegetables! Such luxuries they are and after a short stroll I go to bed.

THURSDAY 9th MARCH

I have a good night's rest notwithstanding I miss the motion of the Ship. My bed is an ordinary iron bedstead without hangings but with Musquito Curtains instead. The Bedroom window looks into a very pretty sort of Courtyard at the back of the Hotel.

This yard is "roofed in" so to speak with vines, trained on wires—it is nicely laid out with a mound of rock work and shrubs:— there is a small Fountain in the middle—a fine Magnolia, and under the Verandah, which runs along two sides (along the whole length of which is trained in neat and graceful festoons, a very beautiful passion flower), are lots of Couches and Sofas for Smokers. In the corner, in a Cage, is a Cockatoo, which is said to be the wonder of the whole Colonies, and a full and particular printed account of his sayings and doings is hung up in a frame beside him. I never heard so clever a bird; and it would be no exaggeration to say, that he could hold a (tolerably) rational conversation with any one for some minutes. He can repeat the whole verse of "Pop goes the Weasel"; imitate a Lady sewing by holding a piece of linen in his claw, drawing the thread with his beak and you hear the click of the needle and of the thimble, etc. and has any amount of accomplishments besides.

The day is rather warm. I devote my time to going to the Post Office, where I receive a Letter from George, and to various Shipping Offices, to try and find out what my future plans are likely to be; and to seeing Melbourne.

FRIDAY 10th MARCH

I discover today that there are Races going on at a short distance, I therefore go with a friend to see what they are like. The course is about five miles distant by train, and tickets for the Grand stand and Railway fare are 12/- each. The Station is situate within a few yards of the Stand which is placed on the side of a hill. I cannot praise too highly the Stand arrangements generally. In front of the Stand is a Lawn from which the noisy "ring men" are excluded. These men occupy the saddling paddock adjoining. Punctuality in starting is well observed and jockeys are fined if they are not at the post in time.

The horses were very good and some of the races were first rate. There was a goodly show of beauty in the Stand—but I cannot but observe that the taste of the Ladies here generally is most vile, as regards the variety of colours they wear at the same time—in other respects they are tolerably good looking and well dressed. The men, as a rule, are very fine fellows, tall and good looking and I doubt whether we can shew either finer, handsomer or jollier fellows, in England.

SATURDAY 11th TO 18th

A daily record would only be tedious. I devote my time to lionizing Melbourne. The streets are good and are all arranged at right angles. Collins Street and Bourke Street are very fine large straight Streets, and the Shops are good. In Collins Street is what is called "the Block" which answers to our Rotten Row, though the Carriages are very poor, and light Buggies are everywhere the fashionable private vehicle. They have a novel mode of watering the Streets; a thing constantly required owing to the amount of dust; there is a first rate natural water supply some thirty miles away.

The water is carried in pipes to Melbourne from the Yan Yean which is at a very much higher level. As the pressure is very great a Scavenger, by merely affixing a short standard and nozzle to one of the fire plugs, is able to water about two hundred yards (in length) of Street at the same time and with the top of his finger on the end of the nozzle, he imitates a very heavy shower of rain. There are a few "Hansoms" and some Omnibuses but the chief mode of conveyance is a two-wheeled Irish Car, with a sort of Oilskin head, in which the people sit back to back, like in a Dogcart. They are I consider rather dangerous and uncomfortable conveyances yet the horses seldom if ever tumble down.

Attached to the University is a very splendid Museum of Natural History, Mineralogy, etc. The specimens of birds, beasts and fishes are very grand, and well classified. There are also very good fossils including the Megatherium the Moa bird and many extinct animals. There is also a perfect Skeleton of a Whale ninety feet long which was stranded in Hobson's Bay a few years ago.

There are also models and sections of all the principal Goldfields in Australia, and the various apparatus for Gold sifting, and crushing the quartz. I took a boat and rowed up the River Yarra for several miles and saw the principal suburbs in that direction. On my return I saw several four-oared boats in training for the Regatta, to be held shortly after Easter. The boats are chiefly of English build, "Claspers" and "Salters" but the art of building racing boats is now becoming well understood in the Colonies, as several English builders have settled there and they turn out very nice Crafts.

Down all the principal streets of the Town there are streams of water running in the gutters; I do not, however, admire such natural drainage, especially as there are no under-ground sewers, as far as I can ascertain. The trains which are frequent and of light construction, are very convenient and the line running to Sandridge Pier was very useful.

I frequently required to go on board "the Suberb". There are several public gardens in which English trees are cultivated with great success; many of our Green-house plants grow out of doors and flower profusely, especially the Plumbago Capensis which is a mass of flower. The shrubs are really splendid, and with most of them I was familiarly acquainted. The Pine tree from Norfolk island is especially lovely and the tree ferns are curiously elegant and pretty.

I was deluded one day to take the train and go to Brighton,

twenty miles away, a miserable watering place on the Sea. I left the place by very next train however a wiser man. The houses have chiefly no upper story; this it is alleged is more economical especially in saving Servants. During the latter part of my stay I managed to catch a severe cold which rather interrupted the pleasure of my visit to Melbourne.

Provisions are very cheap. The common price for a Leg of Mutton is 1/6d. Vegetables are good and proportionably cheap. Fish as a rule is not good except Gar fish and Whiting—Gar-fish are about eight inches long and have a long Bill or projecting lower jaw (say three inches long) like a sword fish—they are first rate eating and very delicate in flavour.

Clothes especially are dear; 50 per Cent I should say dearer than in England; yet they are good and well made and fashions arrive out at Melbourne almost as soon as at home. The Churches I visited were orderly and well conducted: the singing was very hearty and good, but too slow for my modern notions— there was a very large and respectable Congregation in the Roman Catholic Cathedral, which is the finest Ecclesiastical building in the Town; it is still in an unfinished state, and this remark applies to almost every other public building. Altogether taking into consideration the fact that thirty three years ago there was hardly a house at all in Melbourne, I cannot but admire the very rapid progress it has made and the spirit with which the people try to reproduce the Institutions of the Mother Country, which in many instances have been improved by being modern-ized.

MONDAY 20th MARCH

Today after saying good bye to my many friends I embark on board the "Alexandra" Steamer for Sydney. I start at 3 oClock in the afternoon for what will I expect be a sixty-hour passage. During the morning I had plenty to do—sending off one of my Portmanteaus for home with dirty clothes—for the future I expect to be able from time to time to procure proper washing for my reduced stock of garments. I had also to see after my money in the Bank and write some letters for fear I should miss the Mail at Sydney. For the first day the passage was very rough and during the night the Steamer rolled very much. It was a miserably stormy night—rain and sleet with a very strong gale.

I slept on a Sofa quite in the Stern, as I preferred this to sleeping in a Cabin with two invalids, one of whom had a terrible and perpetual cough, and the other was constantly Sea sick.

TUESDAY 21st MARCH

Nothing unusual today except that weather was more favorable and we are out of sight of land during the whole day until about 8 oClock when we sight the light at Cape Howe. I may mention that we had plenty of Grapes on board the Steamer. They were grown at Adelaide and were delivered on board at 2s/6d per Cwt.—they were really very respectable to look at and well flavoured grapes—very superior to *our* own outdoor grapes.

WEDNESDAY 22nd MARCH

This was a nice day and we have a favorable wind, which makes us travel. We are in sight of land the whole day—generally about half a mile away from shore and have a capital view of some two hundred miles of Coast scenery. This at times is very pretty as the "Bush" fringes the Shore at most places. One hill we see called "Pigeon house" is peculiar from its being very like what its name implies, as it has a natural sort of Lantern on the summit.

We sight Sydney Heads about 8 oClock and pass through them about half past.

The place where the "Dunbar" was lost about three years ago "with all hands", is pointed out. She appears to have mistaken in the dark a gap in the Cliffs for the mouth of "the Heads", and in a heavy Gale to have gone with all Sail set, to her destruction. One common Sailor only survived. As it is quite dark and rains in torrents, I cannot describe the Harbour till I see it by daylight. I merely take a few Clothes with me on shore and go direct to Petty's Hotel at which I arrive at 9.30 p.m. being anxious once more to obtain a good night's rest.

THURSDAY 23rd MARCH

This morning I clear my luggage at the Custom House and find that the Mail Steamer from Honolulu is detained owing to the heavy Gale through which we came in the "Alexandra". I devote the remainder of the day to writing letters home and seeing the Town of Sydney.

I find the Mail came in during the night and see by the Papers that the "Wonga Wonga" for San Fransisco is advertised to sail on the 31st. I am disappointed that she should sail so soon as the previous announcements said she would sail on the 8th April and thus my stay at Sydney is curtailed by some eight days. I find a Letter from George waiting for me at the Post Office and I finish my letters for home which require to be posted tonight. At half past One oClock I start with a friend whom I made on board the "Alexandra" for Paramatta Groves, distant from Syndey about fifteen miles. The journey is made either by Rail or by Steamer. I prefer the latter as I thereby have the chance of seeing some portion of the Harbour.

This Harbour is about the prettiest in the World. It is composed of numberless irregular Bays running in all directions. These are fringed with high land, are well wooded, and interspersed with Rock. Amongst these Bays are the houses of many of the "Elite" of Sydney.

To show the extent of Coast-line of these various Bays, it has been computed that a man in a rowing boat could coast round the shores of these Bays in fifteen days. They run in all directions and in some instances, as for instance, Paramatta Bay, they run "inland" fifteen miles, from Port Jackson or the Main Harbour of Sydney. The journey to Paramatta was simply lovely:— one Bay after another discloses itself, each possessing new features of interest.

We pass close to Cockatoo Island, formerly the Main Convict Establishment of Sydney though now no longer used as such. The Guard houses are still standing on the beach, erected in sight of each other and thereby precluding any chance of escape. Our small Steamer calls at various stopping places on the way up.

As we proceed up the Bay the rocky woodland hills with their Gum trees, Iron-bark, stringy bark, native fig trees and tree ferns give place to more homely Mangold trees and rather flatter "home scenery". These Mangold trees grow close to the water's edge and are of thick foliage and reminded me of a thick and tall Rhodendendron hedge. They only grow near Salt water —fresh water would kill them at once. Along the hillsides there are plenty of Orange groves, the fruit of which is expected to be ripe about next June. As the tide is low, we are not able quite to reach the Town or Village of Paramatta, but we land about a mile away, and then get on a "Bus" which deposits us in the Town. We get some Luncheon at a nice small Inn at which as usual, there are two very nice looking Barmaids, and after staying a couple of hours and exploring the rather uninteresting Town we return by Steamer and reach home about 7 oClock at night.

SATURDAY 25th MARCH

This morning I went by appointment to see some friends to whom I had been introduced and with them I visited a large Tan-yard which is on a very grand and interesting scale.

Afterwards I went over some Market Gardens kept by John Baptist and which are considered to be the best in Sydney. Although the shrubs were very good and generally very much finer than in England, yet I did not consider the gardens were equal to what we have in England, as regards their Exotic and foliage plants, and the Gardener himself said that they obtained most of their best seeds direct from home. This was the Afternoon of the manning of the new Forts recently built to fortify Sydney Harbour. Accordingly we made up a party of six and started about half-past one oClock on board a fine steamer "the Colleroy" to see the fun. We anchored after going some miles just under the Forts, and we could see the targets placed in the narrow channel at "the Heads" and which were supposed to represent the enemies' Ships. Against these at a given signal Guns were fired from concealed Forts which were built so as to rake the Heads, and a very fair aim the Gunners appeared to have. After firing for a long time, a Torpedo* with an old boat placed over it, was fired by a Galvanic battery. It contained 800 lbs. of powder and raised an immense column of water to the height of quite one hundred feet into the air. It was a grand sight.

After this a small steamer called "the Thetis" with the Governor (Lord Belmore) and the chief Government Officials on board, steamed out of the Harbour and being supposed to be a Fillibustering Ship such as the Americans were ridiculously reported to be just then fitting out, was the object of attack for

* This device was more a static mine than a moving torpedo, as we use the term today. The static type of torpedo was introduced in 1805 by Robert Fulton. The self-propelling torpedo dates from 1862.

"Some minds improve by travel,
others, rather Resemble Copper Wire or
Brass Which gets the narrower by
going farther."

Tom Hood

In the following remarks which literally
speaking are "Pencillings by the way", and
which are my first attempt at keeping a
Diary, I wish at the outset to dispel the
notion my friends may perhaps entertain,
that I am anxious to write my Autobiography.
My wish for doing so arises from the feeling,
I hold very strongly, that an Autobiography
as a rule originates in an over-estimate,
which the Writer sets, either upon his own
powers of description, or of his usefulness
to his fellow man. At the same time
as some of my friends may not have
the opportunity and, I sincerely trust,
may never have similar reason for
visiting places which in the course
of a few months I expect to visit, I

have at their request, though contrary to my own previous intention and wishes, agreed to from time to time to jot down short Memoranda of incidents in my journey as they occur, and I trust that my simple endeavours to record facts from first impressions, may be a sufficient apology for any want of classification of ideas, or for the crudeness with which they are certain to be pourtrayed.

Green's Ship.
  "The Supert" "at sea" —
  8th December 1870.

A view of the Lincolnshire town of Grantham in 1860. Ten years later our diarist left here on his twenty-eight thousand mile "constitutional".

A contemporary photograph showing Flinders Street, Melbourne, in about 1872. The Port Philip Club Hotel is arrowed. *Photo. State Library of Victoria.*

A contemporary engraving showing the Melbourne race course and stands in 1865.
Reproduced from the "Illustrated Australian News", 25th November, 1867.

A contemporary photograph of Collins Street, Melbourne, looking east. *Photo.
State Library of Victoria.*

A contemporary photograph showing unfinished Roman Catholic cathedral, Melbourne, in about 1871. *Photo. State Library of Victoria.*

A contemporary photograph showing the waterfront and the Queen Street Wharf, at Auckland in the 1870s. *Auckland Public Library Photograph Coll.*

A contemporary engraving of a Chinese theatre at San Francisco. *Reproduced from "American Pictures, drawn with pen and pencil",* c. 1878.

The Bridal Veil Fall. *Reproduced from an American stereoscopic-view photograph of* c. 1900.

Inspiration Point looking down the Yosemite Valley. *Reproduced from an American stereograph photograph* 1904.

An 1870 engraving of a Central Pacific train leaving one snow shed and approaching another. *Reproduced from "American Pictures, drawn with pen and pencil".*

Observation car on Pacific Railway approaching the Great Salt Lake.

A contemporary engraving of the Mormon Tabernacle, Salt Lake City. *Reproduced from "American Pictures drawn with pen and pencil", c. 1878.*

the several field batteries and the Volunteers generally. We followed close in her wake and as a very heavy fire of blank cartridge was directed against the Steamer especially from Fort Denison, a ten Gun Fort in the River distant not more than one hundred yards from our Steamer, it may easily be imagined that the roar of the Guns was rather too loud to be pleasant. Of course all this, is well in its way, and helps to assure the nervous people in Sydney of their being well guarded. I doubt not that a first rate Iron-clad would steam straight up into the Harbour without being very much damaged, even if they knew of her coming. The Guns on the Forts are not very heavy, still they were well served, especially those by the Sailors of H.M.S. Clio which is now in the Colonies. I had some friends to dine with me afterwards and who had lost their dinner by going with me to the sight.

SUNDAY 26th MARCH

By appointment I went to St. James' Church to enquire for Mr B——'s Pew, to whom I had previously delivered my letter of introduction. After some trouble and parading round the Church, being sent from "pillar to post" by the stupid beadles of the Church, I found it. The Governor attends this church and the Congregation was a very well dressed and a fashionable one. Several of the Ladies were very good looking and dressed with much better taste than those I saw in Melbourne.

I remarked this on many occasions of my stay in Sydney, and I believe it to be an allowed fact that such is the case.

After Church and a walk of two miles with Mr. B——, I dined with him and his family and spent a very pleasant Afternoon with them. I enjoyed it much.

The Camelias in his Garden were very fine; they stand out of doors all the year round and there were several of them beautiful and well grown shrubs, twenty feet high, and which shewed a very good stock of buds for next May and June.

The house is pleasantly situate and overlooks one of the numerous Bays called Rushcutter's Bay. For the last fourteen months there has been very little else but rain in Sydney and consequently this fact afforded every apology for the inferior quality of the flowers and fruit at this particular season. In the Evening I attended a Church which was close to my Hotel where

I heard a remarkably good Sermon, quite in the Spurgeonic style, though happily devoid of any coarseness or vulgarity.

MONDAY 27th MARCH

This Afternoon I devoted to seeing the Botanical Gardens which are very tastefully laid out and all the specimens are carefully labelled. In the centres of the Gardens are two very fine Norfolk Island Pine Trees. I should judge them to be eighty feet high: these are most graceful trees and are common in and around Sydney. The Gardens also contain a nice collection of native animals and birds. Parrots and Cockatoos were well represented. There were also good specimens of Kangaroo and the Wallaby tribe. In the Evening I went to the Theatre and saw "All's well that ends well" very fairly acted. The Theatre is not so orderly as that at Melbourne, and the "Gods" take, sometimes, a more prominent part in the performance than is consistent with true pleasure to the Playgoer.

TUESDAY 28th MARCH

I engaged a Hansom Cab today and drove to Botany Bay, which is about eighteen miles from Sydney. As far as I can gather the Convict system was never carried out at this place although the general impression is that such was the case. The neighbourhood of Botany well deserves its name, as I never have seen a more beautiful collection of wild flowers than there is, on the wild Moorland through which I passed on my return to Sydney. Most of the delicate heathers which adorn our Hothouses at home are there growing in wild profusion. White heather is more common than any other colour, and there is every shade of lilac and blue heath, that can possibly be imagined.

These combined with flowering Wattles, tree grasses (resembling Bullrushes and growing eighteen and twenty feet high in their flowering stalk) and brilliant waxlike scarlet cluster flowers, the name of which I did not ascertain, make a very rich "Botany Bay". In the distance is an Obelisk erected on the spot where the great Captain Cook is said for the first time to have planted his foot on Australian soil [in 1770], and when he failed to discover Sydney's pretty Harbour, only a very few miles further on than the place where he happened to land.

WEDNESDAY 29th MARCH

I spent this morning in riding on Omnibuses which went in different directions to the Suburbs of Sydney, and in the Afternoon I went with Mr. B. B. who kindly offered to be my Guide over the University, a very fine building; so fine that I think it rather anticipates the requirements of the Colony. From the top of the Central tower is obtained a magnificent view of the neighbourhood and from that elevation I gathered a very useful lesson in the local Geography of Sydney.

THURSDAY 30th MARCH

This morning I devoted to private business part of which consisted in taking my passage in the "Wonga Wonga"* for San Francisco for which I paid £40 and partly in having my hair cut at "Caffyn's" who has a good shop in George Street, the principal Street of Sydney, and with whom I spent a long time "yarning" on Cricket as played in the Colonies and "at home". His opinion appeared to be that Colonial Cricketers would play better, if they had ever seen *really first* rate Cricket; but that at present they never had seen any, and consequently they were devoid of the "finish", which is the distinguishing mark of our best players.† After arranging my money matters at the Bank I kept an appointment I had made to drive out to Sydney Heads, in a very nice light private Buggy and pair. The Buggy was well appointed, and the pair of Cobs stepped well together, and as the journey was romantic, and our party select, we had a very pleasant afternoon. As we passed the shore we saw some Fishermen netting. We therefore stopped the Carriage and purchased from them some small fish called "yellow-tails" and two "Squid" (which are the "Sea devils" as described in Victor Hugo's "Toilers of the Sea") which were to serve as bait for a fishing day we had arranged for tomorrow.

In the Evening I took a Cab and paid P.P.C. calls upon several friends who had been very kind to me during my visit.

FRIDAY 31st MARCH

This morning my friends and I were "up with the lark" and trudged

---

* "Wonga Wonga", the Australian name of a Pigeon—very swift.
† The England *v.* Australia Test Matches date from the winter of 1876–7. The Australians first beat a full England side in August, 1892.

after breakfast to Woolloomooloo Bay, where we had arranged to meet three friends with whom we were to go fishing. We soon found them and set sail in a small boat in the direction of Shark Island about four miles down the Bay. Having anchored the boat we proceeded to "deep Sea fish" and we soon succeeded in catching a choice and varied assortment of fish; Mackarel; Flatheads; (six and eight lbs. each); Rock Cod (a venomous stinging fish resembling a Perch, made of red coral, but very good to eat); Fiddle fish; a large sort of Mackerel about 4 lbs weight which was cut up for bait; Bream (called "Brim"; both black and red) and several kinds of other fish of every colour many of them peculiarly marked with stripes. In the middle of the day we landed on a small wooded island and having pulled down some dead trees, we made a fire in a crevice of the rock. When the Embers had died down, we placed a quantity of Beef steak upon a Gridiron, and cooked it splendidly and at the same time we roasted some Onions in the fire. During the time this was cooking, some of the party were engaged procuring Oysters on the Rocks, while others were engaged, scaling and preparing some of the fish we had caught, which were to be broiled for our second course.

We then proceeded to demolish the Steak and Onions, which were done "to a turn", and regale the inner man with a copious supply of "Bass". Afterwards we had the broiled fish, by way of dessert, and the dinner on the whole was as great a success as can well be imagined, and hardly to be surpassed for its primitive excellency.

After dinner we caught several more fish of various kinds, and arrived home with a favorable breeze about 8 oClock. I forgot to mention we caught a kind of Shark called a "War-biggen" about fourteen lbs. in weight. As he was a very awkward customer to have in our boat, we pulled him alongside, and after treating him to a very heavy blow on the head with the "Tiller", as his head was on the boat side, we let him sink with the broken hook in his mouth to the bottom, soon doubtless to become a prey to the hundreds of his black brethren who are the scourge and curse to all people who accidentally find themselves in the water of the Bay. So numerous and voracious are they that it is very dangerous indeed to have even your hand over the boat side. In the Bay there are also thousands of the red stinging jelly fish (Medusa) which are also common on our own shores, but which are present here in immense quantities. I ascertained "by accident" tonight that the Steamer "Wonga Wonga" for San Francisco did not start at 9 oClock in the morning, as had been previously advertised, but at 4 to-morrow Afternoon. This delighted me as I had but little time for packing, etc. which I had delayed to do, until the last moment. As originally advertised she was to sail on 8th April but her time of departure had, contrary to my wishes and inclination been altered to the 1st of the month. In this respect I could fully realise "All fools' day" as I lost the best part of my proposed stay in Sydney.

Chapter 3

SATURDAY 1st APRIL TO GOOD FRIDAY THE 7th, 1871

We left Sydney this Evening at 8 oClock for Auckland having about twenty passengers on board. These the Ship could accommodate nicely and there were not more than two in each Cabin. The Steamer is 687 tons Register and notwithstanding that she has been lengthened, is not sufficiently large for the trade for which she is used: for the first three days we have a very rough and disagreeable passage—the Deck is perpetually deluged with Sea water and heavy showers and fog are of frequent occurrence. I am glad to say that about Wednesday we have a change in the weather; and thanks to the lightening of the Ship by the consumption of Coal, we are in better trim and ship fewer "Green Seas" than we did when we started. Most of the Passengers are Sea sick at first, but they gradually recover and appear on Deck towards Thursday. We sight land called the "Three Kings" islands on Thursday morning and after this we steam round the North and East shores of Auckland, the Northern Province of the North Island of the group composing New Zealand.

GOOD FRIDAY 7th APRIL

About half past 8 this morning we are entering the Harbour of Auckland, and a very pretty sight is before us. Although this Harbour is not equal to Sydney, still it has many objects of interest. The surrounding Country is especially fresh and fertile, and presents many traces of civilized cultivation. The town is almost Crescent shape and is built at the end of a pretty Bay. The dwelling houses are generally small and one-storied— hence the principal buildings such as the Court house and the Governor's house shew themselves to great advantage. There is only one principal street which runs in continuation of the landing Pier. The time of our actual arrival is delayed by reason of our Pilot fouling a Brig which was in our track and prevented our swinging properly alongside the Pier. We therefore make a large circuit of the Harbour and on the next attempt we are properly moored to the Pier. It being Good Friday, all the Shops are closed and we therefore are without the opportunity of judging of the merits of the Town. Our only chance appears to be to hire a Carriage and see the Country. This we do, and a R.C. Priest who is one of our Passengers accompanies us. We drive to Onehunga (One-e-hunger) where we leave our Priest with an old College friend of his, who kindly affords us every hospitality and "entertains strangers" like a true Apostle. We have a good view of Manukau Harbour, near to which the Orpheus was lost a few years ago, and we drive on to a small Inn at Otahuhu. Of course being Good Friday, we had fish (Snapper) for dinner, and this combined with other delicacies made for us a fair dinner for so outlandish a place. One of the things which strikes a stranger in the Colonies is the enormous amount of flies which pester you especially at Meal times. A stranger to these parts really can hardly form any notion of their numbers. They constantly settle on your face and "a new chum" is found out at once, as he is constantly brushing them away with his hand, while a "regular Colonist" can let them crawl all over his face without moving, or being tickled in the least by them.

The appearance of the Country is Volcanic and there are numbers of small hills which bear, on the very face of them, evident traces of being extinct Volcanoes, and that too at no very distant time. The soil is particularly fertile and were it not for the Mäories ("Mowries"), who at times are very quarrelsome and treacherous, the squatters would quickly be repaid for their exertions. From the drive we had of some twelve or fourteen miles into the Country we could form a very fair notion of its character, and I confess I was favorably impressed with what I saw of it. Just at this time there is a great Gold fever raging about seventy miles away, in the Thames Gold fields, and the Papers which we procured on our arrival announced that one

57

Claim (the Caledonian) had during the last month yielded no less than "one ton of *pure* Gold"!! The shares in this Mine which were only £12 paid up are now at £103.! In the Town of Auckland there are lots of Mäories to be seen, walking about in ordinary clothes, though their tattooed faces and dark complexions at once proclaim their being Aborigines. The Mäori women are absolutely hideous, yet there are some of the half castes who are very handsome, and who are frequently married to Europeans. The Steamer left the Harbour for Honolulu at 10 oClock in the Evening and although I had every wish to stay longer in so romantic and pretty a Country, yet I could not afford to lose my Passage money and so I once more entrusted myself to the tender mercies of our rolling and over-laden Steamer.

SATURDAY 8th APRIL

At Auckland we received a fresh number of Passengers (over twenty I believe) the consequence is that four are stowed away into each small Cabin of the Ship, and as two Cabins join at one Washstand it is a work of considerable time, and at a loss of some temper, that one's ablutions are performed in the Morning. Yet I believe in the old saying of "More the merrier" and as most of the Passengers have travelled on many previous occasions they are well used to "endure" things which cannot be "cured". We have in all one hundred and two passengers of which number about fortyeight are in the Saloon. During last night we were forced to stop the Engines for four hours owing to the dense fog which prevailed, and we were too near land to steam with safety. The day was rather rough and unpleasant.

SUNDAY 9th APRIL—EASTER DAY

We had Service this Morning and a very fine day indeed. Lat: 33.00 S. Lon: 178.30 E. Dist: 220 miles.

MONDAY 10th

This day we pass close to an active Volcanic rock called Curtis' Island. Smoke was issuing from the side of the rock. Afterwards we pass another fertile island called Macaulay's island on which there are said to be large flocks of Goats; these are of great service to the various Whalers who frequent these grounds and who go on shore to catch them. We distinguished some Goats on the island, which was about three miles away. About 7 oClock in the Evening we pass "Sunday island" which about six months ago was subjected to a violent Earthquake and Volcanic eruption which rent the whole island. There were two white men on the island and one woman. The two men quarrelled seriously, and each went about (one American) (one English) with Revolvers determined to shoot each other. The Volcanic disturbance put an end I hear to one of them. There were volumes of smoke still issuing from it. The men lived by growing Cabbages and Potatoes which they sold to the Whalers. Lat: 30.12. Lon: 178.25. Dist: 231 miles.

MONDAY 10th ANTIPODES DAY

It appears strange to have two Mondays in one week yet such is the case with people who go round the world. A simple explanation appears as follows:- Imagine a fly walking round a Grindstone. The Grindstone makes say one hundred and eighty revolutions and the fly walks once round the Grindstone during *this time*, i.e. he makes one hundred and eighty one revolutions in the same time—hence if he were walking towards the East he would see the Sun one hundred and eighty one times or have one hundred and eighty one days, while in reality, the Grindstone would have only gone one hundred and eighty times round; hence I (the fly) have *to insert* one day during my tour round the World, in order to keep the proper date of the month, when I arrive in America. Lat: 27.21. Lon: 175.47 W. Dist: 210 miles.

TUESDAY 11th APRIL

Splendid weather—quite calm. Lat: 24.30 S. Lon: 173.34 W. Dist: 219 miles.

WEDNESDAY 12th APRIL

Fair and calm—smooth as glass.

We have a Fiddler and a Girl playing the Harp on board. In the Evenings we have any amount of singing and dancing. Choruses are the great institution and several of the Officers and Crew sing well. Lat: 21.31. Lon: 171.39 W. Dist. 208 miles.

THURSDAY 13th APRIL

Awoke at 6 oClock. Savage Island about fifty miles in circumference is four miles to "leeward". We can easily distinguish the Missionary Station, a large white building, with its Flagstaff. While we are gazing landwards we see through our Glasses several Canoes putting off from shore. The Captain kindly consents to stop the Engines for half an hour. Presently the Canoes some dozen or two, each with four men, paddle up alongside. The Canoes are propelled by four copper colored "Carnaccas" with short spade-like paddles—there are long outriggers, boomed out at the side of each Canoe, to keep them steady—the outriggers stretch out about twelve feet from the side of the Canoe and float on the water.

The Men are well proportioned and finely made. Their dress consists of a Straw hat and a sort of Shirt, and they bring for barter lots of War instruments, also Cocoa nuts, Bananas, Water Melons and a few curiosities. Some of them can speak a little English and an American Captain we had on Board on addressing one of them and asking for "Cocoa nuts" received the reply "Hand on a minnit" spoken very distinctly and very quickly. One of them asked "One pound" for something he had —he was offered half a Sovereign but it was suggested it were better to offer a one shilling piece which he preferred to the half Sovereign as there was more of it in bulk, and when two shilling pieces were offered, he closed at once with the bargain. We got several Cocoa nuts in exchange for small pieces of Tobacco, which they prize greatly, much more so than money. In one of the canoes there was a Native woman who was tolerably good looking and dressed in a sort of Man's Shirt—this dress while satisfying all the requirements of decency, disclosed beautifully turned bare limbs, such as any English woman might justly envy, or might without vanity be proud of.

Less than fifteen years ago the Islanders were barbarous and cannibals, and it was unsafe for travellers to land at all. Ships never went near it, unless they had a strong wind, for fear of being attacked. Now there is no fear if you want to barter for provisions. We sent the Missionary some of our newspapers. The Engines were turned ahead whilst three of the natives were on board our Ship, still bartering. As the Canoes had drifted a mile away astern, our Captain took up a rope's end and laid it about them; whereupon they quickly got over the side and all three with one consent, took the water like so many ducks, and floated away still holding their valuables high above their heads. I expect their Canoes would pick them up; if not, we were then not more than two miles from shore and they appeared to be quite at home in the water.

I forgot to mention that some of the men's backs were bare, and on these the flies had settled as thick as could be; no doubt being fond of Cocoa-nut Oil, with which they rub themselves. They reminded me of a Dog in Summer, who has been rolling in something, which attracts the flies' attention. Our stock of flies on board has greatly increased in consequence of the visit we received from these Islanders.

FRIDAY 14th APRIL TO SUNDAY 23rd APRIL 1871

[The diary records only the Latitude and Longitude and the distance travelled each day, a total mileage of 2,053 miles in ten days sailing.]

MONDAY 24th

I have previously described a long Sea Voyage and I don't find anything particular has taken place during the days I have just recorded together. We are now approaching Honolulu and expect to arrive on Tuesday night or Wednesday Morning. The first part of our journey from Auckland was remarkable for the fine weather we enjoyed. We had no South East Trades to speak of, and what wind we had, was against us. The North East Trades are also against us, and are very strong and they cause us a good deal of rolling and tossing. Before we passed the Equator we had very hot weather and our Cabins were stifling and intolerably close. We are also very crowded at Meal times. In fact the "Wonga" is not equal to the Trade for which she is engaged, and they must have larger Steamers or they will lose credit. The food is just bearable, but all "drink" is bad and very dear. Lat: 16.45. Lon: 157.54. Dist: 210 miles.

TUESDAY 25th APRIL 1871

The great inconvenience we suffer from, want of Air, is caused by the Ports being too low in the water; and consequently we are never able to have them opened; therefore our crowded Cabins are unpleasant. The Main Deck is higher than the Stern, hence the Second class Cabins are better than ours, as far as fresh air goes. Our intention last Thursday was to have touched at Fanning Island but, it being very low land, we found ourselves fifteen miles away to windward, and as it was so far out of our course, the Captain could not stop at it, though he wished to have done so.

There are very few birds to be seen in the Pacific. We have seen some Tropical or Boatswain birds. They are White birds and have only two long narrow feathers nearly a yard long for a tail. This has a funny appearance. We have seen several "Boobies" and also some "Man of War Hawks". Flying fish of a larger size abound. We also saw a dead Whale floating past us about two hundred yards from us. Towards the latter part of our journey the food becomes nauseous and we long to get on shore. During Tuesday morning the 25th April we have land in sight for some time, viz. the two small islands of Mawi and Molokai.

Lat: 20.39. Lon: 157.34. Dist: 234 miles, or 39 Dist. from Honolulu.

Hawaii which is the largest and most Southernmost of the Sandwich islands Group was some distance East of us. This island is remarkable for being the highest known island; it is 13,760 feet high or five hundred feet higher than "Mount Cook" in New Zealand. On this island is also an enormous Volcano called Kilauea, twenty-three miles in circumference, said to be the largest in the World. We were unable to visit this spot, however, as it takes more than a week for the small local Steamer to go round the islands.

About one oClock we sight in the distance "Oahu" the island on which Honolulu is situate.

We make the land very slowly, as we have a high Trade wind and a rough Sea running against us. When we get nearer the Shore we have also a very heavy rain and fog, which unfortunately hides a very pretty picture from our view. Honolulu* lies at the bottom of a high circle of hills about 4,000 feet high. Its appearance is most picturesque. There are a few Spires of

* The capital of Hawaii. The islands were annexed to the United States in 1898 but became an independent state in 1959. The American naval base of Pearl Harbour is here situated.

Churches dotted amongst a number of wooden houses, and amongst these there are numerous Cocoa-nut and Palm trees, besides other very beautiful trees. The hills are remarkably green and boldly Conical and are mostly covered with a bright green "scrub". There is a Wharf, to gain which, we go through rather an intricate Channel; and our Pilot, who does not appear to know his work very well, ran us against the Pier and destroyed a large portion of the Woodwork.

We find that the "Moses Taylor" for San Francisco is not yet in, and so it is impossible to estimate the length of our stay in the island. There really is no Hotel in the Town, and although a party of four of us, agree to stay at the "Globe Hotel", yet this in reality is merely a Lodging house.

Eventually we stay here six days and I was most agreeably surprised with the place.

There is a King Kamehama the 5th who is Brother in law to Queen Emma. There is also a good Government quite a miniature Edition of our own form of Government. The laws of the Country are practical and good. A very heavy duty is imposed on Spirituous liquors of all kinds, and an Excise License costs £200 a year. Hence there are only six Public houses or "Drinking Bars" in the place. At only one Shop do they sell Opium and the License to do so costs £2,000 a year.

The Education is under [the] Government and so excellent are the provisions of the State that every Man and Woman is said to be able to read and write. I visited some of the Schools and heard the method of teaching, and I must say, that both the Teachers and the taught, were much better up to their work than our English Schools generally. Their Arithmetic and Parsing were first rate. The Natives are remarkably clean; men and women (as a rule) bathe themselves two or three times a day. Of course the "Carnaccas" are very dark, yet they are by no means repulsively ugly, and the women especially, have intelligent eyes and look clean and neat. The half castes are as a rule very good looking.

One of the provisions of the State is that before a White man can obtain a Seat in the Government, or be entitled to be a "good Citizen", he must marry a Native woman—hence there are plenty of half castes. The Women dress in a long sort of long Smock, which reaches the ground and is pleated from the Shoulders, and hangs loosely: it is generally made of black serge, or else of some very gaudy print—they do not wear Shoes (as a rule); and they all walk, and carry themselves, remarkably well. The women ride on horseback "straddlewise", like the men—the proper riding dress is a short "body", and trousers, coming high up the waist, of different colours, and from each leg they have a flowing skirt or habit; they ride very well and very shortly you become quite accustomed to the unusual style they ride in, as they sit a horse remarkably well. Queen Emma has a nice house in the Town, and they have a very fair Military Band, which has been taught by an Englishman. The people are especially civil and polite to Englishmen, and although I went amongst the lowest, as well as good Society, I never met with any incivility or rudeness.

On the day after our arrival we were pleased to find that an English Ironclad "the Zealous" the Flag Ship of the Pacific Squadron had called at Honolulu and proposed to stay there some days. My present travelling companion (who is an Officer in the Royal Engineers and a "Magdala man") and I made the acquaintance of some of the Officers and exchanged with them complimentary dinners and similar civilities. While we were dining on board we had the opportunity of thoroughly inspecting the Ship and were introduced to most of the Officers and left Cards on the Admiral.

Whilst I was reading in a local paper the names of the Officers, I discovered that the Chaplain was The Revd. Henry Alexander and upon enquiry I found out that it was my old friend the Vicar of Shelford.* It was by the merest accident I discovered him.

As the Officer from whom I enquired informed me that he was just then on shore, I went to the Wharf and intercepted him, as he was leaving to go on board again. The natural upshot of this was another invitation to Luncheon, on Sunday, and my friend (who also received an invitation from another Officer) and I had the Steam Launch sent for us at 11.30 A.M. especially to convey us to the Ship, which was lying some two miles away; there not being sufficient water for her to come inside the Bar. The Officers were exceedingly jolly, and I greatly regretted that time would not permit us to accept the many and pressing invitations we received, to enjoy a free passage with them to San Francisco. I had however taken a through ticket, and as they

* Near Nottingham, some twenty miles west of Grantham.

were going a week later than we were and "under sail" I could not sacrifice a month of my time, reserved for seeing America, even to enjoy the society of such hospitable and jolly fellows. During my stay I had several long rides across the island and into the Country—there are but few roads and those are not good.

Sugar is cultivated extensively and one Planter said, that owing to the stringency of the Excise laws (which prohibited the making of Rum) he annually poured into the Sea £5,000 worth of refuse from his Sugar Mills, which he might otherwise have converted into that amount in value of Rum.

The principal Native food is Paui (Pow-e) which is made from the Yarro plant. This is a bulbous plant with a leaf like the "Calladium" or Arum, and is planted in large beds which are constantly irrigated and kept flooded.

The root is dried and baked by the Natives. When ground down and mixed with water it forms a thick white fluid. It is then put into Calabashes, or large Pumpkins cut longitudinally, and which are suspended by Network bags from the two ends of a stick, and carried about by Natives for sale.

It has a sour and disagreeable taste, and the idea that the Natives eat it with their fingers, and have a habit of constantly taking "sly sips" at it, and then licking their fingers, does not tend to heighten one's desire to join them.

The Chinese (as is common everywhere as far as I can discover) are here too very enterprising and industrious. I dined and fed every day at a Chinese Restaurant. The Cooking was clean and good and very English like—they evidently affect our style as much as possible.

As regards money, the American Coinage prevails here, though your "change" comprises money of almost all Nations.

English Silver is sadly at a discount—you can only get 1s/6d in value for a two shilling piece, and about 1s/9d or 2s/- for 2s/6d; and you lose 1s/- in each Sovereign. Any one, coming from America, can buy our Sovereigns at 19s/- each. Shillings however are better and go as quarter dollars, and no glass of drink is sold under a quarter dollar a glass.

I would recommend any one who wishes to bring money from England, to bring it out, for general purposes, in the shape of sixty day Bills of Exchange, drawn on London; as upon these you lose only 10 Cents or less than upon any other kind of money. If the Bills are for £20 or for £25 (say) they are nearly always negociable; even Merchants will take them from you, at current rates of exchange if there are not any Banks in the Town where you happen to be staying.

The Natives out of the Town of Honolulu live mostly in Grass huts—they easily manage to live without fires—Honolulu being in the same latitude as Calcutta. They never, as far as I could discover, use Chairs; but men and women "squat down" on their haunches for any length of time—this is also their mode of sitting, indoors as well as out, especially the common people. The women smoke as much as the men, and you may see black beauties, who have only one pipe on the Establishment, take about five puffs and then pass the pipe to their next dark friend, and so round the domestic circle. I must however add that the inelegant amount of spitting, which succeeds the five puffs of Tobacco, is not in character with the superior education I have before mentioned, and is out of proportion to the amount of Tobacco, each "laughing-eyed beauty" has indulged in.

On Sunday Evening I attended the English Church. When I first looked through the Church Porch and viewed the interior, I fancied that we had made a mistake and had arrived at the Roman Catholic Establishment, as there were Candles and a large Cross in front of the Reredos. I went in, however, and during the Service I failed to discover anything more of the High Church character, than is usual in English Churches, and from what I could judge, the Service and the Parish work generally were well attended to.

MONDAY 1st MAY 1871

The Steamer "Ajax" which had taken the place of the "Moses Taylor" was advertised to sail today at 6 oClock—this Steamer was originally built as a Gunboat for the United States Navy, and, being just finished at the end of the War, was sold with several others for the Passenger trade. She is after the American plan and is very high out of the water, having a large Hurricane deck built upon her Aft Main Deck. Hence she is able to carry many extra Passengers. She is a great contrast to the "Wonga Wonga" having plenty of room and good ventilation. The arrangement as regards Stewards is also very good, and their waiting at Table is first rate. Everything is remarkably clean and tidy. The Stewards who wait at Table all move at the signal of a bell, which the chief Steward rings at various periods of the Meal. These signals they instantly obey and by so doing they manage to bring the meat hot to Table. They are also very civil and obliging and although I heard very bad accounts of the way "feeding" was conducted on board, I must say I am most agreeably surprised. The Steamer is not rapid yet she appears to be tolerably safe and seaworthy, though I must confess we have not had any bad weather to try her. The food also is very good especially the various kinds of Corn Cakes so much in vogue in the "States" and which we indulge in with Treacle or "Golden Syrup" at Breakfast. The drink on board however is very dear and not good—the reason alleged as to the high price of liquors is the enormous protective duty on spirits, etc. imported into the States.

We brought about ten lean Cattle on board from Honolulu. One of these is killed each day. This rate of butchering is not too great considering that we have two hundred and fifty grown up people on board. During our Voyage we have nothing very unusual occurring. The Ocean called Pacific does not belie its name and with the exception of the constant rolling of our lofty and apparently disproportioned Ship, we never experience anything but a calm Sea with a heavy swell, rolling up on our beam. The Voyage as a rule is almost devoid of interest in objects of Natural history and we scarcely see any birds. On one occasion in the 10th of May we ran through, for a distance of about fifteen miles, an innumerable and unusually large shoal of diminutive "Portuguese Men of War" which covered the Ocean, far and near, like Snow flakes. They were very small about the size of one's Thumb-nail, and speculation said they were young ones; at all events they were much less in size than those I saw in the Atlantic which were as large as my fist. We also saw numerous floating fish which were said to be a species of Barnacle. They were first supposed to be a sort of Sea weed and from the Ship's Deck appeared to float in the water, like the head of some flower (say a brown rose) but on closer examination they were found to be crustaceous fish, with spreading tentacles which expanded and disclosed numerous small feelers, which they extended and withdrew at pleasure, and with which they can attach themselves to any object. During the last four or five days the weather has become quite chilly and we have once more assumed our Winter Clothes.

[The diary records only basic details from the ship's log for the period 2nd May to 11th May. During these ten days 1,853 miles were covered.]

Chapter 4

THURSDAY 12th MAY, 1871

About 12 oClock today we pass some small rocky islands called South Farallons (Faral-y-one), which are protected by a substantial Lighthouse. On the largest of them, we can see a great number of what are said to be Seals (but which in reality are Sea Lions) basking on the rocks. They are generally six feet long and are of a yellowish brown color. They dash off the rocks into the water, and swim about at pleasure. They are very common on this Coast. We also saw large flocks of birds mostly divers, Sea Parrots, and Shag, besides numerous other birds whose names I was not able to ascertain.

About two miles outside the far famed Golden Gate, the entrance into San Francisco Bay, we had to cross a long Bar of Sand and Mud, caused by the settling of the Mud and Drift Sand from the Gold Fields, at a certain place.

The most remarkable phenomenon connected with the Bar was the distinctness of the line of demarcation, as shewn by the different color of the water on either side of it. This was said to be not usual, except in certain winds. At times the wind causes the water on the Bar to be very rough, and many a Ship which has braved the perils of Ocean, has had her boats washed away in crossing this natural breakwater. On your right before you enter the Golden Gate, stands a large White House well placed on the high Cliff. It is properly called "Cliff House". It is the resort of most of the "holiday-makers" from San Francisco who go there, more especially to obtain a nice view of the Sea, and also the numerous semi-tame Sea Lions, which congregate

69

on the rocks and which are not allowed to be hunted or disturbed in any way. I am now passing through the far famed "Golden Gate", which consists of two picturesque rocks on either shore* and after steaming some eight miles past several Forts and up the Bay, we arrive at the Pier.

A large Steamer being in possession of part of our Wharf causes us an hour's delay in getting alongside. Eventually we do so and after the Custom House Officers have minutely examined our Luggage we take a Coach and go to the "Occidental Hotel" about a mile away in the Town of San Francisco. There are four good Hotels in San Francisco, the Grand, Occidental, Lick House and Cosmopolitan. They are built on the usual American plan—the front of the Ground floor is devoted principally to Shops. There is a very fine Hall or Vestibule in which smoking is allowed, and where men appoint to meet one another. The Bar is distinct from the Hotel and you pass through a splendid Billiard room to it. The Billiard room has thirteen American Tables in it. The Carpet cost £750 and was made expressly for it. There is a convenient "Lift" from the Hall which is greatly in request. In the large Dining room there are many Ladies dining with their husbands, or "without" as the case may be. Many families live entirely at Hotels. After a good dinner with Ice and Strawberries and Cream (to any extent) we went in search of a Chinese Theatre. It is a dirty place. We had the plot of the Play interpreted to us by a young Chinese—but one Play lasts for many Evenings. The Music was horrible, yet it was the chief part of the performance. Some of the "Swells" in the Boxes took off their Boots and sat with their feet over the side of the Box, a rather inelegant proceeding (to say the least of it). The Chinese quarter is one of the lowest that can be imagined.

SATURDAY 13th MAY

The greater part of today I spent in making calls upon friends to whom I had letters of introduction, and in arranging and planning our Excursion to Yosemite for Monday. This was most perplexing, for no sooner had you made up your mind to follow one Man's advice, than another came up directly and gave your first adviser "the lie direct" behind his back and assured you most plausibly, and with evidence which you had no power to

* The famous Golden Gate bridge was not then built; it was completed in 1937.

confute that his was the only feasible plan. As there were something like six different routes, we were greatly vexed and eventually very uncivil to any one offering gratuitous information. This question continued to vex us until we had taken our tickets, and thus put an end to further uncertainty.

In the Evening we went about 7.30 to a large and elegant Skating Rink at which was advertised a Grand Bal Masque to be given by the Members of the San Francisco Skating Club.

The Hall or Dancing floor of the very finest board was some 300 feet long by 150 broad.

A Gallery and Seats are all round the Hall and these were filled with several thousands of nicely dressed people. There was a nice Band playing in the centre. At the given time seventy-five couples, in Skates on small Wheels, came hand in hand down the room headed by The Master of Ceremonies. Many of them were dressed in Costume, the M.C. being dressed as a French Zouave. Then they danced a pretty Skating Cotillion, which lasted about half an hour and which consisted chiefly in a sort of "follow my leader" through very intricate figures and constantly, with great precision, emerging in long line each to rejoin his own Partner— Ladies and Gentlemen each following in distinct lines.

After this came some good "fancy Skating" altogether, and then all the Skaters gave way for Miss Carrie A. Moore said to be "the finest Lady Skater in the World".

This was a good looking and well dressing young Lady, the "Professional" of the Rink.

She was beautifully dressed in Blue trimmed with Swans' Down and a pretty Gipsey hat and had a moderately short dress on. The elegant way in which she danced and skated surpassed anything I ever saw or perhaps shall see; and I willingly confess, that for Ladylike grace, and elegance of posture and everything else, I never saw any Ballet Girl who is fit to be compared with her, or any public performance which I applauded with more genuine pleasure.

SUNDAY 14th MAY

All Shops etc are open today as usual; so are the Theatres. The Japan Steamer "The Great Republic" having arrived last night I was anxious to go on board her and confirm the good accounts I had heard of this line of Steamers. She is the largest and most comfortable Steamer I have yet seen, and allowing for the height she is out of water, I should consider her a pretty good Sea-Boat. She is admirably fitted up with every appliance for escape in case of fire, or other emergency, and her whole appearance betokens great care and cleanliness. In the Afternoon I went to "Cliff House" by a road used as the great trotting road of San Francisco, on which I saw plenty of Trotters and smart Buggies.

At Cliff House I had a good view of the Seals or Sea Lions, but I was rather disappointed in the view, as a dense Sea-fog unfortunately prevailed while I was there. The Sea Lions are preserved from molestation by a Special Act of the Legislature in their behalf.

MONDAY 15th MAY

After depositing my heavy luggage and surplus Cash in the baggage room of the Occidental Hotel, to await my return from Yosemite, with three friends I crossed over the Bay of San Francisco to the Station of the Central Pacific Railroad. I only took a small Valise and my Field glasses. We left San Francisco at 4 p.m. for Lathrop, where we changed for Modesta, 102 miles from San Francisco.

On arriving at Modesta at 9 p.m., after great difficulty, we secured beds and retired very soon as we had to be up early. At one Hotel so great was the rush of people that eight men were supposed to sleep in one room.

TUESDAY 16th MAY

Up at 5.30, and started with nine other passengers on a Coach and four Horses, for Coulterville distant forty nine miles. The first part of the journey was rather flat and dusty and through an immense tract of undulating and parched up Corn fields. There was a "Track" and that is about all you can say for roads. Our Coach was the common Stage of America, having a low body on low wheels, and on this account it is not easily upset. At the first change of horses we had a fresh and unbroken horse, which refused to draw at any price. It lay down, then backed and reared, then lay down again, and would not start, until the driver by flogging him over the head, and my belabouring him behind, as he lay sulking, with a thick rope halter, for several minutes we fairly cured his bad temper and got him on his legs again. After the driver had driven him round quietly a few times, we got under weigh and the vicious brute afterwards did his work very well. About noon, we cross the Tuolumine River by a very capitally constructed ferry boat, which was attached to an iron rope, run across the Steam, by two Pulleys, fore and aft, which glided along the smooth iron rope. These Pulleys were attached by ropes to the Boat and by lengthening the ropes (or the distance between the pulleys and the boat) the latter could be steered to the greatest nicety while the Current propelled the boat across. The arrangement was decidedly ingenious and took our fancy greatly. We were now for the first time introduced to California Gold fields of which more hereafter. We had our dinner at "Le Grange" a small Village close to the River and in an hour proceeded on our way. This being only the second trip of our Coach this Season, and as we went straight across a Mountainous Grass Country, interspersed here and there with stones, and watercourses, now for the most part dry, you can imagine our ride was not of the smoothest character.

After changing horses again we had very hilly roads, some of which were very steep and by no means pleasant to drive down yet we arrived at 6 oClock at the Town or Village of Coulterville. In the palmy days of Gold digging, this was a flourishing place but now many houses were empty, and property had depreciated from the enormous prices paid in the "Golden Age". We slept for the night at a quiet unpretending Inn, and went to bed as usual early and very tired.

WEDNESDAY 17th MAY

We left Coulterville this morning at half past 4 oClock without Breakfast.

After a long walk up hill, where it was impossible for the Horses to drag the Coach with any people inside it, and after a long ride of twelve miles, we arrived for Breakfast at Bowers Cave. This is a remarkable place, and the Cave consists of a large hollow in the rocks, with a crystal pool of water about forty feet deep at the bottom of it.

Here we found, in rich profusion, some Alpine plants especially House leek in full flower. We had a good Breakfast à la Français at a small Inn kept by cleanly disposed French people. Their Omelettes were very good and the Meal may, in

American phraseology, be fairly styled "a square meal". We then started up a long zig-zag drive on the side of steep Mountains which were at times unpleasant to look down, especially for those who have any ideas of turning "giddy". This drive continued for about fourteen miles, the greater part of which was, as I say, on the extreme verge of steep hills. This led us over the top of Pilot Peak, which is the highest in that Neighbourhood, being over 10,000 feet above the Sea. The top was partially covered with Snow, and the Pine Forests which covered the countless Peaks on either side, for miles distant, made the scenery remarkably grand and wild.

The Coach road was very narrow and allowed only six inches on either side of the wheels and as it was built up in many places with logs of timber and earth, and overhung the sides of the hills, which were cut to furnish the ballast for the road, and as the turns which we invariably took for safety's sake at a swing Canter with four horses (the leaders galloping) were very sudden and sharp, our ride to Hazle Green, which we reached about 2 oClock was quite exciting enough to be really interesting. As we were rather late in arriving at Hazle Green which is merely a Log Hut in the midst of dense Forest, we proceeded at once to get Saddle horses and place our luggage on the back of a pack Mule which we drove before us. We had now five miles to ride to Crane Flat for Luncheon so we galloped, whenever the steep descent did not compel us to get off and lead our horses. On arriving we found that the Proprietor of the Wooden Shanty which they were pleased to designate an "Hotel" had only arrived the previous day, and it required a great deal of "blarney" and coaxing on our part to induce a bad tempered Irishwoman to give us anything at all to eat. Good words in the end prevailed, to induce her to furnish for us some Mutton Chops. I unfortunately drew down upon myself a great storm of female abuse, because I took some Bread and Jam which were placed on the Table as preliminaries to our more formal meal and to which I helped myself without our sharp-tempered Hostess' leave. Hungry men however can put up with almost anything, and after making her a lot of polite speeches, she so far apologised to me as to say "she had had some *civil* Gentlemen there yesterday who knew how to behave themselves" and then she afterwards added "she thought I was like one of them in the face". I put the best construction I could upon this equivocal compliment which

74

caused a great laugh, at my expense, from my jolly companions. After a rough ride we arrived in day light at the descent into the Yosemite Valley. Here we all got off and led our horses two miles down a very steep and ugly zig-zag.

The horses are trained and follow very well but it is very steep and in places the stones and rocks are troublesome.

The horses brought up in these parts seldom slip with their fore-legs, which save their blundering hind legs very often. I thought nothing could have saved one of our horses which slipped its hind leg between two large stones, right up to its hough, as it was going down a very steep and winding way; it however had the sense to stop and draw its leg straight out, and then proceed quietly on its journey.

When we arrived in the Valley, we had still six miles to ride (making a total of twenty three miles on horseback by the "Coulterville Trail"). It was now growing dark, our party became divided, and as I unfortunately was in the division which was without a guide, we lost our way and also the trail. By keeping close however to the bank of the River Mercèd, which we knew ran in a certain direction through the Valley, and making some enquiries from the wretched Indians, we at last came to the Sentinel Hotel kept by a Mr. Black. Here we had a good Supper, and after smoking out of doors round a good Pine log fire, which the Guides, and "hangers on" generally, had made for their own benefit, we went to bed.

THURSDAY 18th MAY AND FRIDAY 19th MAY

When so many people have failed adequately to describe the natural grandeur and the romantic scenery of Yosemite Valley, I cannot really think of attempting it—yet there may be some features of interest which may be amusing although not portrayed in the usual Guide Book style.

The Valley itself is about ten miles long and varies in width, from half a mile to a quarter of a mile: it is 4,060 feet above the level of the Sea and through it flows a very pretty stream, full of Trout, called the Mercèd. The soil in the Valley differs in various places, and though in a portion of it some attempts are made towards cultivation such as growing Peaches, Grapes, and Strawberries, yet as a whole it is entirely covered with lofty Pine, Cedar, and other coniferous trees, of every stage of growth, up to 200 feet high and even upwards. For curiosity I measured several trees, which I found to be over twenty feet in circumference—these were Red Cedar trees and Norwegian Pine, also Sugar Pine, Arbor Vitae and many others. The only habitations are three Hotels in the Valley, and Indian Wigwams; everything which comes into the Valley is necessarily carried on the backs of Mules for forty or fifty miles, including Beer and Wine and Eatables generally, and while we were there the usual Mule train came in, which carried (of course in several sections) a modern luxury in the shape of a Billiard Table which was to be put up in one of the Hotels. On either side of the Valley there arise sheer precipitous rocks of every shape and form. The highest of these "Clouds Rest" is 6,450 feet above the Valley or 11,010 above the Sea and the lowest is about 2,500 above the Valley, the average being about 4,000 feet. Hence it is said, that if a flock of wild Geese once got into the Valley they never could find their way out of it again.

The Mountains surrounding the Valley are nearly perpendicular and in many places are quite so: and a fair idea of the Valley may be gathered by imagining that a "huge landslip" (or sinking) has at some time or other occurred in the midst of a very Mountainous Country, leaving the perpendicular sides of the Mountains as if they had been cut with a Knife, and when it had settled some 6,000 feet, the Valley representing the original tops of the Mountains worn down by time almost level. The South Dome 6,000 feet, Captain 3,100 feet, Sentinel Dome 4,500 feet, Three Brothers 4,300 feet, above the Valley are some few of the principal rocks. The principal objects of beauty and admiration are the Waterfalls and Cascades.

Of these there are seven. The Vernal Fall which I rank first in beauty, and which surpasses anything I can ever imagine is only 300 feet high. It is a clear fall, with a large volume of water, which appears to start in four Columns but these quickly blend into one sheet of transparent spray.

Above this on the same River is the "Nevada Fall", 700 feet, which is identically the same as regards the amount of water but which loses somewhat the grandeur of the Vernal Fall, flowing as it does between a very splendid Mountain Gorge, and helped up with a lovely background of trees and rock. Near to the Vernal Fall is a rock called Lady Franklin's rock; so called from its being the favorite seat of that Lady during her three months stay in the Valley two years ago [1869], and from which you may gaze on the Vernal Fall till you are fairly lost in silent amazement.

The Bridal Veil 940 feet is wonderfully grand, and by some is preferred to the Vernal.

It is a clear and well defined Fall, with a large body of water flowing over it. The only idea I can give of the beauty of water flowing so many feet, is of a countless succession of bouquets of crystal rockets, which burst in regular order and in one continuous stream; and when you have traced one towards the bottom, your eye instantly detects another shower of bursting liquid ready to succeed the former one which you have lost in mist ere it reaches the ground.

The Yosemite Fall which is directly opposite my Bedroom window is very grand. It is 2,634 feet high and in three compartments or divisions. The first is 1,600 feet, second 434 feet, third 600 feet. At first when you enter the Valley you feel disposed to criticise the measurements of everything, and to imagine that the whole is one gigantic Barnum-like exaggeration.

This idea I fancy prevails in the minds of most men, and is I think to be accounted for by the extreme clearness and rarity of the Atmosphere of the Valley. When however you are credibly informed that a Pine tree, on the top of (say) the "Glacier Point" (over 5,000 feet high) which to you appears as large as a tree in a Child's Box of Playthings is (by actual admeasurement) two hundred feet high and five feet in diameter, and that another tree, growing in a niche on the side of El Capitan, about 2,000 feet from the ground, is by survey found to be ninety feet high, you then have no difficulty in realising that the facts and figures with which you have been furnished are really correct, and that you have hitherto failed to realise the gigantic grandeur of this extraordinary place. Besides the Falls I have alluded to there is the Sentinel Fall 3,200 feet, The Virgin's Tear about the same height and The Royal Arch Fall 1,800 feet. I spent two whole days in the Saddle, riding about from one point of interest to the other in the Valley; and though the rarity of the air and my consequent want of breath at such lofty altitudes would not permit of my climbing the very lofty mountains with my more venturesome companions, yet I may say I saw everything I well could see.

On the 19th May we were up at 5.30 and rode three miles to see Mirror Lake and the very beautiful reflection of the Mountains, which are literally photographed on its surface.

The water of the Lake is very clear, and we saw lots of splendid Trout at the bottom of the Lake, which are sometimes to be taken with a Fly, when there is some wind. We also rode to the Bridal Veil Fall to see at 3.30 in the Afternoon, the splendid Rainbows caused by the Mist at the bottom of the Fall and seen at that hour—they were three in number and were extremely brilliant and fine.

SATURDAY 20th MAY

Our party of four, with three very jolly young Americans, who joined us through this trip, and our Guide and Pack Mule started at 8 oClock for a ride of twenty three miles to an Inn called "Clarke's", which is out by the Maraposa route. After six miles ride in the Valley we had to ascend nearly opposite to the side we came in and by a similarly zig zag trail. It is hard work riding either up or down such steep places, but I must say this trail is easier than the one by which we entered. We again ascend and go out of our way so as to have one more and grand general view of the Valley from "Inspiration Point".

It was from this place that in 1852 (I think the year was) the Valley was first discovered by some White Men who were chasing the Indians. The Indians had robbed the White Men of their Horses. When the Whites suddenly stumbled upon "Inspiration Point", no wonder they were struck with awe at the beauty of the scene before them. After this point was passed, our ride as usual at this time of year lay through large quantities of Snow, and it was with difficulty that we could in many instances keep our Horses from sticking fast, as the Snow was rapidly thawing and we rode as straight as we could. On this occasion as well as many others where Snow prevailed we found many "Snow Plants". These were very extraordinary Plants and are only to be found with Snow. They are about one foot high, of a brilliant red or lake color, and before the flower opens they much resemble the common Rhubarb before it goes into flower. When the Snow plant opens, the flower resembles our Hyacinth in form and with a pocket knife you can detach the whole Plant from the ground. It is always found growing in or near a Snow drift, the melting of which discloses the Plant to view. Several Tourists tried to preserve them in mugs, and round Biscuit tins filled with cold water, but they quickly withered away in Water. After a ride of twelve miles we arrived at a Wooden Shanty called "Mountain View House" the half way house on this trail. Two parties of Tourists were before us and we had therefore some time to wait till our turn for dinner came. When it did, we enjoyed our Venison and other good things and were glad to find that we could indulge our tastes with English Bottled Porter, though at ruinous prices. In one of the parties we met on the road, we discovered an old Lady, of some sixty Summers, riding straddlewise and with a Parasol up!

With this way of riding I find no fault, as it is decidedly the best and safest both of woman and beast, who have much Mountain climbing to do, especially if they dress in Bloomer Costume, as they ought to do; but a Parasol in the midst of Snow, and to protect the Ladies' remnant of what appeared to be (even at its best) a not very lovely complexion, seemed ludicrously out of character. After a further ride of eleven or twelve miles, the latter part of which was very dusty and steep of descent, we cross the River and arrive at Clarke's where we put up for the night. Our Supper consists of Grizzly Bear Steak and Venison. The former is rather strong and very tough. The latter good and full of taste. The man who shot the Bear told us, that made the forty-ninth he had killed and bagged in the neighbourhood, and I believe him. They are plentiful all about the district we have been in, and they are very fierce if you cross their track. If you do not offend them they will run away and not harm you.

They are particularly tenacious of life and seldom it is that they are killed "dead" on the spot.

SATURDAY 21st MAY

We are up this morning before 6 oClock and on horseback for the Maraposa group of Big trees. They lie in a dense Forest and are about seven miles away.

We have to ride slowly with our Guide as the grade of the trail is bad in many places. Our horses too are all strange and quite unaccustomed to mountain work. Mine was by no means up to his work, and the Guide said he had never been on the trail before, hence he manifested a careless desire to run my leg against ledges of rock and trees whenever he could : and thus I had always to be "riding him" instead of the correct style, of letting him take care of himself as they very soon learn to do. I forgot to mention that at Breakfast we again had Bear Steak, Venison, and delicious small Brook Trout. We reach the trees in time and well they repay us for our trouble. There are some four hundred or more of them. They are the Wellingtonia Gigantica or "Sequoia Gigantica" (if the latter term is preferred). I think it is the more correct of the two and the Yankees foolishly kick at "Wellingtonia". The largest of the trees is the "Grizzly Giant". We measured it with String and found it to be over one hundred feet in circumference or thirty four feet in diameter. Its first arm, or branch, is forty six feet from the ground and is about six feet in diameter (nineteen feet in circumference). At a distance of twelve feet above the ground the tree was twenty eight and a half feet in *diameter*. These are facts I can vouch for. This is not the only large tree. There are many others between twenty feet and thirty feet or more in diameter. They are generally single trees, or in groups of four or five, and you have to ride some distance between the trees in order to see them all. One large tree had been blown down and was now hollow with age. We all rode our horses through it for several feet. To do this we only required to stoop our heads slightly. In another tree we had eight horses sheltered together, in its hollow stem which had been burnt out with fire as it stood, though the tree was still alive and green. We also rode through two or three of the more dilapidated ones. There can be no doubt as to these facts, and I cannot but wonder at the extraordinary size of such trees. The trees have all fancy and appropriate names. One "Bob Sawyer" and one "Longfellow" seemed to imply jokes if you can see them. After we had seen the last of the trees, we halted at the purest spring of water I ever met with, at a height of 5,639 feet above the Sea, which made Brandy remarkably good when mixed with it. Artists are especially fond of this water, it being so clear and pure for painting purposes. After a very brisk ride we arrived home about 11.30 a.m. We then indulged in a good dinner—Bear meat as usual furnished a chief dish. About 1.30 p.m. we start on a Stage Coach for Maraposa, distant about twenty eight miles. At starting we are 4,220 feet above the level of the Sea. In the first three miles we ascend 1,700 feet and in the next seven we descend 2,700 feet. To do this of course the grades are very steep, and it is slow travelling. We arrive at a good Hotel "White & Hatches" at five oClock and there we sup sumptuously, before we proceed on the remainder of the journey. This is a remarkably nice clean and comfortable Hotel, and amongst other names in the Visitors' Book I saw that of Abraham Lincoln in 1869. It was now getting dusk so we light the Coach lamps, and start at a rattling pace for Maraposa, which we reach safely notwithstanding that one of our lamps goes out just as we are in rather a critical place of our bad road, where we had an unpleasant Precipice on one side of us for some few miles. We reach Maraposa about 10 oClock and after securing places for the next Coach, we get to bed as we have to be up again at 3 oClock in the morning.

MONDAY 22nd MAY

Up at dark, it being 3 oClock in the morning. We drive away through miles of worked out Gold fields, until 8 a.m. when we arrive at Hornitos for Breakfast. The Country all around bears the traces of being worked for Gold, or rather what is termed "Placer Diggings". This is *shallow* working, and generally the Gold stratum lies some three to ten feet below the surface. These are frequently very productive diggings, and where there is plenty of water, they are easily managed. Without water it is not possible to wash the dirt away from the Gold. The water is conveyed in Channels, and the mixture of Clayey matter with the streams, causes all the small and large rivers in the Golden localities to have a very red and dirty appearance. Besides "Placer" mining, there is the quartz-crushing, which necessitates regular and systematic mining, sometimes to a very great depth. The only Placer Mining is now carried on by the indefatigable Chinaman, who appears upon the scene at every turn you take and who from his industrious and penurious habits, finds a ready living where White men would starve. They are greatly disliked and hated by the White Laborers, as they will work for very small wages, and thus have reduced the exorbitantly high rate of wages, which used to be paid in the neighbourhood. There is also another very extensive system of mining carried on by hydraulic means but this is practised more inland or "up Country". The water is passed through tubes, often for a long distance, and at a high pressure is forced against the sides of Sandstone rock. This rock it gradually wears away and the dirt and silt in falling down, run into Channels made at the bottom of the rock, while the heavy Gold sinks to the bottom of the channel and is caught in the various tanks and traps, which are made so as to let the water and dirt escape by flowing over the top of them. Although in many places the entire face of the Country is changed, and the land is rendered useless by the diggers, who have upturned the Sand and Gravel and left it untidy like so many enormous Moles would have done; yet there are still many new Companies being started to dig in places as yet inaccessible to individual enterprise, and who doubtless will be well repaid for their labours. The tales we heard of horror and blackguardism, which occurred in the midst of the numerous places we passed, and which now looked so orderly, would take up too much time and space in my Diary; yet I was credibly informed by several different men, that they themselves lived for months in places where it was the usual thing for five and even more deliberate murders to be committed each week. Such was the state of ruffianism and lawlessness to which Gold, Gambling and Drink reduced the digger, who as a rule comprised in their numbers many of the greatest scamps unhung. I was happy to hear that in one especially rough Town through which we passed, and in which there was a terrible gang of some twenty five lawless ruffians, they had all within a couple of years either been shot by their Comrades or been lynched by that fine Institution of redressing ruffianism "A Vigilance Committee". At the time when these Committees sprung up the Country was so unsettled as to be entirely without the administration of any kind of justice, or if there was any shew of justice it was so tardy of being carried out that the Culprit, who was readily let out on bail, generally escaped at his Trial by reason of the difficulty in procuring evidence, owing to the lapse of time, or the murder or abduction of some principal witness. Hence "Viligance Committees" sprang up. They were the respectable portion of the Community and were sworn to secresy, and when any ruffianism occurred, the Offender was privately tried by them, and was either shot or allowed only a few minutes, during which he was to quit *for ever* that part of the Country. If he neglected to quit at once, or if he ever came back he was shot to a certainty, or

A contemporary engraving of the Sherman Hotel, Chicago. *Reproduced from "American Pictures, drawn with pen and pencil"*, c. 1878.

The Suspension Bridge at Niagara. *Reproduced from an American stereoscopic photograph of* c. *1890.*

Niagara Falls from Prospect Point. *Reproduced from a stereoscopic photograph of* c. *1900.*

A picturesque walk on Goat Island, above the Falls. *Reproduced from a stereoscopic photograph of* c. *1890.*

The Thousand Islands.

A contemporary engraving of Central Park, New York, as featured in the "Leisure Hour" magazine, 30th September 1871.

Running the Lachine Rapids.

A contemporary engraving of Broadway, New York, as featured in the "Leisure Hour" magazine of 4th February, 1871.

Cunard S.S. "Russia".

The Adelphi Hotel, Liverpool. *Reproduced from a contemporary engraving in a Victorian railway-guide.*

Having partially recovered from a
severe attack of spitting of blood which since
the middle of last October had prostrated and
entirely incapacitated me for all kinds of business,
Dr Wilks the eminent Physician whom I was
advised to consult in London, gave his decided
opinion that the only means of restoring me
permanently to my former good health,
lay in my taking a long Sea Voyage. —
Accordingly I decided to visit Australia and
at once took measures to insure as far as
possible the Doctor's predictions being verified.

After personally inspecting several Ships
which were advertised to sail about the
beginning and end of December and taking
the advice of an old friend "in the Shipping
line" I proceeded to inspect "the Superb" one of
Green's Ships then lying in the East India
Docks at Blackwall. She was the largest Ship
then in Dock being about 1700 Tons Register
and of which Captain E. Jones was the
Commander.

After trying in vain for several days to
induce the Owners to lower the price they
originally asked for a whole Cabin, I had

perhaps hung up as a warning to others; whichever mode of dealing the Committee chose to adopt. In whatever way he was disposed of his death was an absolute certainty and he knew it.

I am not sure whether or not I have yet noticed that on this drive as well as many others you see lots of what would appear to be Rabbit burrows: they are inhabited by the Ground Squirrel.

This Animal is invariably accompanied by a small Owl, who lives with him, flies to the hole at the approach of danger and warns the Squirrel of it. These two have generally another queer companion, a Snake, and they three, bird, beast and reptile, join at the same house and live together in harmony. The fields are full of these holes and the Brown Squirrel, which is rather larger than our Squirrel, soon becomes no novelty whatever.

Another thing I must notice is the extreme beauty and profusion of the wild flowers of California. They are on every roadside and every Corn field, and as I have always taken an interest in flowers, I have especially done so in my journey through California and I may say America generally. I have no hesitation in stating my belief, that I have seen every flower (as far as I can recollect) that we grow in our Gardens in England, growing wild and luxuriantly somewhere or other in America. Lupins (Pink, White and Blue) as well as Larkspurs, and Escholsias (Yellow smelling flowers) are a perfect nuisance to the Farmer and actually smother out his Corn Crops. The Lupins were as large and fine as ours at home. There were wild Geraniums, with flowers (of one colour) much larger than a Shilling, and the plants stood eighteen inches high; Nemophyla (White Blue and Macculata) was quite common, especially in the Pine forests:—the Blue was superior in size and colour to anything we have at home. In coming over the Prairies, near Omaha, there were any amount of Sweet Williams (Pink variety and rather smaller than ours). I cannot go through the whole Botanical category, but my firm and fixed impression is that every flower we grow, is to be found in a wild state in America, besides many "beauties" I saw, which I was unable to name, or to gather, owing to my being either in a Train or on the top of a Coach.

This made a very great impression on my mind and proved to be a great source of amusement to me, as well as to others, to whom I was able to give some information on a subject, they had never previously taken any interest. After leaving Hornitos about 8.30 a.m. we proceeded on our journey in a large Coach and six first rate horses.

We have twenty Passengers in the Coach which is quite full. The coach is of the English type and the Coachman who is a great Swell and one of the best drivers in that locality, is quite in keeping with the fine Coach. After passing over a hilly and stony Grass Country we come to a fertile plain called "the Valley of the Mercèd". This is remarkably productive—there are peach Orchards and Vineyards in abundance, and fruit of all kinds is very plentiful; so much so, that in the Season, the Owners will allow strangers to eat as much as they can without paying for it. The Peaches are used principally for making Peach Brandy, this being one of the ways in which they dispose of their surplus crop. The River Mercèd a few years ago, caused great destruction by overflowing its banks and flooding the Country for miles round. This flood which proved very disastrous to human and animal life, also caused the river to change its course, and the old river bed is to be seen in many places. After this fertile region we come to a long sandy undulating Plain covered with Corn Plots. These are of enormous size, and I was sorry to find that this is now the second year that the Crops have been destroyed by the unusual drought. There were acres of Barley not more than six inches high; some in ear, and some quite ready for cutting, and in fact, being cut, but I am sadly afraid it was prematurely ripe, and would prove a sad loss to the Farmer. I must here mention that the mode of reaping Corn is somewhat peculiar. A Reaping Machine with six horses is driven along at a good pace and merely cuts off the heads of the Corn, which it delivers into a large low Dray or Waggon, which is drawn by two horses alongside the Reaper. When this Waggon is full it is replaced by a similar one. Thus the Corn Stacks represent nothing but the heads of Corn, and the Straw being of no value is burnt, as the Homesteads are not constructed for utilizing it or turning it into Manure. At present the land is made to grow Corn year after year. This style of farming will I expect some day or other come to an end. I forgot to mention that the Corn is ready and quite dry enough for stacking as soon as it is in the Waggon. The remainder of our journey to Modesto, was the most tedious and uninteresting I ever travelled. We were at times almost Axle deep in Sand, and the surface of the Country being very undulating we had to travel in clouds of dust very slowly. Happily all things have an end and having crossed the Tolumine River in a Ferry boat, which was large enough to hold our Coach and six, besides other vehicles, we arrived at Modesto at 4.30 p.m. thirteen and a half hours Coach ride in a blazing Sun, and cramped up in a Coach, is rather tiring work. We left Modesto for Lathrop the junction of the Main line at 5 oClock p.m.

Here we had a good dinner and after parting with some of our friends for Sacramento, we lay down in the Waiting room till 12 oClock and went to sleep. Our Train for San Francisco came up at Midnight, and we retired to our Sleeping Car, for which we had previously telegraphed from Lathrop. A Sleeping Car is a very luxurious contrivance. On each side of a Car, which is some sixty feet long, are arranged two tiers of berths, similar to those in a good Ship. These have Curtains which are drawn at the side, and hide (or are supposed to hide) the Passenger from each other. Each lower berth (there are two berths, top and bottom, they being styled a "Section") is provided with the cleanest of Sheets and Pillow Cases and is capable in the day-time of being converted into two Arm Chairs, one to be appropriated by the several occupants of the "Section". The upper berth by ingenious mechanism is made to fold up and represent the Cornice of the Car, while all Bed clothes, etc. are hidden away along with the Curtains in the top or upper berth. Thus every vestige of Sleeping Apartments, is removed as soon as ever the Passengers get up in a morning, and this is generally not later than 6 oClock.

Ladies and Gentlemen sleep in separate berths, though there is no part of a Sleeping Car set aside for the former. This arrangement is productive of scenes, more easily imagined than described, and I doubt not would cause at first a great distress and annoyance to some of our excessively proper English Ladies; yet American Ladies are very Cosmopolitan in their ideas, and readily adapt themselves to all circumstances of life. A Black Steward attends each Car and makes up the beds with great neatness. He is also on guard during the night and is supposed to act as a Sentry; at the same time he cleans your Boots and attends to your general wants.

We turn into our berths and sleep quietly and soundly till we arrive at San Francisco at 7.30 a.m.

After a good bath, and making other alterations to our travel-stained toilet, and a good Breakfast at the "Occidental", we set out to procure our tickets for the Overland route to New York. I call upon Mr. H. and afterwards arrange to dine with him at the Union Club at 6 oClock. We had a pleasant dinner at a very comfortable Club, and as previously arranged I go with him to call upon three young Ladies. We find them at home keeping house for their Brother-in-law. They certainly were as I told them "awfully jolly" and lived in a very nice house indeed.

We amused ourselves by dancing in the large Hall, while one of them played for us, and very well they danced. If all the Girls in that part of the Country were as good looking, and nice as they were, I hardly suppose that any Ladies would unintentionally remain Old Maids.

This morning we go and visit the Mint and see them rapidly turning out 20 Dollar pieces, which are certainly a very handsome Coin. Afterwards we go by special invitation (as we really are "Australian Passengers") to a grand Champagne Luncheon given by the Owners of the "Moses Taylor". This Steamer sails at 12 oClock for Honolulu. She is the Sister Ship to the "Ajax" in which we came over. Our old Stewards now again transferred to the former Ship, recognise us and help us liberally to Champagne, and we endure many long speeches, which are principally to the praise and glory of Mr. Webb and the founder of this line of Steamers to New Zealand. In the Evening Mr. H. dines with me and we spend a very jolly Evening afterwards at various places of amusement. My impression of San Francisco is that as a whole the general aspect of the Town surpasses Melbourne. The Shops are good and the buildings, the fronts of which are mostly of cast iron painted Stone colour, are lofty and elegant. Yet the solid stone of Melbourne public buildings, is conspicuous by its absence in San Francisco. The Town to all appearance is quiet and free from the ruffianism, which I heard prevailed. If a Man keeps sober, and avoids the numerous and insiduous invitations to gamble, with which he is beset by very Gentlemanly, well dressed, and smoothe spoken scoundrels, he is tolerably safe from being shot with a six shooter or some other outrage committed upon him. I cannot but think that it is, as a whole, the most irreligious and bare-faced immoral Town

I have ever seen, and this it appears they make little (if any) attempt to conceal. Having seen it thoroughly both by Day-light and Gas-light I may I think be entitled to form an opinion on the subject, and I confess that Paris as regards morals is very subdued when compared with San Francisco.

Chapter 5

We start this morning at 8 oClock for Oakland Station, having previously provided ourselves with a good Luncheon basket, and having checked our heavy luggage for Omaha.* The system of checking luggage, as practised in America, cannot be too highly praised for completeness and comfort to the Traveller. You present your Railway ticket at the Luggage Office, as also the luggage requiring to be checked and you receive a Brass Check with a number stamped on it. The Counterfoil Brass number with a Leathern strap affixed to it is looped to your luggage:— after that it is placed in a through Baggage Car, and the production of the Counterfoil alone entitles the bearer to receive his luggage at the end of the journey. The system is the best and most perfect possible and ought to be adopted in other Countries as it relieves a Passenger of all anxiety as to his luggage. We arrive at Sacramento about 2 oClock the weather being rather hot. There is only a single line of rails and there appears to be very little ballast to the Sleepers. The rails are merely held down to the Sleepers by hooks which are driven into the Sleepers and there are no "Chairs" the same as on English lines. The track across America is remarkably easy and the running very smooth.

The land continued to run tolerably level until we arrived the other side of Sacramento. After passing Sacramento, and

---

* San Francisco was, until 1869, largely cut off from the rest of America, the trans-continental railway being only opened in that year. In 1876 a line south to Los Angeles was opened.

especially about Colfax, we ascent 7,042 feet in about a hundred miles before we are able to cross the Sierra Nevada Mountains. This ascent is effected by running the line of Railway along the sides, or rather, winding round the corners of the Mountains. We had two powerful Engines attached to seven or eight Cars. The Scenery as we began to ascend was in many places very grand while the high and dense Pine-clad Mountains were generally covered with Snow.

Previously to our arriving at "Cape Horn" we go into what is called the Observation Car. This is a large open Car attached to the end of the Train so as to enable the Passengers to obtain a capital view of the surrounding Country. There it is that in turning off to the left we see before us on our right a wide deep chasm and apparently impassable. How we get over it at first puzzles us, yet we can discern the line of Railway on the other side to our right—by a clever and bold feat of Engineering skill, and by winding up one side of the ravine, then by crossing a very high and dangerous looking *curved* tressle Bridge several hundred yards long, we gradually find we have turned a very acute angle and are just beginning to round Cape Horn. This is a wild and bleak headland which stands out boldly before us and round its precipitous face we travel along:— often we are 2,000 feet above the Valley below; and the track in some cases appears to overhang the sides of the hills.

Of course the objects in the Valley as seen from this height look very small, and the scenery generally is grand.

It is in this part of the journey that the hydraulic mining or washing for Gold is carried on. Water for this purpose is often conveyed in Wooden Aquaducts for many miles: and the immense power is obtained by running the water to the top of a hill near where it is required, and then conducting the stream into an iron tube sometimes two hundred feet high. Of course the pressure obtained from a column of water two hundred feet high can be appreciated by any one, who knows sufficient of hydraulics as to understand the "hydrostatic paradox". When we are nearly at the summit of the Sierra Nevada, we have to pass for thirty-five miles through continuous Snow sheds. These are all made of pine boards and appear to be roofs, reared as Lean-tos and on a level with the sides of the Mountains and in some cases are regularly built Sheds, extending right over the very tops of the Mountains. By this means the Railway

89

tracks are kept clear and open even during the heaviest Snow storms in Winter. As the Snowfall in Winter varies from sixteen to even twenty feet, these Sheds are indispensable. The dense atmosphere, impregnated with *Wood* smoke from the Engines, produces a very disagreeable sensation on your Eyes and Nose in a Tunnel thirty five miles long, and we were highly delighted after two hours inconvenience once more to find ourselves in fresh air. We continue to pass several deep and thickly wooded Cannyons (a common word in America, similar to our ravines).

Night approaches and no doubt we shall unconsciously in our sleep travel past many very interesting places.

Lake Domer for instance, famous for the awful catastrophe which befel the unlucky Train of 82 Emigrants, who full of health and spirits, encamped on its shores, and yet who, by slow degrees, died of starvation by reason of their being suddenly yet nevertheless securely, imprisoned by a deep fall of Snow.

FRIDAY 26th MAY

It is not my intention to devote this Diary of mine, to the purposes of a Guide Book, as I have one in my possession, which gives in minute detail every particular of the various Stations and objects of interest we pass in the train: to this I would refer any person, who takes the trouble to read these remarks, "for further particulars".

This Morning after a tolerably good night's rest in the Sleeping Car I awake and find we are just opposite what is called Humboldt Sink, a large Lake into which the River Humboldt empties itself.

This Lake was at one time supposed to have no outlet, yet one is now found at its Southern end into another Lake of the same name. These Lakes dry up in Summer. Some say that there are underground Channels, but most probably, evaporation in the Summer months, is the true cause of their disappearing. The river Humboldt follows us for two hundred and fifty miles and winds in and out and across our track.

On all sides we see nothing but Sandy plains in which Wild Sage is the only vegetation. We soon now come to the forty one miles Desert which really deserves its name.

During the whole of today's journey, the dust is simply intolerable and follows the train in dense clouds. Such a Country is quite devoid of interest. Endless Alkali Plains, very few (if any) flowers, and no vegetation, except the wild Sage.

The train pulls up at the principal Refreshment Eating Stations, three times a day; (say) 7 oClock for Breakfast, 12 oClock for Dinner and 5.30 or 6 p.m. for Supper. Beer is a "luxury" and paid for, as such.—2s/– a Pint 4s/– a Quart. Bourbon or Rye Whiskey is tolerably cheap, and generally good. Take your own Brandy with you is the best advice I can offer! The charge is one Dollar for each meal.

The sole features of interest we pass, are here and there, the Graves of several poor white men and women, who at no long distance of time have fallen victims to the treachery of the Indians, who for many hundreds of miles through which we are passing still continue to infest the Country. They are ugly, idle, good-for-nothing, and cruel scoundrels—too idle to work though not to beg; as they may be seen soliciting alms at almost every Station where the train stops. I fully disbelieve in the noble "Pathfinder" and "Deerslayer" of the "Railway-Library-Shilling-Novel" type. Such creatures only exist in the fertile brain of some fanciful Author who draws largely on his imagination. I am happy to think that in a very few years what with Whiskey, Smallpox and the contact with the White Men, many of these merciless and treacherous abortions will have gone to the "happy hunting grounds", never again to repeat atrocities, which are not surpassed for horror, even by the Indian Mutiny. I must again refer to the Guide Book for a full description of the various tribes of Indians.

SATURDAY 27th MAY

We arrive this morning at 7.30 at Ogden the junction for Salt Lake City. This may also be taken as the end of the Central Pacific Rail Road. The next division being the Union Pacific Rail Road: It is as well to set your Watch here one hour and twenty minutes faster, as Salt Lake time is forty minutes ahead of the Central Pacific Rail Road time and the Union Pacific Rail Road forty minutes ahead of Salt Lake City time.

We take the Branch line for Salt Lake City* distant about

* The railway from Salt Lake City to Ogden had only been opened in the previous year.

thirty six miles. Throughout this journey we continue to run in sight of and along the shores of the Great Salt Lake. The Lake is about one hundred miles long and greatest width is forty five miles. The Railway runs round the Northern and Eastern sides of the Lake. Salt Lake City is situate at the South Eastern corner of the Lake, though at a short distance from it. On the Lake there are several islands, the largest Antelope Island, is fifteen miles long and six broad.

As we approach Salt Lake City, the Valley between the Lake and the foot of the Wahsatch Mountains, becomes very fertilised and productive: these Mountains are very high and are capped perpetually with Snow. From these flow to the Lake many streams of water, and this water is turned to every possible account in irrigating the small Farms of the various Mormon Settlers, who thrive in the Valley. Their Farms flourish and look extremely well, while their meadows were covered with luxuriant, but a coarse kind of grass. On the right lies the Great Salt Lake. Its waters are extremely brackish and contain 25 per cent of solid Salt. Look across the Lake, and you see Antelope island and the other islands rising some 3,000 feet high above the Lake (that is a total of some 8,000 feet above the Sea) and covered with Snow. These form quite a pretty Swiss picture, while the waters at their base, of the purest and deepest blue, serve as an admirable foreground. We arrive in Salt Lake City about Noon, and unfortunately for us the wind was unusually high, and drove the dust along in blinding clouds.

After depositing our luggage at the Townsend House we went to call upon or rather "interview" Brigham Young. We sent in our Cards and were introduced to him, and at the same time to one of the Elders, a Mr. Smith. The latter personage did most of the talking for Brigham, who was suffering from a Cold and sore Throat. They both were affable and talked on various subjects. One of our party, who is in the Royal Engineers was well "up" in irrigation, as practised in India, and this subject served as a very good source of conversation.

After this we walked through the Town and inspected it. The City is very pleasantly situate at the foot of the Wahsatch Mountains, and they may also be said, to surround it on three sides. The Streets are set out the unusual width of one hundred and thirty two feet; they are parallel to the points of the Compass, and have plenty of Boulevard trees on the "side-walks".

Down several of the Streets there are pure streams of running water, which give the place an idea of being tolerably healthy. The blocks in the centre of the City, each contain ten acres of land, and these again are subdivided into smaller Allotments.

Almost every house stands in its own grounds, and has a pleasant Garden attached to it. Over most of the Shops there is a Sign board with "Holiness to the Lord" written above it, while underneath there appears a Painting of God's Eye. The real Eye of God probably, grieves over the unjust transactions of many a Mormon Shop Keeper or I am not a judge of their true character and dealing. The Shop is then styled probably "Zion's Co-operative Store", or some other Scriptural name is brought in, by way of a sign, similar to the fashion of Advertising English Shop Keepers who style their Shops by some fanciful name.

In the Evening, we took tickets for the Mormon Theatre. This is a large and spacious building larger than most of our Country Theatres.

It is dimly lighted with Oil Lamps, which are of course inferior in effect, to Gas. Brigham Young, however, for some reason or other, objects to Gas, and he is Lord Paramount in this part of the Country. The pieces we saw acted were "Louis XIth" and "Milky White" and the Performance, by a Company of Actors from New York, was highly creditable. Sitting in the Stalls, an Elder, was pointed out to me, having (as I was informed) sixteen wives. He was Grey headed and so many wives in his case appeared sadly out of place.

Brigham is said to have eight Wives and forty eight Children. His wives (I don't mean his "Spiritual "wives) live in two large houses, quite distinct from each other, as far as I could ascertain.

A full description of them and of Mormons generally is given in Hepworth Dixon's "New America".

A large body of American troops are stationed a short distance from the City, at Camp Douglas, which is a strong Fort or Barrack and overlooks the City. In a very few minutes the United States Guns, would make the City untenable by the Mormons.

As an instance of Brigham's keeping the upper hand over his flock, I observed that all the Telegraph wires go directly into his private Office, and thus he alone receives the "latest intelligence" which he doles out at pleasure to the other Saints.

I also observed numerous spies of his, who "hung about" the various Hotels, and pick up scraps of conversation. If Visitors unguardedly express their Anti-Mormon feelings too strongly, it is highly probable they receive a polite notice to "quit the City" and it is well for them if they attend to the warning at once. Instances are not wanting, in such an outlandish place, of people "disappearing" mysteriously, and never turning up again or being heard of at all.

SUNDAY 28th MAY

This Morning at 10.30 we went to the Tabernacle, but we found that the Service was to be conducted in a smaller room, which stood in the Tabernacle grounds, the Tabernacle being reserved for the Afternoon. There was a large Horse-shoe shaped Platform at one end of this smaller room. On this Platform sat many of the Elect or Elders of the Church. Some wore their hats— others read the Morning Paper published in Salt Lake, and others chatted audibly with their neighbours. They all appear to be "great" at giving the "right hand of fellowship" and thus they invariably shake hands every time they meet. The Congregation (on this occasion mostly Gentiles) sat in the body of the room and at the extreme or West end there was a small nicely toned Organ and a choir of some twenty or thirty voices. The Choir were led by a Conductor with a baton, while on the Organ above the Keyboard was a Looking glass in which the Organist could observe the movements of the Conductor, similar to the arrangements in the Crystal Palace Organ. At the commencement of the Service, one of the Elders from a Reading Desk got up and said "The Choir will please sing the Hymn on Page twenty four". Accordingly the Choir did, by themselves, sing the Hymn, while the whole Congregation sat down unconcernedly and as a rule, talked and chatted with their neighbours.

The Choir I must say were very well trained but they sang too slowly; yet (but for that fault) they sang in first rate time and tune. The Hymns were to very old English tunes, such as I remember in Village Churches, as a Boy; and they were properly sung in parts, and no "liberties", whether "Tallissian" or otherwise, were taken with the original score. After the Hymn we had a long extempore Prayer, chiefly thanking God for his goodness to the Mormon Cause, and praying that "their's" the only true and "saving" Religion might flourish in all the World; and so on. Afterwards by special invitation the Choir were "pleased" to sing another Hymn, which they did without any interference, or interruption, or attempt at joining in with them, by the Congregation.

Then came a very eloquent and Scholar-like Sermon, though without any text, for an hour from the Revd. George Q. Cannon, who dwelt principally on the persecutions the Mormons had undergone, and he trumpeted forth the praises of Mormonism generally. After he had finished, Brigham Young rose and was received with marked attention on all sides. He criticised the remarks of Mr. Cannon with regard to the persecuted Mormons, and with great ingenuity and tact, he argued that the general rule in life was, that the persecuted turned the tables on their persecutors. He then gave an outline of Mormonism, quoting (as did Mr. Cannon) 14 Rev: 6th Verse to shew that it was reserved for the latter days, for God to send the Angel, having the "Everlasting Gospel" (i.e. Mormonism) to preach to all the World. That the Gospel was the Revelation, as preached to Joseph Smith, to whom it had by "the Angel" been revealed, *what was the true and original purity of Divine worship*. The Bible he affirmed was true, yet it was to be supplemented and assisted, by Revelation, direct from God, through Jesus Christ.

Brigham Young is a sharp, shrewd, though uneducated man, having a great fixity of purpose. He is uneducated and unable to speak correctly or even in tolerably good Grammar. "Air these things true" "They is true", was a favorite way of winding up his sentences. He has any amount of pluck and fearless impudence, and by shrewd cunning, is much more than a match, for the majority of his poor deluded followers, over whom he reigns as "*Prophet* Priest and King". The Mormon men as a rule, are up to the standard of well-to-do-Agricultural Labourers, who are satisfied to jog along without trouble or anxiety. The women are, as it appears, reduced to a state of absolute slavery, while in the "upper classes" they have little else to do than—

"to suckle fools and chronicle small beer".

They have a most jaded and hang-dog look; their eyes are cast down to the ground, and though we tried to make some of the young girls we passed in the street smile and look pleasant, yet we invariably failed to do so.

They are a very unintellectual class of females, especially the older women, who wear long Coal-scuttle Bonnets, with a large Curtain to keep the Sun from their necks, very similar to the fashion amongst old women here twenty years ago.

In a word, I have visited Salt Lake and I never wish to see it again, nor do I ever intend to remain longer than is absolutely necessary, in that part of the Country, in which such blasphemous Imposters hold sway.

In the Afternoon we paid our exorbitant Hotel Bill and returned by train to Ogden Station so as to be in time to start by the early Train on Monday morning.

We stayed at a small Public House in Ogden, I cannot call it an Inn. Ogden is also a Town frequented by Mormons, being in the Utah County.

When I say that at this Public house there were Bugs enough in my Bedroom to have eaten me up bodily, had I ever ventured to go to sleep, you may easily imagine my night's rest was not refreshing. At first I slew them vigorously—very soon however, from disgust, I "sheathed my gory sword", and bade them live on, as long as they would, on Mormons and such monstrosities.

I forgot to mention, that after Service at Salt Lake, we went into the Tabernacle, which is a wonderfully large building in the shape of an Elipse, capable, they say, of seating some fourteen thousand people—the seats at the far end of the building rise Amphitheatrically, and a large Gallery runs round three sides of the building.

The Acoustic properties of the building are very good. I never remember to have seen a larger public building. A Temple, said to be larger, is now in course of erection in the other portion of ground reserved for Religious buildings, and its foundations are already laid.

But as "The surplus tithes" are the only source of revenue from which the building fund is supplied it is probable many years will elapse before the Temple is completed.

MONDAY 29th MAY

We left Ogden this morning at 8.30 and indulged ourselves in the luxury of a Drawing room Car.

This is the end Section of a Saloon Carriage with a passage

96

for general passengers' use at the side of it. It holds four people and is a very cosy and comfortable way of travelling a long journey. It is perfectly private, and it also serves for sleeping in, as well as living in, during the day.

The first few miles after leaving Ogden are very pretty: afterwards it is very dreary for a long distance.

In the Afternoon a Passenger accidentally fell off the train whilst it was going tolerably fast. As soon as it was discovered, we ran back and picked him up, about two miles off, and beyond a severe shaking, he was none the worse. This is the first practical instance I have seen of the use of the Cord communication in Railway trains.

A smart intelligent Boy, saw the Passenger tumble off, and he at once pulled the rope and stopped the train. In the meanwhile the Conductors of the various Carriages passed the word along to the Driver who thus knew what to do, when the train *had* stopped.

We continue over 7,000 feet above the Sea for a long distance.

TUESDAY 30th MAY

During the night our altitude is great, as we are proceeding to cross the summit of the Rocky Mountains.

In the night I was awoke by Snow coming into our Car and on my bed, through the open Ventilators, and in the morning the ground was quite white over with Snow. About mid-day we arrive at Sherman Station, which is 8,242 feet above the Sea and the highest on this line of Railway. Here it was very cold and cheerless. Snow drifts are lying in all directions.

There is nothing very particularly remarkable at the top of the Mountains. Cold and poor grass-land, interspersed with occasional small rocks or stones! In a few miles we shall be out of the "Indian" Districts. Up to now, we have been passing through a Country infested by them. The only way they are kept in check is by the United States troops. These are stationed in Forts, detached at intervals of (perhaps) ten miles along many miles of the Railway and there are still frequent fights between the troops and them. I do not say the Forts were built expressly to guard the Railway. but as the Railway track (as is commonly the case with main roads in England) runs nearly parallel to the old Emigrant-road, which is visible in many places, and is the only sign of the Country being at all Civilised; these Forts *now* come in useful to guard the Railway.

Unless troops were in the neighbourhood, the Railway would soon be closed. The United States Government have formed a sort of Regiment of a tribe of Indians. This Regiment they use against their former and most bitter enemies the Sioux ("Sew") Indians, who are a numerous and very hostile tribe. When they meet each other it is certain to be "War to the Knife". The Regiment is armed with Rifle Carbines and Revolvers; they cannot however be induced to discard their own Bows and Arrows, etc., hence they load their poor ponies most unmercifully, by carrying two sets of fighting gear.

By way of concession to the Indians, it was permitted them to ride on any train (or rather I may say on freight trains) but if there is only one or two they often ride on the Engine of Passenger trains. They ride as a rule on a Goods Waggon.

We found several Indians riding on a train which was shunted for us at a Station. One of our Passengers, in a fit of curiosity, got up on the Indians' Carriage.

One of the Indians, in a moment, fetched his Revolver and buckled it on and the Passenger who was conversant with Indian life generally "skedaddled" off the truck in a hurry, as he told us, that they were just as likely to shoot him as not if they imagined he was going to interfere with them at all.

Towards night we began to strike the "rolling Prairie". Antelope are now very common and we see herds of them grazing in the distance. We also see Prairie Hen, but there are no Buffalo, so far north as this. They are generally in the Kansas and Colorado Country, South of this.

WEDNESDAY 31st MAY

We get up this morning by half past 6, which is about the usual time, especially as Breakfast hour at the Refreshment Station is always arranged to be about 7 oClock. We are now fairly in the rolling Prairie.

The land appears to be especially rich and fertile and the flowers are exquisite. The ballast ditches on either side the line are full of them; as also the fields are.

I say "Ballast Ditches" but I am wrong; the Americans do not ballast their lines at all. But I ought rather to say, the ditches from which the "spoil" is taken, to raise the line above the ground level.

This is just the correct season to see Nebraska (which may be styled Prairie proper) to perfection. The fields of Maize look remarkably well, and Agriculture generally is in full operation.

The Country reminds me very much of good English Fen land (without the Ditches), yet there is more rich grass land than there is in our Fens. The more you go East, the more fertile and civilized the Country becomes.

We arrive at 3 oClock at Omaha. When it was a Railway Terminus it was a large Town—since the making of the Pacific Railway it has ceased to be a Terminus, and thus its inhabitants have followed the traffic and trade which has gone West.* Here we get out of the train, and say "Good bye" to the Pacific Railway. The distance from San Francisco to Omaha being 1,913 miles. At Omaha we and our heavy luggage—which we had not seen since San Francisco and which we find all ready to our hand—are conveyed across the Missouri in a large Steam Ferry boat.

This contrivance will soon be laid aside, as they are now, with usual American enterprise, building a large and splendid Railway Bridge across the River; thus connecting Omaha and Council Bluffs, the Town on the opposite Bank of the River. We start at half past 4 oClock in the afternoon for Chicago, by the Chicago and North Western line. There are no less than four lines of Railway from Council Bluffs to Chicago.

Since we left San Francisco we have quickened our pace of Railway travelling. As far as Ogden we travelled only eighteen miles an hour; afterwards twenty two, and now we are going about twenty five miles an hour—the distance to Chicago is 491 miles.

THURSDAY 1st JUNE

We fail to obtain a Drawing room Car, so we use the ordinary Sleeping Car. Our friends diverged from us at Council Bluffs, having tickets for the Rock island route. The Sleeping Car was fearfully hot, and close like the weather, and we got up very early, tired and without being refreshed at all.

We are passing through a very rich Country; it is well

* Omaha was founded in 1854, it became a city in 1867. In 1900 the population was over a hundred thousand, in 1960 it had risen to 301,598.

fenced and laid out in Farms—there is still much land requiring to be reclaimed. Some parts are very pretty. Especially when we came to a small Tributary of the Mississippi where there was a charming view of a Bridge and a Mill, and a small pretty river. The place was called "Cedar Rapids". It is not at all connected with the St. Lawrence River Rapids of that name. Here the view, looking up the River, surpasses anything I remember on the Rhine. We now travel at a good speed and have two sets of Rails. At Clinton there are three splendid Bridges by which we cross the Mississippi. One of them is made of iron, and is remarkably light and elegant. I suppose the Bridges are in all some two or three miles long. Great precautions are taken against the Wooden Bridges at this, as at every other place on the Railways, catching fire from passing trains; and a Signal Man is stationed on every important Bridge. It is his business to walk over the Bridge, as also through the Snow Shed (as the case may be) after each train and guard against fire. The dust and heat of this part of the journey were simply intolerable and the Brown Holland Wrapper I brought at San Francisco (which by the way gives one the appearance of some Cattle jobber at a Country Market) came in very useful. We arrive at Chicago at 3.30 and at once proceeded to Sherman House, a very large Hotel. Here we try with plenty of Soap and Bathing to remove the clouds of dust, which had fairly pervaded every portion of our Skin and Hair and made us feel miserably dirty.

We dine at Table d'hote, and here for the first time we suffer the infliction of Black Waiters. A more stupid, lazy, thick-headed class I never saw. Preserve me from Servants of the Uncle Tom style! They will even stop to argue with you, as to whether or not you have ordered them to bring Viands, which, in their opinion, forsooth, are or are not incongruous. What impudence to impeach or cast a doubt upon a "Britisher's" Knowledge of the Art of Gastronomy! We stroll in the Evening through the Town, and failing to find any amusement, we are sent to bed rather early through a severe thunderstorm.

FRIDAY 2nd JUNE

The great sight I wished to have seen viz. the place where Pigs are killed wholesale; where, as they say, thousands of Pigs in the course of a year walk up through a fatal trap-door to their own

100

destruction, and in less than five minutes, appear at the other end of the building in the shape of Ham Sandwiches and Hair Brushes, was not unfortunately just now in operation; the weather being too hot for the bloody business.

We obtain permission to inspect a Corn Elevator. This is 'a large Warehouse one hundred and fifty feet high. In this one building alone, which we saw, sixteen Million Bushels of Wheat are dealt with in the course of one year. The Maize or Corn grown in the Neighbourhood, is brought by the Farmer to Town to a duly appointed Inspector of Corn. It is his business to classify the Corn according to its quality. Having done so, he gives the Farmer a Certificate that the Corn he has deposited in the Warehouse is so many bushels, and of such and such a class or quality.

This Corn is then allowed to be mixed with other Corn of a similar class and when the Farmer sells the Corn, which he can do by producing to the buyer the ticket, he the Buyer is entitled to receive so much Corn of that Class from the Proprietors of the Elevator in which the Corn was stored.

Steam Shovels in two and a half minutes clear the loaded Corn-trucks which stand on the adjoining Railway. The Corn is then elevated, in the usual way, to the top of the Building, and deposited in huge Garners, from which it can be let off into the Ships, docked in the Canal below, by means of long "Shoots" or pipes.

There is an immense amount of Machinery in the building, and there are many "Journals", or parts, where the Axle of some fly wheel or other Machinery, revolves in its accompanying "bearing".

As friction upon these "Journals" is necessarily very great, and the greater portion of the internal work is of Wood, there is danger of fire from heated journals.*

To guard against this each Journal has an Electric Wire attached, and these wires all converge to one spot in the building, which is a large board similar to that used for Electric Bells. When any journal is heated, the Electricity at once detaches its own special number on the board, which flies out, and thus the man told off for this important purpose, *in an instant*, detects the place where Oil is wanted; more quickly than he could by any

* Just over four months after this was written the City of Chicago was ravished by the Great Chicago fire, which broke out on October 8th, 1871.

other means. This Machinery is simple and very interesting.

I also visited the Water works which are newly erected and in which the Machinery is supposed to be very excellent.

In a fine Billiard Saloon, into which I was told to go, there were no less than twenty eight Tables, a larger number than I have ever seen before in one room.

The Town on the whole is pleasant; at the same time, it is entirely a business Town, and not one to please Tourists. It is principally built on land reclaimed from Lake Michigan and large buildings, which were originally built on too low ground, have had to be raised considerably. The appliances to do this are no doubt ingenious, but I cannot describe them; yet it is not more "curious than true" that a large portion of the Town (and there are splendid and large buildings in it) has been elevated "*bodily*" some eight or ten feet. We pay rather extravagantly at our Hotel; six Dollars and a fraction for a good day's board! We start at 5.15 for Detroit and Niagara and by way of experiment we have our Supper in a "Pulman's Car". I hear there is a great desire to discontinue these Dining Cars, as they are very heavy, with all their Cooking apparatus, and it is very questionable whether or not they can make it pay. Besides this, they interfere with the legitimate trade of the Refreshment Rooms along the railway if such swindling places can ever rightly be styled "legitimate".

We find it to be a very good Car, and we join our party to some of our former English friends, whom we have picked up again at Chicago, and we spend a very pleasant and merry Evening.

SATURDAY 3rd JUNE

At Chicago I forgot to mention we checked our luggage through to New York, although we went by a different route. This we did through our friendly Ticket Agent. About 4 oClock in the morning we pass over a Ferry at Detroit. The train is put on board a large Steam Boat and conveyed across. This is certainly a gigantic and clever contrivance, and one which does credit to the Canadians, who first started it. During this time, the Custom Officer searches your baggage, and marks it, but they are only particular about Tobacco and Spirits. We find the Country is very woody, though a great portion has been reclaimed. The baggage master called at our Carriage early this morning to know whether we held Checks, corresponding to the numbers of certain Checks, which he held in his hand. To our dismay we find that all our party had lost some article of personal luggage, but no one could find out what.

He informed us that the baggage car had caught fire during the night, and that our luggage was badly burnt, or injured some way or other. This caused us great anxiety and trouble, particularly as none of us knew the extent of his loss. At first, we were told that all was badly burnt, but the evidence one way or other was very conflicting and we could not ascertain anything until we arrived at Suspension Bridge, the Station for Niagara.

The Suspension Bridge is double barrelled, (so to speak), on the top of it run the trains, whilst Carriages and foot people pass over in the underneath Platform of the Bridge.

The Falls are not visible from the Bridge which is three miles away. We arrive at the Bridge, and then I discovered to my delight that my "Main Trunk" was tolerably safe *from fire*. I asked permission of the Baggage Master to open it, as I saw it was very wet. I did so, and by a fortunate coincidence, I had placed my Macintosh on the top of everything, and thus kept many things comparatively dry. I removed a bundle of wet things and had them dried when I arrived at Niagara. My Rugs and Great Coat I found were amongst the "Missing".

We were an hour late in arriving, and were glad enough to sit down to Dinner about 3 oClock at the Cataract Hotel, a very comfortable and not very extravagant house.

After the Dinner we walked to view the Falls. We obtained a good view from Prospect Point, which is on the American side of the River.

There are two Falls of water; the Canadian 162 feet high which is the same as the "Horse Shoe Fall", and the American Falls 158 feet high. The Falls are especially remarkable, for the immense and inconceivable volume of water which is continually passing over them. This and the distance across the Falls, or rather the distance occupied by the water in falling over, rather diminishes the grandeur of the height of the Falls. This *body* of water, can only be appreciated by seeing the immense river, both above and below the Falls, which must necessarily pass over some 150 feet of sheer rock. Both the Falls are very grand; sublimely so; and each claims for itself peculiar features of interest. I prefer the American Fall, as it is easier to be seen, and the view you obtain of it gives a better impression of its grandeur. We go into a small house, where we find a Carriage drawn up and down a steep incline plane, some 200 feet high, and by which you reach the Ferry, at the bottom of the high rocks. Of course we try the experiment of going down in a small sort of open Omnibus, and we are gratified with the sensation of a kind of "gliding down the roof of a house" at a rapid pace. We cross in a small open Boat, just below the Falls and obtain a very good view. The water there is profoundly deep, and perfectly smooth, without stream.

After a hard walk up hill, we go to Clifton House, a new Hotel on the Canadian side the River, from which the best view of the Falls is obtained. Here we stumble on an old fellow traveller, with whom we "quaff the flowing bowl" to the extent of American iced drinks, as usual, "all round". We return over the new Suspension Bridge (not the Railway Suspension Bridge I have before mentioned). This new Bridge is built in one span and in sight of the Falls. It is 1,300 feet long, and 190 feet above the water, and is used for Carriages, as well as foot people. It is extremely elegant in Structure and the view from it is fine—of course there is the usual "Niagarian Toll" of half a Dollar, to pay.

SUNDAY 4th JUNE, 1871

This morning, we pay the customary half a Dollar, without which you cannot stir in Niagara, and we go over the Bridge which spans the Rapids or Cataracts above the American Falls and leads on to Goat Island.

From this Island you obtain a fine view of everything, and it is this Island which divides the two Falls.

The Island is kept up nicely, and adventurous Tourists can put on bathing dresses, and get wet through in an imaginary pleasure trip, under the actual water of the Falls.

I did not go, and my friends who did so, assured me positively that there was nothing to repay them for their trouble in going under the Canadian Fall. We accompanied some of our party to the Station "en route" for New York and after Dinner, we again visited Goat Island, and spent the afternoon on three smaller islands, which are connected with it by rustic iron Bridges. These three islands are called the Three Sisters. They are situate in the midst of the Rapids above the Falls, and have been picturesquely laid out in Walks, etc.

The Grandeur of the Rapids, or "The Cataracts" as they are called, in my opinion far exceeds that of the Falls themselves:— they are about two miles across and some miles long, and the waters leap over every obstacle with headlong fury, until eventually they tumble over the Falls. There is something very fascinating in watching the ever varying and rapacious stream running as it does at such an awful pace, and the question is where to? In the Evening at half past seven I went to Church. The service was short, and appreciable in proportion. We had the American Prayer Book, which is founded on the English one, but which is abridged very considerably. What a pity it is that it should not be adopted in this Country and that our Church Authorities, should not immediately be forced to "swallow their pride" and adopt it in its entirety for our Services. The forms of Morning and Evening Prayer are about half the length of our own, and the abbreviations which have been made are well timed and worthy of the attention of all those who love the Church, and at the same time wish to preserve her usefulness and "entirety" in an age of *inevitable* "Church Reform".

Chapter 6

MONDAY 5th JUNE, 1871

This Morning we left Niagara Station, at 10 oClock for Lewiston a Village a few miles distant.

Our route lay for the most part along the sides of the rocks, above the River and below the Falls. Having arrived at Lewiston, we had a famous view of General Brock's Monument, an Obelisk most conspicuously placed on the side of a very pretty hill or promontory on the Canadian shore.

We take the Steamer "City of Toronto" for a forty seven mile trip along the Southern end of Lake Ontario as far as Toronto.

We arrive in the Harbour of Toronto, somewhat behind time, owing to our having to convey and also to unload at a small wayside Station the whole Camp Equipage of a Canadian Regiment of Militia, which was to encamp there next day; this delayed us so much, that instead of spending a couple of hours at Toronto, we merely have time to see the "Corsican" (Mail Steamer) which is to convey us to Montreal, steaming out of the Harbour. This causes us some disappointment as we had expected to have had a couple of hours at Toronto. After some signalling, in which at first we believed we should not be successful, the "Corsican" allayed our fears of having to wait twenty four hours at Toronto, by stopping her Engines in order that we might come alongside. Accordingly we with an immense herd of other Passengers, proceeded on board the already crowded Steamer. After an awful "squash" at the Steward's window, my friend and I succeeded in procuring good berths in the stern of the boat, which had the great advantage of opening to daylight, or rather, they looked out both as to door and window on to the open Lake; Our entrance being, along a narrow gallery or passage, which ran round the stern of the Steamer. Here really for the first time, we came in contact with Canadian Ladies, and the difference in appearance and manners, between them and the tawdry, "over-jewelled" Ladies of the Western States, of whom we had lately seen so much, was very refreshing and English-like. The Men too looked "jolly" and as if they had something to live for, and we all were gratified and pleased, at seeing once more the English Ensign on our Steamer, and that the Hotels, and other public buildings, were not ashamed or afraid of prefixing the word "Royal" to their Signboard, a word which must be unknown, and I am sure unappreciable, to the Democratic and Republican Vocabulary of the United States. We had on board a large number of Clergymen, who were going to attend a Synod at Quebec. Some of them were *"real Gentlemen"*, but I must confess that they all were very ready to take their meals before any one else (Ladies not excepted) and as we had three sets of Tables, in succession, for each meal, I was surprised and by no means pleased, that they always and most persistently tried to monopolize the first and "highest room". In this particular, I regret to remark, that the Canadian Clergy, are not peculiar. I cannot fail to express the opinion I hold (viz) that the selfishness of many of that Cloth, counterbalances the commendable, retiring and gentlemanly conduct of the few. During the Evening, we pass along the Western shore of the Lake, and occasionally stop at various small Towns. The Shore scenery was quiet, yet very pretty and some of the Towns, especially "Port Hope" must certainly be ranked amongst the loveliest and snuggest spots I have seen.

TUESDAY 6th JUNE

Up very early this morning and found that the Steamer was waiting at Kingston for the Mails, which did not appear to be ready for us; anyhow we waited for them some time. About half past seven we commence to pass through what is called "the Thousand Islands", the beauty of which must be seen to be realised.

Islands of every conceivable shape are on all sides of you,

as far as the eye can reach. There are supposed to be from 1,500 to 1,800 of these islands, and they extend from forty to fifty miles down the river which at this part varies from six to twelve miles in width. The Navigation is doubtless at times very difficult and small wooden Lighthouses are placed on many points to guide Rafts and the Steamers.

The effect of this Scenery, heightened as it was, by a beautifully clear and sunny day can better be imagined than described. Suffice it to say, that by staring, with both eyes widely open, I feel sure I failed to take in one half of the beauties of nature I passed by in a quick going Steamer. After we pass Prescott we begin the Rapids. About six miles below are the "Gallop Rapids", then the "Rapids du Plat", afterwards the "Long Sault", nine miles in length, and divided by an island in the centre, into two Channels, The American and The Lost Channel.

Then there are three sets, the "Cotean du Lac", the "Cedars" and the "Cascades" which in eleven miles descend eighty two and a half feet; of course this descent is not gradual, but you go, as it were, by jumps, during some of which the Steamer travels *very* fast, without being under Steam at all. The last and most exciting is "La Chien Rapid" where the Stern of the Steamer appears to grate along a rock for some distance, and then shoot through a narrow Channel, which is just wide enough to admit her, and is only seven feet deep. To shoot this requires a "Pilot" and there are only two Indians and one White Man, who can officiate in that capacity.

Taking the Rapids altogether, there is more made of their danger than really exists; Yet they are still very remarkable, and it will require a man to know well what he is going to do before he tries the experiment of shooting them. I should doubt whether an open boat would live in some parts of them. We also saw several Timber Rafts of enormous size. Wooden Huts are built on most of them, and in them the Crew of sometimes twenty or more men live during the time they are floating down to Quebec or other places. Long Oars or Sweeps are fixed at each end of the Raft and by such means they are steered. Having safely passed "La Chien" we are in sight of Montreal and the famous "Victoria Bridge" by which the Trains on the Grand Trunk Railway cross the St. Lawrence. It is but a few yards short of two miles in length, the two Centre Arches being 382 feet span, and the remainder being 282 feet span. It certainly is a magnificent

Tubular Bridge, and its extreme length takes off from its otherwise, heavy and massive appearance.

We land at half past six oClock at Montreal, and proceed to the St. Lawrence Hall Hotel for "high Tea", and finally wind up the Evening by having "half price" at a tolerably good, though small Theatre.

WEDNESDAY 7th JUNE

Unfortunately this morning turned out to be a rainy one. After waiting some time in the hopes it would clear up, we decided on taking one of the numerous pair horse Carriages which were plying for hire, and having a good drive round the neighbourhood of Montreal. We accordingly hire a Carriage, and drive round Mount Royal, a distance of nine miles and the fashionable drive, where we have a view of very fine Landscape scenery, and at the end of our drive we again see "La Chien" Rapids. The houses in the Suburbs are some of them very fine, and must have cost a considerable sum of money in building. Their appearance however is not improved by the Green Sun Shutters, which I understand are kept shut, throughout the Summer months:— This gives the Town a forlorn appearance, rather as if "the whole of the inhabitants, were at the Sea side, and their servants on board wages". The principal buildings are mostly old and very good and are the work of the "French" Canadians. The Convent of St. Anne's, which the "Canadian Boat Song" immortalizes, is a fine building. In fact most of the buildings are French workmanship:— there is a fine English Cathedral of modern Architecture, which we were not able to obtain a view of, as the Sexton was at his dinner and being an old man "he could not be disturbed".

One of our friends had an introduction to a retired Scotch Banker at Montreal, and we met them, as they were often strolling about. The Banker's hospitality knew no denial and we were all five or six of us, invited to come at once and taste some genuine Scotch Whiskey "which he had had eleven years in bottle". As our host, who was one of the kindest I ever met, would insist that we at 12 oClock in the day, should drink Whisky and iced water in proportions known only North of the Tweed, and we each had two full glasses, we were disposed to have the most amiable impression of what we saw of "men and manners" in Montreal.

We had an early dinner at our Hotel, and our kind friend and a friend of his joined us, and good fun we had until they saw us off by the Train at 4 oClock, en route for Lake Champlain and Saratoga. In leaving Montreal our route lay over the Victoria Bridge across the St. Lawrence.

We arrive on the Shore of Lake Champlain at 10 oClock, and started by Steamer, the "Adriondack", about half past. In this arrangement we were sadly disappointed, as for the first time we discovered that we should not see the beauties of Lake Champlain by daylight.

The Steamer we were on, was certainly a marvel, in the comfort of its arrangement, and the beauty of its decorations. Each Cabin (and there was room for one hundred first Class Passengers) was a perfect gem of a Bedroom, and after so much knocking about it was only natural that we should have a good night's rest.

THURSDAY 8th JUNE

I was up about half past 4 oClock, and it being perfectly fine, I had a good view of the tail-end of the Lake, or rather of the river, which in most places is very narrow. From what I saw, I have no doubt I should have been very pleased with the Scenery on the Lake, and I regretted very much that in two days later, we should have succeeded in coming by the "day" boats, which were advertised to start to run on the 10th instant.

In the Neighbourhood, we saw many small Grave-yards, with White Head stones, all neatly railed off and fenced in. At first I imagined they were private burial grounds, as they were amongst the hills, and in queer sequestered places.

After enquiry I found out they were spots where a skirmish, or may be a small battle, took place in the War of 1812 and thus posterity has commemorated the event.* The idea commended itself to me from the Piety displayed by those who originally placed the stones there, as well as by those who continued to keep them in repair. We arrived at a small Station called "Whitehall" at 5.50 this morning and at 6.10 we started for Saratoga where we arrived at 9 oClock. The only incivility I met with in Railway travelling occurred in this short journey. The party offending was the Paper-boy, who was backed up by the Brakesman in an act of rudeness. They were both young men,

* Author's marginal note: See also "Legends of the Black Watch" by Grant.

apparently under twenty years of age, and it is the *Youth* of America (in my humble opinion as well as in that of many other people) who are the most ignorant, self-opinionated, and despicable "Cads" I ever met with. I pity a Country which blindly entrusts the suffrage into the hands of such "unlicked cubs", as soon as they are out of their "teens": and then for want of a better name calls it *"Manhood* Suffrage". What Men!

We stay at the Congress Hotel at Saratoga.

The Hotels here are most Leviathan in their dimensions. This one and "The Union" opposite make up about sixteen hundreds beds nightly between them.

In the front of the Building runs a splendid wide Corridor I believe a hundred and eighty feet long; and this again is nicely protected by the "Shade trees" which are in double rows down the Streets on each side. There is every accommodation for Visitors at this, the "Queen of American Fashionable Watering places". The Season had not commenced and very few Visitors were in Saratoga as yet.

Of course there are plenty of pretty walks and drives about the place, and six or eight different kinds of Springs, which are all "free" and have proper Attendants to give Glasses of Water. There is also a nice shady Park, or Pleasure ground of some sort, where I spent several hours in the heat of the day. From what I hear, the extravagance in the dress of American Ladies, who devote two whole months in preparing to "look fine" at Saratoga, is beyond anything we can imagine in England and frequently beyond the Pockets of their husbands. I was told on good authority by a Lady, whose word I can rely upon, that it is quite a common thing for Ladies to wear four and even five new dresses, each day of their visit at Saratoga. The "soiled dresses" I heard, were taken back by the Haberdashers, of course at an enormous sacrifice, and they were sent to Australia as "Second hand". I doubt very much however whether our friends in Australia would quietly allow such a statement to go uncontradicted if they were to hear it.

By the merest chance, we discover at the Railway Station, during the Afternoon, that to catch the day Steamer at Albany, we must leave Saratoga this Evening. A general hunt is instituted immediately for the "stragglers" of our party, who are sauntering about under the delusion we were going to stay all night at Saratoga, and in fact, we had arranged for our beds.

111

We start at 7.30 and arrive in Albany at 10 oClock. There we have supper, and after strolling through the Town, we enjoy the excitement of a fire, which attacked some Workshops, but was speedily put out, almost before we could well get there. In what part of the Town it was, I cannot say, as I merely followed a Crowd who were attracted by the various Fire bells of all the Churches in the place, and who went "helter-skelter" for a mile or more in one direction.

FRIDAY 9th JUNE

This Morning at 9 a.m. we get on board the "Chauncy Vibbard" Steamer on the Hudson and start for New York, a hundred and sixty four miles away. Of the pace of this Steamer, I think it will be sufficient to say, that she has been known to run twenty seven miles an hour—her pace on this occasion, including several stoppages, the delay of stopping the Engines, warping her to the Pier and starting, and of being compelled to go "half Steam" past all the strings of Barges we met, was over twenty miles an hour throughout.

The accommodation for Eating, etc. is of course good as usual, and we have a capital Dinner while we are on board.

By this time I am almost satiated with Scenery, yet the eight hours' ride we had, and especially the latter part of it, is I think equal if not superior to any other river scenery I know. Of course it is homelike and not wild and rugged yet there are the Catskill* Mountains, West Point and the Military Academy there, and the ten miles of "Palisades" near New York; and besides these the banks of the river are of considerable height, throughout the whole journey. I cannot describe the places successively along the route, yet most of them are very pretty, especially near West Point where General Grant was then reviewing the Cadets. As you approach New York, on the left bank of the river, there are many miles of pretty Villa residences, well shaded from the River by trees, and each Villa is apparently quite different from the rest. On the opposite shore are the famous "Palisades" which are high, sombre rocks, rising precipitously from the water.

* Author's note: Catskill (or Kaatskill) Mountains are famous, being the scene of the Tale of "Rip Van Winkle".

These have an air of barrenness and sterility, which contrasts pleasantly, with the rich partèrres of flowers on the other and civilised side of the River. We also pass the State Prison of Sing Sing.

On the banks of the river, at frequent intervals, there are very large buildings like Warehouses, with a long "shoot" attached to each. These I discovered were Ice houses, to supply New York Market, during the Summer, with Ice. The extraordinary quantity of Ice consumed in America, is truly marvellous, and can only be appreciated when we see the immense provisions made for supplying New York alone. We land at the 5th Avenue Hotel, from one of the Piers at New York about 6 oClock. This is a very large Hotel and apparently well conducted.

It is on the usual American plan having its ground floor devoted chiefly to Shops. Hence you might furnish yourself with an Outfit for a Voyage round the World, without going "off the premises". The Entrance Hall or Vestibule, serves as a sort of Exchange or place of assignation to meet one's friends, and it is usually full of men smoking and transacting ordinary business. The Clerks, at the Office in the corner, are shrewd men, and they can tell you anything you require about almost anybody. The "Cars" which run on the Tramways are a very safe agreeable and expeditious mode of progression. They run past the door every five minutes and take you to the very heart of New York.

I am decidedly in favor of Tramways, after what I have seen in America generally.

Persons of ordinary activity can readily get on and off the Cars without their stopping and they run without any unpleasant vibration or noise. Five Cents is the price whether for one yard's ride or for five miles.

If ever you enter a Car, it is five Cents, and in paper money (in which there are Notes as low as five and ten Cents); it is easily collected. They have powerful brakes and can stop in very few yards.

There are also Omnibuses, the same as in England which charge ten Cents (or –/5d English money)—these are more "select" though not more agreeable as far as travelling goes. Cabs in New York are a monstrosity, and the Drivers swindle on all sides. A Cabman would hardly look at you under five dollars. Hence they are too dear for any one to ride in, and the

Cabbies most grossly over-charge whenever they get a chance of doing so.

In the Evening I went down "Broadway" and strolled into Niblo's Theatre, where I saw the usual blood and thunder style of acting, with the "bowie knife" well up before the Footlights, eight or ten times during a short Play.

SATURDAY 10th JUNE

This morning I went to call at my Kind friend A.— W.—, whose business place is in Beckman Street. Having a small pocket Map in my possession, which I had torn out of a Guide Book, I found my way about New York quite easily. In his Office I found "in waiting for me" the Baggage Master of the Michigan Central Railway, "who was anxious", he said, "to settle on the spot my claim against his Company for damaged luggage".

We made appointments to see each other during the day and were both prevented keeping them. Thus it happened that the whole day was spent before we came really to the business part of the matter.

When we arrived at this, the proceeding was so straight that we settled it with my friend's help for fifty Dollars, which compensated me for the loss of my Rug and other damage, and at the same time was, I believe, the fair thing for a Railway Company to do under the circumstances.

My fellow travellers also claimed and recovered adequate compensation.

Altogether the Company behaved very honorably in the matter, and set a good precedent for English Companies, who would probably have lugged me into a Law Suit, instead of treating Gentlemen as such, and meeting them in the proper spirit.

This Afternoon I went to visit my friend A.— W.— in Brooklyn, and stayed with him during my sojourn in New York. My stay in New York extended till Wednesday the 21st of June.

During my visit, which owing to the kindness of my friends, was a very pleasant one, I saw most of the principal sights of the place. The "Central Park" is one of the great sights .To reach this you have to go through the most fashionable part of New York. It is situate at the extreme or as we should say "West end" of 5th Avenue.

The houses at this end of the Street, which is about four or five miles long, are generally *very* good and well built. They appear to me to be as substantial, and ornamental, as any houses in London, and the rents paid are enormous. Many of the houses are built of a dark red Sandstone which is easily worked, and even to a newly built house, it gives an air of more or less antiquity. I must say I admire the taste as displayed in Architecture. I also saw the house of Mr. Stuart, a very rich "Dry Goods Man", which was barely finished, and is built on the most extravagant and costly scale. It is of White Marble, and as I saw it in hot weather, there was an unpleasant glare from the Marble, which I am afraid will look cold and sepulchral in Winter.

The Central Park is laid out in long drives, which are beautifully kept, and extend through prettily arranged Landscape Gardening. The principal drive is about nine miles long, and along the whole distance, speaks for itself, as to the taste displayed in laying it out, and the marvellous way in which the trees and shrubs have grown. The small supply of water too, has been turned to good account, and there are several little Lakes, on which you may be rowed or paddled about either in a Venetian Gondola, or even in a crazy Indian Canoe, or in any other known style of frail or fanciful Ferryboat. After you have driven across the Park, during which time the regulations are, that your speed is to be limited to seven miles an hour, you may either turn round and come home by another route, or else proceed to the straight trotting road, where there is no restriction as to pace, and where the "Upper ten" and the Young "Swells" who affect fast Trotters, may be seen perched upon Skeleton Buggies giving every now and then their fancy trotters what they call "breathers" or "spins" for a quarter of a mile or more at a time. I happened to see several well known trotters while I was there.

One afternoon I received an invitation to go a long drive with a gentleman and Lady to whom a friend of mine and I had been introduced.

We had a pair of nice horses, and after driving through the Park we proceeded to "Jerome Park" where the Races are held, and we also had a *Land* view of the numerous Villas, I described as I came down the Hudson. At some of these we called, and I found that Gardening and Hot house fruit growing were becoming more fashionable than formerly in America. One remark applies to the Central Park, as well as to the equally pretty Park, I saw at Brooklyn and it is this—It appears to me and I should say, to every stranger, a very absurd proceeding, that the paths for foot people are purposely placed as far as possible from the Carriage drives. Thus the great beauty of the Park, viz. the Carriages and their occupants is entirely lost to foot people. I cannot say that I have any pleasure in walking in a Park, merely to see Nursemaids and Perambulators, while "the Beauty and fashion" both as regards horse (and human) flesh is wasting its sweetness "unheeded and alone".

Perhaps the Authorities were of opinion that "distance lends enchantment to the view". I cannot however think that they purposely could pay, the many nice looking Girls I saw during my stay, so poor and undeserved a compliment.

Greenwood Cemetery which is of immense size is well worth a visit. The Screen or Facade at the entrance is of richly carved red Sandstone and in very good taste. The grounds are open for Carriages, and if so mournful a place can be made pretty, the attempts at making this place so, have been attended with considerable success. Many persons it appears, on the death of a relation, erect a sort of Mausoleum to put the body in, and wherein they hope, at some time or other also to be buried themselves. Many of these small yet extravagant follies (I have no better word for them) are built round a very pretty little ornamental Lake, and act as a good *"Advertisement"* to the bereaved parent or Father, as the case may be, who has perhaps half ruined himself by such a piece of useless ostentation. On the other hand, you may take it, if you please, that this is one of the few *provident* acts which the Ephemeral Yankee, who is often "a man today and a mouse tomorrow" is guilty of: as he thereby insures for himself a "roof over his head" even when he has "gone". I would mention that the funerals are largely attended by "friends of the deceased" in Carriages. The Hearse is drawn by Grey horses, in Gilt harness, and altogether is not a melancholy sight. The weather was invariably hot in New York during my stay. I noticed in America that every house had one and frequently more Lightning Conductors: this appears to be requisite, as during the Summer and Autumn, scarcely a day elapses without Thunder and Lightning. Many of the Shops in New York are splendid, but all the articles are outrageously dear.

Broadway is the principal Shopping Street hence it is the principal resort of female beauty of all descriptions. Talking of

Beauty, I should say that in Broadway for instance, in walking down it, you would hardly pass any woman who was not tolerably well dressed and ordinarily pretty; yet the same style of face prevails amongst the whole of the American Ladies. Good Eyes, and a nicely cut nose; yet a *firmness* and *squareness* about the mouth and too great a length of lower jaw and Chin, which at once gives a sullen and rather bad-tempered look; and extinguishes in the expression, the whole of the vivacity and "merry twinkle" of their keen dark eyes. The rosy-lipped and not "over-jawed" English Girl, of the present day, forms a pleasing contrast in this respect to her American Female "Cousin".

By way of diversion, and of descending from the "Gay" to the "Gutter", I would remark, that the Sanitary arrangements of the Streets, and the number of Scavengers employed, is not equal to the wants of modern cleanliness. And again throughout the whole of American Towns, they indulge in the very selfish and disagreeable practice of monopolising a large portion (sometimes even the whole) of the "side walks" (as they call them) with articles exposed for sale; so much so that I remember instances, of my having to turn out into the Street as it was impossible to walk on the Pavement. On discussing this question in New York, I am told that the practice is quite *"contrary to Law"* but that the "Jack-in-Office" whether a Town Council Man or an Alderman or whatever Municipal personage he may be, has the power of granting or obtaining a License to these Tradesmen, *thus* to use the footway; and were he to refuse to grant or obtain such consent, he would probably lose the support of the Tradesman at the next Election and thus the abuse creeps in, and becomes a general thing, and the people who make the greatest profession of utilitarianism, suffer a most glaring, and disgusting public nuisance to go uncorrected. At San Francisco it is equally bad, and at Chicago (if possible) worse than it is in New York.

The New York style of living appears to be, to dine in the middle of the day, and to come home to "high Tea" at 6 or half past. After this there is no further meal in the shape of Supper, as *we* have. Besides, you cannot manage to eat so much *Animal* food in hot Countries. There are plenty of good Restaurants where food is good and tolerably cheap. The Churches, which on every side abound, are well attended in Winter, but I hear, they are very close and "stuffy" in Summer. Hence few people go to Church during Summer months, notwithstanding the fact that cheap Fans are provided, free gratis, and are constantly used by the Members of the Congregation.

At first sight it is somewhat peculiar to see every person fanning himself, or herself in Church. The general effect produced, reminded me very forcibly of the waving of a field of turnips, whose leaves are violently agitated by a strong breeze. One day we formed a party and took a nice, light Sailing Boat (of the Centre-board build) out of the Harbour as far as the Sandy Hook Light Ship. There we indulged ourselves in fishing for Blue-fish, which rather resemble in shape a Salmon and run six and eight pounds.

The way they are caught is by hanging a line over the Stern as the boat is sailing fast, to which is attached a bright piece of Lead and a large Hook. The fish then take it, like our Spoon bait, and there is good fun and trouble in hauling them on board.

Frequent fires break out in the City. To meet these efficiently, the *Volunteer* Fire Brigade has been (at the advice and instigation of our Captain Shaw) disbanded, and the system has been re-modelled on the London Plan, which I am told works very well. The jealousy and fights which occurred between the various Corps of Volunteers, were very prejudicial to the unlucky individual whose house was in flames; and a fight by rival Firemen, beside a burning house, was a more common occurrence than any effectual attempt to extinguish it. I found that I must now do my best to return homewards and accordingly I secured by good luck a passage on the "Russia" for the 21st instant. On the whole I had a very pleasant time in New York, and although my staying with kind friends prevented my seeing much of the gay Theatres, and places of general resort in the Evening, yet I was introduced to many excellent people who like my Host and Hostess appeared only to vie amongst themselves in making my stay in New York as agreeable as possible.

WEDNESDAY, 21st JUNE

At 8.30 this morning I go on board the Steam Ship "Russia"*

---

* Lloyd's Register records that this vessel measured 358 feet long and was of 2,960 tons gross. In 1880 she was renamed "Waesland" on being sold to a Belgian firm.

118

lying in the Cunard Dock on the other side of the Harbour, and we sail from Dock about 9 oClock. She is one of the first Class Steamers, which carry only *Saloon Passengers* and one of the fastest on this line. We have one hundred and seventy Passengers on board and amongst them many very nice people. As I go on board, I accidently pick up one of the friends I met at Yosemite, and with whom I travelled occasionally as we crossed by the Pacific Railway. I also through him discovered, another friend from my own part of the Country, and we three make up a tolerable party by ourselves. The first part of our Passage was tolerably smooth. About Monday afternoon however the 26th June it blew a regular Gale, such a one as I have not yet seen. It continued to blow all night and seriously disturbed not only the rest but also the stomachs of most of the Passengers. I am glad to say I was not sick. Although the wind was with us, yet we ran with only close reefed Topsails set, and the Steamer rolled very heavily for many days.

All I can say of the comforts on board and of the discipline of the Crew, is that they were *first rate*, and I would recommend the "Cunard Line" to any one who wishes to visit America.*

We landed our Mails and Passengers at Queenstown on Friday morning 30th at half past 3 and arrived at Liverpool about 10 oClock the same Evening, the Passage being 9 days 5 hours.

This time is reckoned from Sandy Hook (eighteen miles from New York) to the "Bell Buoy" on the Bar at Liverpool. Considering the fact that one Blade of our Screw was damaged when we left New York, and that the distance is a trifle over 3,000 miles our pace was very good, and we had a very delightful trip across. After inducing the Custom House Officers to examine our baggage so late at night, we made up a party of six of us to go to the Adelphi Hotel in Liverpool, where after Supper, which was pleasantly delayed till midnight, we retired to rest.

The next day I started on my way home and with the exception of our Train coming into violent Collision at Sheffield with another Passenger Train, thereby Knocking over three of

* At this period the Cunard Line had ships sailing to New York twice a week, every Tuesday and Saturday. The 1st class fare was only £26. An interesting contemporary account of a voyage from Liverpool is contained in *The Leisure Hour* magazine of January 21st, 1871.

their Carriages and seriously cutting several heads and bruising the poor people who were in them, I arrived home without further accident.

I am glad to say I found my friends in a very "tolerable state of preservation" and the kind welcome I received from every one on my return, was to me more gratifying and pleasant, than any incident which has occurred throughout my long, and to me, indeed (and as I trust it may prove to any one who may have patience enough to peruse these hastily written pages) not altogether uninteresting journey.